Chip-Wrecked In

LAS VEGAS

COVER PHOTOGRAPH

Downtown Las Vegas glitters on a balmy spring evening in March of 1994. In the background is Union Plaza Hotel and Casino, named after Union Station, where the trains used to stop. This site was the birthplace of Las Vegas. Photography by Daniel R. Mead.

Other Books From Mead Publishing Company

■

Chip-Wrecked In

LAS VEGAS

A COLLECTION OF STORIES WRITTEN BY
Barney Vinson

PHOTOGRAPHS SELECTED AND CAPTIONED BY
Daniel R. Mead

MEAD PUBLISHING COMPANY ▪ LAS VEGAS, NEVADA U.S.A.

First Printing
October 1994

Published By
MEAD PUBLISHING COMPANY
1515 SOUTH COMMERCE STREET
LAS VEGAS, NEVADA 89102-2703

ISBN 0-934422-07-9
LIBRARY OF CONGRESS CATALOG CARD NUMBER 94-77468

Printed in the United States of America

Table of Contents

Other Books By The Author

■

Las Vegas Behind The Tables
Las Vegas Behind The Tables - Part Two

■

Published By
Gollehon Publishing Company
Grand Rapids, Michigan

Opening Monologue

I NEVER WAS A gamblin' man. Before moving to Las Vegas, the biggest bet I ever made was five bucks on the All-Star game, and thanks to Whitey Ford throwing a slow ball to Rocky Colavito I lost that one.

One thing I never really understood was blackjack, which sounded simple enough until I tried it. I sat waiting for my two cards as the initial hand got underway, rehearsing over and over my how-to-win strategy. Hit anything under 17, stand on anything over 17. When the dealer came to me, he stopped. "You didn't make a bet," he said. He sounded like a traffic cop talking to a motorist he had clocked going fifty-five in a school zone.

"Of course I didn't make a bet," I replied. "I haven't seen my cards yet."

The dealer sighed. "You have to make your bet before you see your cards."

I almost laughed out loud. Sure I was from Texas, but that did not make me a country bumpkin. I wore shoes and socks, just like people in New York City. Giving the dealer a paternal glare I said, "What kind of idiot would make a bet before seeing what he's got?"

Alas, it was true. The players, I learned, actually did make their bets before getting their cards. It was certainly nothing at all like poker.

Poker was a man's game. You either bluffed or you called or you folded. I mean, can you imagine Wild Bill Hickock, sitting in the back of that bar in Deadwood, looking down at a seven and deuce, and saying, "Hit me?" That's not a dead man's hand. It's a dumb man's hand!

Apparently I was wrong again. Blackjack has become the

most popular card game around. In Las Vegas, visitors spend a third of their day at the blackjack tables, which doesn't leave much time for eating, seeing shows, or wiring home for more money.

I am told that the reason no other live game can backtrack blackjack is because of all the player options. The player decides if he wants an extra card, or if he wants to split pairs, or if he wants insurance. In some casinos he can even surrender half his bet after seeing his first two cards, which is something else that never made sense to me. Why didn't he just bet half as much to begin with?

There's high-stakes action at the Northern Club in this 1935 photograph. There are steel eyes and solemn faces at the table as an excited crowd gathers to watch a big game, or are they posing for the camera? At any rate, casinos have come a long way since the plumbing ran along the walls and single-bulb lamps hung by their cords from the ceiling.

About the only option not available is one that I think would make the game even more popular: "Triple pay on a blackjack if you are at a table where the dealer speaks *English*."

The wheel of fortune spins lazily at the Apache Casino, which opened in 1932. This photograph was probably taken in 1939 or 1940. The Apache closed in 1941 and reopened in 1945 as the S.S. Rex. Owner Tony Cornero had previously operated gambling ships (one was named the *Rex*) off the southern California coast, but resettled in Las Vegas after several confrontations with Earl Warren. The S.S. Rex became the Eldorado in 1948, and finally Binion's Horseshoe Club in 1951.

At the dice table, the player can only bet on a certain number, then stand there and pray that it comes up. Keno was invented by the Chinese, and once you play it you realize why there have been so many wars in the Orient. They just wanted a little excitement after playing keno. Baccarat is a classy game, but I always feel that I should be as well-dressed as the dealers.

Since I cannot afford a tuxedo, how can I afford to even play a game that I'm not sure I even know how to pronounce?

Then there are the slot machines. When I first came to Las Vegas, slot machines were just a nifty little way of getting rid of one's pocket change. After hitting a $100 jackpot, one woman reportedly got so excited that she accidentally drank half a cup of nickels. When she got home, she probably asked her friends, "Do you notice any change in me?"

Nowadays, million dollar jackpots are so commonplace that the winners hardly even make the newspapers anymore. When I was writing my book, *Las Vegas Behind The Tables Part Two*, I interviewed the lucky stiff who won a Megabucks jackpot of five million dollars. He told me he was thinking about writing his own book, something along the lines of what it was like to win so much money.

"Forget it," I told him. "There are only two people who would read it. You—and your IRS agent."

I don't know if he ever wrote his book or not, but at last report "I Won Five Million Dollars" was not in the literary top ten. Come to think about it, neither was *my* book.

Early Times

LAS VEGAS WASN'T ALWAYS this chrome-plated spider web that stretches across the tip of Nevada. In fact, the whole state might never have been more than a blank page in an atlas . . . if it hadn't been for the railroad.

Nowadays when we see a train, most of us let loose with a string of curses under our breath. It will probably cut us off at the next crossing, and we'll have time to do a crossword puzzle while it inches past.

But when Abraham Lincoln was president, the railroad was king. One of Lincoln's dreams was to link California and the territory of Nevada to the rest of the country with a transcontinental train line. There was a reason for it, and it wasn't patriotism. Gold had been found at Sutter's Mill near Sacramento, and at Virginia City the Comstock Lode unearthed enough silver to pay for the Civil War.

Still, those were hard times for people out west. To give you an idea of how popular Nevada was, anyone who wanted to live there could get 160 acres of land just for the asking. All he had to do was homestead for five years, and then it was his—free and clear.

Then came the railroad, that mighty iron horse of nineteenth century America. Central Pacific was looking for a place to build a town for its depot, and it was in a hurry. Arch-rival Union Pacific was already heading west from Omaha, and Central wanted to beat the other railroad to Nevada so it could get all the good right-of-way land. An army of 4,000 Chinese laborers laid track twelve hours a day, seven days a week, finally reaching the Truckee River in 1867. That's when Central Pacific scouts came face to face with Myron Lake.

Lake owned a toll bridge spanning the river—which was

the only way miners could get from the Carson Valley to Virginia City, where the silver was. He also owned a trading station, a tavern, a hotel and some nice big chunks of homestead land. Lake made the railroad an offer it couldn't refuse.

In exchange for a depot and townsite near his bridge, he would give Central Pacific 80 acres of land. Oh, but there was one catch. They had to deed half the lots back to him. It was the best offer the railroad got, so six weeks later the new town, named after Civil War hero Jesse Reno, went on the auction block.

Meanwhile, history was being made in Arizona Territory, where the Las Vegas Valley was located. (It would be deeded to Nevada in 1867.) A visionary with the improbable name of Octavius Decatur Gass had turned an old Mormon settlement called the Las Vegas Ranch into a popular way station for travelers. It would eventually be sold to Montana Senator William Clark, who also happened to own the San Pedro, Los Angeles and Salt Lake Railroad. The railroad wanted a town there because that's where the nearest water was, and it offered investors free train rides to Las Vegas for its big land auction. It was enough to make the auction a success, and Las Vegas was put on the map.

In 1905, the final spike connecting Salt Lake City and California was hammered into the ground about 30 miles south of Las Vegas. In contrast to the symbolic driving of a gold or silver spike, and the usual array of parades and speeches and banquets, the Las Vegas ceremony was almost anti-climactic. Since there were no gold spikes around, the wife of the railroad manager had a tiny one made. At the appropriate moment, the chief engineer fished the ornament out of his pocket—and stuck it in his tie. Oh, well, Las Vegas always did march to the tune of a different drummer.

By this time, silver had petered out in Virginia City, and the

---

(Right) As Nevada's mining boom moved south, saloons and casinos were among the first businesses to follow. This photograph of a gambling operation in Searchlight—about 50 miles south of Las Vegas—dates back to the turn of the century.

Until the 1950s, Reno was Nevada's hot spot. This 1931 photograph shows the first major "Biggest-Little-City" sign at the intersection of Commercial Row and Virginia Streets. The sign has been changed many times over the years.

mining boom had shifted to the southern part of the state. Reno and Carson City were old news. New towns were springing up wherever the miners went . . . Tonopah, Goldfield, Searchlight, Rhyolite.

According to Daniel Mead, in *Loose Change* magazine, "a wandering runt named Frank 'Shorty' Harris took a swipe at a quartz boulder with his pick. As the boulder separated, it exposed a bullfrog-shaped chunk of gold as large as a man's fist." Thus begun the saga of Rhyolite (and The Bullfrog Mine), just a stone's throw from Death Valley.

"The quartz was just full of free gold," Harris said in a 1909 interview with newspaper publisher E.R. Clemens. "Talk about rich! Why, gee whiz, it was great. We took the stuff back to the spring and panned it, and we certainly went straight up. The very first boulder was as rich in gold as anything I had ever seen."

By this time Rhyolite was the third-largest city in Nevada, with a population of 10,000 people and three railroads to serve them. But the gold got harder and harder to find, and soon Rhyolite was just another ghost town. Publisher Clemens closed down the *Rhyolite Herald* and left in 1911, riding a steam locomotive to another developing area in the southern part of Nevada. The place, Spanish for "the meadows," was Las

By 1947, Reno's Virginia Street was firmly established as Nevada's gaming center. Harrah's, now a nationwide operation, started out as a bingo room at this location in 1944. Two years later, Lincoln Fitzgerald's Nevada Club opened down the block; it is still in the same location, and has scarcely changed over the years.

By the early 1940s, Reno's "Biggest-Little-City" sign had been updated to neon. The Reno Club, shown in the previous photograph, finally closed its doors in 1940. Harolds Club—which opened in 1935—took over the property and named it Harolds Roaring Camp.

Vegas.

Nevada had always attracted men with spirit—cattle ranchers, miners, prospectors, gamblers. Yet when the first territorial legislature met in Carson City in 1861, the first thing it did was pass a law prohibiting games of chance. Nevada's men of spirit ignored that law. In 1869, the anti-gambling law was repealed, but that didn't last, either. Four years later, the legislature passed a law prohibiting gambling everywhere but on the second floor of buildings, which was like saying, "Yes, you can," while saying, "No, you can't." Then in 1910, gambling was again ruled illegal in Nevada, and the *San Francisco Examiner* reported smugly that "legalized gambling has drawn its last breath in the United States."

Enter again Nevada's men of spirit, notably one Phil Tobin, a freshman assemblyman from Humboldt County. The year was 1931, and aside from the proposed construction of a dam on the Colorado River, things were looking pretty bleak in Nevada. The state needed tourists, and the legislature came up with two ways to get them. First, it passed a bill changing the residence requirement for divorces from three months to six weeks. Then Phil Tobin stood up on the assembly floor and introduced Assembly Bill 98, better known as the "wide-open gambling bill."

"I had two reasons for introducing that bill," Tobin later remembered. "First, illegal gambling was prevalent. Everyone had a blanket and a deck of cards, and it was getting out of hand. Some of these tinhorn cops were collecting 50 bucks a month for allowing it. Secondly, the state needed revenue. This way we could pick up the money from the license fees for the games."

Tobin himself never gambled, and only visited Las Vegas once during his lifetime. "I don't like gambling," he admitted. "The extent of what I got from introducing the gambling bill was three bottles of Scotch," which he promptly gave away.

March 20, 1931: The Friday edition of Reno's *Nevada State Journal* carried the following items on its front page: President Hoover was spending a vacation at sea. A tornado killed three people in Oklahoma. A racketeer was slain in Los Angeles. A Zenith radio was on sale for $77.50. But the headline across the top of the page said it all: "GAMING, DIVORCE BILLS SIGNED."

And so Nevada entered its modern era of gaming, becoming the only state where people could gamble legally. Most of the nation's press believed Nevada's "experiment" was doomed to failure, and in truth the gambling industry got off to a sluggish start. In fact, the first gaming license in Las Vegas was issued to Northern Club proprietor Mayme Stocker, allowing her to op-

(Next Pages) Welcome to Harolds Club! As you can see in this 1937 photograph, slot machines were not the public's favorite game of chance during the late 1930s. Can you find the dog in this picture?

erate the grand total of two slot machines.

The turning point came when underworld figure Benjamin "Bugsy" Siegel opened the Flamingo outside the city limits of Las Vegas on the highway to Los Angeles. This was Nevada's first major resort, and it radically changed the whole complexion of gambling.

Writer John Scarne, who interviewed Siegel shortly before his assassination in California, had another theory. "I believe," he said, "that his [Siegel's] murder gave the Flamingo so much

(Above) Extensive worldwide advertising put Harolds Club on the map. By the mid-1950s, you could still get a mighty fine 50¢ Tom Collins to sip while playing keno for a $25,000 payoff.

(Right) Harolds Club, under the leadership of ex-carnival barker Harold Smith, began billboard advertising in the late 1930s. Twenty-three hundred light-hearted, cartoon-like signs spanned the United States and other locations throughout the world. Soon everyone knew where Harolds Club was.

(Above) "Make This Four Lanes." The message was clear! Interstate 80 over Donner Summit was the scene of bottle-necked traffic as irritated motorists tried to make their way to Reno from Sacramento and San Francisco. When the snows—commonly reaching depths of 25 feet—closed this road in the wintertime, Reno became a ghost town. "Pappy" Smith initiated the movement to link California and Nevada with a four-lane highway that would stay open year-round.

nationwide publicity that everybody heard about it. Even in death Bugsy Siegel helped turn a chunk of Nevada desert into the now-famous Las Vegas Strip . . . that is unmatched anywhere in the world."

In 1982, Harolds Club (now owned by the Summa Corporation) dropped its western motif and expanded northward to Commercial Row. By this time, Reno was facing heavy competition from Las Vegas, which was quickly becoming the Nevada tourist's end destination.

Historians agree, however, that the state's most innovative gaming pioneers were William Harrah and Harold Smith, both operating out of Reno. Harrah was the first to run his businesses like a corporation, and the first to build a high-rise hotel. His initial venture in gaming was a Reno bingo parlor in 1937; it closed six weeks later. He opened and sold several other bingo clubs until he amassed enough money to buy the Blackout Bar in 1942. Now he was in gambling big-time with

20 slot machines, one craps table and one blackjack table. By the time of his death in 1978, he had created a multi-million dollar empire that included the world-famous Harrah's Club in downtown Reno and Harrah's Tahoe at South Lake Tahoe, as well as the world's largest collection of vintage automobiles.

From equally humble beginnings, Harold Smith opened Harold's Club in 1935 with the following gaming attractions:

One eight-foot penny roulette wheel,

One nickel slot machine,

And one dime slot machine.

"We began to boom in early '41," Smith recalled. "We added games and machines and expanded upwards, downwards and sideways. We couldn't train employees fast enough. Finally I saw my own name in lights, an illuminated sign that soared three stories straight above the sidewalk."

In those days, casinos were dreary places. The lighting was bad, the walls were bare and the clientele (mostly male) were lucky if they didn't trip over an electrical cord or somebody's dog on their way through the casino. Harold Smith changed all that by offering such unheard-of amenities as air conditioning, escalators, elevators, parking garages and 24-hour action. He was the first to hire women dealers, saying that women "would bring gentility and refinement" to casino games.

He was also the first casino owner to advertise, and 2,300 of his famous roadside signs dotted the world's landscape. "Harold's Club Or Bust," the signs read, each decorated with some kind of cartoon character headed for his magical gambling mecca out west.

There were 500 billboards in California alone. In Casablanca, camel riders saw signs reminding them they were only 10,648 miles from Harold's Club. Signs were built at an elephant's eye-level in the Congo, while penguin eye-level signs in the Antarctic reminded brave souls they were only 8,542 miles from Harold's Club.

It paid off big-time. In fact, Smith once joked that the signs generated so much business that neighboring casinos made millions off his customer overflow. True or not, the fact is that Smith's massive advertising campaign gave Harold's Club—and

Reno—national recognition.

One of the secrets of Smith's success was his emphasis on the Wild West. That theme was plastered from one end of his casino to the other: hanging wagon wheels, gun collections, dealers dressed in cowboy outfits and ten-gallon hats. It worked fine for a while, and Reno ("The Biggest Little City In The World") cashed in on it.

By the mid-1980s, however, the whole urban cowboy subject had become boring. As one spokesperson for Harold's Club put it, "We were in the West selling the West to westerners. People didn't like it anymore. The boots hurt and the pants were too tight."

(Below/Right) Nevada's very first gaming license was issued to J.H. Morgan and Mayme V. Stocker (shown here posing in full costume for Helldorado Days in 1934) on March 20, 1931. Ms. Stocker's Northern Club was taken over by a Mr. Stearns in 1933, then by a Mr. Sorber in 1935. Sorber changed the name to the Monte Carlo Club in 1943. A long line of owners followed, including Wilbur Clark (from 1943 to 1945). Later the facility was called Club 15, probably because its address was 15 E. Fremont Street. On September 4, 1970, Don Pettit purchased the property and named it the Coin Castle. Present owner Herb Pastor bought the property July 1, 1977.

STATE OF NEVADA
COUNTY OF
CLARK

No 1

GAMING   LICENSE

NOT TRANSFERABLE

$ $1410.00   Las Vegas, Nevada,_____

____Mayme V. Stocker & J. H. Morgan____ having paid to the License
Collector of Clark County the sum of___$1410.00___ Dollars, is hereby entitled
to conduct a_____Gambling & Slot Machine (2)_____ business at
_____Las Vegas_____ forTHREE MONTHS ending
___June 20th___, 1931, in conformity with and subject to the provisions of law.

COUNTY TREASURER   COUNTY AUDITOR

RECEIVED PAYMENT IN FULL ON ABOVE LICENSE

By_____puty   _____
                                                        SHERIFF

The cards had been dealt, though, and Reno was playing its hand—wooing the same ragged customers that Harold Smith romanced 50 years before. "We didn't offer enough besides gaming," a Reno official said. "People don't want to gamble all the time. We don't have things like Las Vegas, which is pushing theme parks, water parks, golf."

It was like the old joke about the man who went to the doctor, and was told he had only a year to live. The man shrugged. "Well, then, I guess I'll move to Reno."

"Reno?" the doctor cried. "Of all the places in the world, why would you want to spend your last year in Reno?"

The man replied, "Because it will *seem* longer."

In 1932, casinos were strictly a man's domain, as this photograph of the Northern Club in Las Vegas illustrates. Notice the embossed tin ceiling and exposed plumbing.

After gambling was legalized in Nevada, operators wasted no time setting up operations in Las Vegas. On April 1, 1931, the Las Vegas Club opened next door to the Northern Club, as shown in this 1940 photograph. After a series of owners, the Las Vegas Club moved to the corner of Main and Fremont Streets, its present location.

Las Vegas, meanwhile, soared to unprecedented heights as the gaming capital of the world, due mainly to the fact that it was easier for tourists to get there. Before an all-weather four-lane highway was completed, motorists going to Reno took their lives in their hands every time they crossed precarious Donner Summit. The congested two-lane road was slow in the summertime and dangerous in the wintertime. Sometimes snow would be piled so high on the roadway that it had to be blasted away with dynamite before traffic could continue. By

(Above) In 1941, the first resort hotel and casino—the El Rancho—was built on the Los Angeles (L.A.) Highway just south of Las Vegas. It was located on the southwest corner of Sahara Avenue and Las Vegas Boulevard South . . . now known as the Strip. Renamed the El Rancho Vegas in 1944, it burned to the ground in the summer of 1960 and was never rebuilt.

(Below) On October 30, 1942, the second resort hotel was opened on the Strip. Named the Last Frontier, the property—built on five acres of land costing $1,000 an acre—became the New Frontier in 1955.

By 1947, the Las Vegas Club's decor included neon lights, air conditioning and an in-house tobacco stand.

the time the new highway was finished in 1964, Las Vegas was far and away the state's greatest gambling oasis.

In the beginning, however, many people saw Las Vegas not as a future resort, but as another San Fernando Valley of fruit orchards and chicken ranches. In fact, in 1930 the Greater Las Vegas Club issued a prophecy that "truck gardening and fruit growing have an unparalleled future in this fertile spot." Other boosters suggested that fruit canneries would be a chief industry in the town's future.

It was even said that Las Vegas would one day be the center

(Next Pages) The train station on Main Street at the foot of Fremont Street was the birthplace of Las Vegas. This 1941 photograph was taken in front of the train depot, looking east down Fremont Street. Today the Union Plaza Hotel and Casino occupies this site.

In 1946, a former California bellhop named Wilbur Clark decided to build a resort hotel on the Strip. This photograph of the construction site was taken from the rooftop of the Last Frontier.

of the country's wool industry, since the town was closer to the sheep ranches of the West than were the mills of New England. Even as late as 1948 the publisher of the *Las Vegas Review Journal* looked upon Southern Nevada as an industrial complex lying in the shadows of Los Angeles. A.E. Cahlan's forecast was that "Las Vegas can become the Buffalo of the West." (Someone should have told him that the buffalo was practically extinct.)

Few people know this, but in the beginning there were actually two unofficial towns of Las Vegas. The first was settled by prospector J.T. McWilliams in 1905 in the area around the

Here is a happy Wilbur Clark . . . laying bricks? Oh well, there's nothing like a little publicity prior to an official opening. It is generally unknown that Clark held part ownership in other Las Vegas casinos before the opening of the Desert Inn. These included the El Rancho Vegas, the Green Shack, the Player's Club and the Monte Carlo Club.

Las Vegas Ranch. The second was established later the same year on property nearby that was owned by the railroad.

When the railroad conducted its land auction, a mass exodus from McWilliams' townsite along Railroad Street began. Everybody was moving to the new Las Vegas, and the original townsite became a hangout for bums, drifters and others down on their luck. They called it McWilliamstown, and Old Town, and Ragtown.

Wilbur Clark's Desert Inn opened April 14, 1950. He ran out of money before the project was finished, and a group of Las Vegas "associates" lent a helping hand. When Clark couldn't pay back the loan, the Desert Inn had new owners.

In 1955, the Last Frontier gave way to the New Frontier. By this time, big-name entertainment was commonplace at Las Vegas resorts. The city was becoming respectable, and wives were now accompanying their husbands on gambling trips.

Then on September 5, 1905, Ragtown came to a fiery end. Nobody knows how the blaze began, but the entire settlement burned to the ground. *The Las Vegas Times* reported the fire in editorial fashion:

"As the fire swept and blazed and rushed, it left in its trail destruction and ashes of what once had been the scene of vigor and life. It is but to relate the original Las Vegas has had its day. The demon fire gave it the finishing touches. Railroad Street, the once busy business mart, is but ashes. No hope that, Phoenix-like, it will rise again. The fire came, the fire saw, the fire conquered. Thus ended, the 'old town' is but a memory."

A year later, Block 16 was established in Las Vegas, the only area in the town where the sale of liquor was permitted. The best-known attraction in this rowdy district was the Arizona Club, "the niftiest house of joy on the Pacific Coast."

In 1907, electric power came to Las Vegas, and that same

Las Vegas is not only a Disneyland for adults; it can be a bargain as well. For those not content with 99¢ breakfasts, there is downtown's Lady Luck Hotel and Casino. Lady Luck will give you a room, wine and dine you, provide you with limousine service and give you complimentary tickets to almost any show in town. The only thing you have to do is gamble—with Lady Luck.

year the town's first artesian water well was drilled. Electricity, water, a "house of joy"—what more did a town need? As the old saying goes, the rest is history.

All In A Day's Work

IN THE EARLY DAYS of gambling, craps players at an illegal club in Kentucky kept their chips in front of them on the table. During one hot and heavy hand, which had been going on for almost an hour, the dice bounced down the layout—one landing on a three and the other nowhere in sight.

A player at the end of the table, nicknamed the Iceman because he owned the local ice house, looked down to see the missing die lodged between several stacks of his chips. Since he was the only person at the table who could see what the number was, it was up to him to call the roll.

The Iceman had more money in action than any other player at the table and was in the enviable position of calling out whatever number he wished. But he was an honest man, and shaking his head sadly, he announced, "Loser seven," tossing the die back to the stickman. Dice are unpredictable little objects that are liable to land anywhere. Ask a dealer who has been around for a few years, and he can tell you about the time one disappeared down a woman's low-cut dress or up a player's sleeve, or the time one went flying down the table and shattered a woman's "diamond" ring. A player once took a swallow of his drink, then brayed in disgust as he spit out a red ice cube. He looked closer and noticed tiny white spots on it. Handing the die to the dealer he said, "I believe this is yours."

Then there was the player who threw one of the dice off the table just as a man walked by with a cup of coffee in his hand. The man stepped on the die, and both feet flew into the air. He landed flat on his back, still holding the cup of coffee, then got to his feet and kept on walking. He never did find out what he stepped on, but he didn't spill a drop of his coffee.

In 18 years, one dealer said he saw the dice land on top of

each other only twice, and both times were on the same day. Another dealer remembers when a player threw the dice and one of them lodged itself in the rubber molding at the far end of the table. Since the shooter was the only player at the game, the stickman decided to have some fun with the pit boss.

"Call it," he said to the pit boss.

The pit boss, seeing only one die on the table, said to the dealer, "Where is it?"

Pointing with his stick, the dealer showed him the other die embedded in the table molding. "Loser seven," the pit boss said, walking away with a smile. Of course, it wasn't a roll, but it did prove one thing. Pit bosses have a sense of humor, too.

Dice are not the only objects with minds of their own. A woman tossed a $5 chip to the stickman for a proposition bet, and the chip broke in two when it hit the table. The boxman,

Shortly after the railroad arrived in Las Vegas, saloons and gambling establishments set up shop. This 1905 photograph shows a couple of burros escaping the summer heat inside a wood-framed tent building. As the mines petered out, prospectors often set their burros loose to fend for themselves. Today their descendants roam the desert . . . sometimes begging food from tourists traveling Nevada's back roads.

The problem is, our slot machines are just too liberal! This 1980s publicity photo from Harolds Club "proves" that their dollar machines were so loose that shovels and wheelbarrows full of money had to be used to refill them.

who had never seen this happen before, said that moments later the woman threw another $5 chip to the stickman. When it landed on the table, it broke in two.

Roulette balls are liable to go anywhere, as a well-dressed gentleman playing in one of Nevada's plushest casinos will verify. While leaning over the table to place his bet, the croupier gave the roulette ball a good hard spin. The ball rocketed off the wheel, striking the gentleman in the most tender and private of places. You might say this was one man who didn't have a ball in Las Vegas.

One of the biggest peeves of all dealers is a noisy player. At a blackjack table one day there was a woman who talked so incessantly that the dealer finally said to her with a wave of his hand, "I'll bet you can't keep quiet until I go on my break." With that, she clamped her lips together and never said another word.

Fifteen minutes later the dealer got his break, but as he turned to leave the table the woman finally spoke up again. "Wait a minute," she cried. "Where's my hundred dollars?"

"What hundred dollars?" the dealer asked blankly.

"You bet me I couldn't keep quiet until you went on your break, and you pointed at a $100 chip, and *I want my hundred dollars!*"

Hearing the commotion, the floorman came rushing up. "What seems to be the problem, ma'am?"

"This dealer bet me a hundred dollars I couldn't keep quiet until he went on his break, and I WANT MY HUNDRED DOLLARS!!"

The casino manager had to settle the dispute and there was only one way to do it. He gave the woman a hundred dollars.

On another occasion, a young man approached the casino manager with the following sad story. He had been gambling all day, he said, and finally accumulated one $100 chip. As he was going to the cashier's cage to cash it, the chip fell from his hand and rolled out of sight. The casino manager, who must rely on gut feelings in such matters, believed the young man to be telling the truth and gave him another $100 chip.

Of course, there are always other ways to make money. Security guards at a plush Strip resort nabbed two men that were charging tourists $5 a head to use the casino's people mover. The man who tipped off security had told the two, "I came here on the people mover yesterday and nobody charged me." The men replied, "That's because we were sick yesterday."

Caesars Palace executive Glenn Gordon tells one of the strangest stories in Las Vegas folklore. According to Gordon, it happened when he worked at the Fremont Hotel. A blind man,

---

(Right) Now you've seen the celebrated "floating craps game." It was all part of the fun in the summer of 1953 at the Sands Hotel swimming pool.

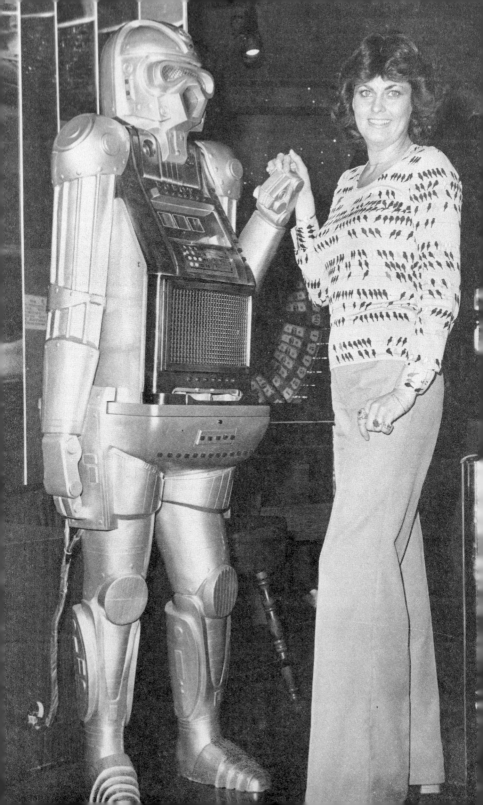

(Left) It's Robbie the Robot, a slot machine that talks! Built by the late John Caler for the Orbit Inn of Las Vegas, Robbie's tummy was a real slot machine. He talked you into playing, and kept talking while you played. The Orbit Inn, which opened in 1964, went through several owners and finally closed its doors for good in 1987. It is not known whether Robbie wandered away or was kidnapped by Darth Vader.

accompanied by his seeing-eye dog, approached the Big 6 wheel. From a blue bag strapped to the dog's body, the man retrieved a stack of bills which he exchanged for chips. Then he pushed the chips in front of the dog, who by this time had jumped upon a stool next to the blind man. While the man dictated to the dealer which numbers he wanted to bet, the dog cocked its head and watched the wheel turn. If the wheel stopped on one of the numbers which the blind man bet, the dog barked excitedly. If the wheel stopped on the joker, which paid 40 to one, the dog would howl.

After an hour of this, the blind man and his dog had won several hundred dollars. Hoping to entice the pair to stay until the casino won the money back, the pit boss asked the blind man if he would like to have dinner in the coffee shop. The blind man declined the offer but said, "You could bring my dog a nice bone if it's not too much trouble."

A few moments later the waiter appeared with a plate. On the plate was a slice of prime rib, cut into bite-sized pieces, surrounding the biggest bone the dog had ever seen.

When the dog finished his meal, he hopped off the stool and led the blind man to the cashier's cage. The blind man's winnings were counted out, with the money placed inside the dog's blue bag. Then the dog led the blind man out of the casino, and another Las Vegas success story was launched.

All You Can Eat

FIRST THE DINNER SHOWS in Las Vegas be-
gan to get phased out. Then slot machines overtook the table
games. Now the latest episode in the ever-changing Las Vegas
soap opera: the slow demise of the gourmet restaurant.

Today in Las Vegas it is the age of the buffet, and no wonder. In some candle-lit gourmet restaurants, prices are not even
listed on the menu—which is like playing Russian roulette
with a knife and fork. The thinking seems to be that if you've
got to ask what it costs for the Foie de Veau Saute Gigi, then
you're better off hitting McDonald's.

The following story will prove my point. A friend of mine is
a newspaper reporter, and one of the perks of his job is getting
a free meal every once in a while at some fancy eating estab-
lishment. On one such occasion, he and his wife invited another couple to join them at a Chinese restaurant inside a Strip
casino, and the sumptuous meal was awaited by all with eager
anticipation.

The waiter snapped to attention as he presented the velvet-
encased menu. "May I suggest a variety of dishes which the
chef will prepare personally?" he asked.

"Sounds good to me," my friend replied, the other three at
the table nodding in agreement.

"And perhaps a bottle of vintage Bordeaux from our wine
cellar?"

Well, it was a wonderful dinner, my friend admitted later.
The food was excellent, the wine was excellent, and the service
was excellent. Yes indeed, everything was first cabin all the way.
Then the check arrived, which came to $600! Fortunately, it
was stamped "complimentary," else my friend would have embarrassed the waiter, the wine steward and his three dinner

companions by having a coronary right there in the restaurant.

Six hundred dollars! You could buy a used car for $600. You could buy five acres of land in Pahrump for $600. You could spend 15 minutes with a lawyer for $600.

My friend let out a sigh of relief, which suddenly changed to a gasp of despair. The tip! He was going to have to leave a tip. He and his friends emptied their respective pockets and purses, coming up with the grand total of $62. Never mind the standard suggested tip of 15 to 20 percent. In this case, the

The buffet at Arizona Charlie's in Las Vegas is one of the best bargains in town. Even better, join Arizona Charlie's birthday club. Then on your birthday you'll get a historic picture postcard inviting you and a friend to the buffet . . . all on the house!

waiter was lucky to get 10 percent.

Of course, when you go to a Las Vegas buffet, you don't hobnob with the same type of clientele as you find at gourmet restaurants. In gourmet restaurants, jackets and ties are required. In buffets, shoes and shirts are required.

As this goes to press, there are 42 buffets in and around Las Vegas, with breakfasts averaging about $3 and dinners about $10. Beverages are not included at some buffets; at others you get your choice of drinks. Depending on the buffet you choose, these range from coffee, tea, milk, soft drinks, wine, beer and frozen cocktails to even champagne.

Children under 12 eat for half-price in some buffets, children anywhere from 4 to 10 get their meals for half-price in others. At Palace Station, children under 12 get $1 off their meals, children under 4 eat free at the Rio, children under 7 eat for half-price at the Sahara, while at the Showboat a kid practically has to be an adult to figure out the price structure. Lunch for adults is $4.45, for children under 12 it's $3.95. Dinner is $6.45 for adults, $4.95 for children under 12. Weekend brunch is $5.45 for adults, and $4.45 for children under 12.

With all the competition for couples with children, it's surprising that some casino hasn't geared its advertising toward couples *without* children. After all, this takes in about half the general population, which would probably beat a path to a buffet which advertised:

CHILDREN UNDER 12 NOT ALLOWED

Another point to remember is that Las Vegas buffets are unlike any other buffets in the world. They are gastronomical emporiums with appropriate names like Wild West Buffet, International Buffet, Big Kitchen Buffet, Sultan's Buffet, Round Table Buffet, Paradise Buffet, El Grande Buffet, Emperor's Buffet, Carnival Buffet, Uptown Buffet, Captain's Buffet, Warehouse Buffet, and of course The Buffet. Caesars Palace has the Palatium Buffet, which (at $6.50) is the most expensive breakfast spot on the buffet circuit. Still, it draws its share of diners, most of whom have no idea what Palatium even means. One tourist was overheard saying to friends, "Hey, why don't we try this Plati-

(Right) Stepping up in the world of all-you-can-eat will bring you to the carving station at the Stardust Hotel's buffet. The Strip casino advertises itself as "A Quarter Mile of Fun." But after a bout with this buffet, you won't be able to walk that far. Las Vegas has buffets for every taste and pocketbook.

---

num Buffet?"

The cheapest breakfast buffet (at $2.99) is at Circus Circus, which also has the cheapest dinner buffet ($3.99). The most expensive dinner buffet is at the Sands, which charges $17.95 a person and includes three live Maine lobsters. At one time, there was no limit on the number of lobsters one could consume at the Sands, then somebody ate 14 of them and that was the end of that.

This seems to be a universal problem at Las Vegas buffets. If the owner isn't careful, people will eat him right out of business. Vacation Village once advertised all the crab legs you could eat for $7.95. They might as well have thrown a live chicken into a pond full of crocodiles. At last report, the price was $11.95, with a two-pound limit—including shells.

Most people have very sensible eating habits, but it's a different story when they get to the head of a buffet line. Then it's every man for himself, with plates piled so high that they need periscopes to find the way back to their tables. Buffet managers are resigned to such sights, and usually just unlock the doors at opening time and dive out of the way.

But the buffets draw the people, who have to go through the casino, and that's what it is all about. Except for the cost of the food, it's a fairly inexpensive proposition as far as the hotels are concerned. The plates are cheap, the silverware is cheap, and the only upkeep involved is mopping the floors and changing the light bulbs.

Gourmet restaurants run the hazard of people breaking plates ($65 apiece) and stealing gold-plated silverware ($90 a set). At a buffet, you're lucky if you can find a fork with all the tines pointed in the same direction. Of course, buffets do have their share of problems. One buffet in Las Vegas was losing $2,000 worth of silverware a month, which caused management to become quite concerned. After an investigation, it was

discovered that the busboys were the culprits. When clearing the tables, they would deposit the dirty plates in the appropriate bins. As for the silverware, they just tossed it into the trash can. Hey, the tables got cleaned in record time, didn't they? What did these bosses want?˙

At any rate, buffets seem to be the wave of the future in Las Vegas. One word of caution, however. Don't be like the man who called a buffet the day after consuming half his weight in rolls, eggs, blintzes, cheeses, fried chicken, salad, fruit, pasta, mashed potatoes, corn on the cob, roast beef, ham steaks, barbecued ribs, pastries, ice cream and champagne. "You guys better check your food," he said. "I woke up this morning sick as a dog."

Video Poker Mania

THERE ARE MORE PEOPLE playing in Las Vegas, but they are playing slot machines. So says Chairman Bill Bible of the Nevada Gaming Control Board. Recent figures back up Bible's statement. A study by the Las Vegas Convention and Visitors Authority shows that 71 percent of tourists who gamble play some type of slot machine, while only 29 percent opted for table games such as blackjack or craps.

So what happened? Twenty years ago slot machines were considered the wayward stepchild of the gaming industry, and the big money was won or lost on the green felt tables. Then a host of things happened almost at once. The economy took a nose-dive; corporations moved into Las Vegas and started courting middle-class America; computer chips were perfected, which allowed slot machines to set up varied and more frequent jackpots; video screens were developed to replace slot machine reels; and a slot machine engineer perfected a video poker machine.

According to Dwight Crevelt in his book *Video Poker Mania,* (Gollehon Press) the innovation of video poker was the most significant contribution of all. "It combines the skill of an age-old game of draw poker with the ease of playing a slot machine," he writes. Consequently, "It is now deemed more respectable to participate in a game of video poker than to pour money down the hungry gullet of a plain slot machine. Making choices gives players a sensation of control and power over the outcome; they are not entirely at the machine's mercy."

When video poker was first introduced, it was tried on an experimental basis at Sam's Town in Las Vegas. The industry was astounded by the results. Players were waiting in line for a spot at one of the twelve machines, itching to try their skill

Progressive video poker machines pay a certain percentage of each coin played into a constantly-growing jackpot. This photograph shows a carousel of video poker machines at the Gold Strike Casino outside Boulder City. Boulder City was born when construction of Boulder Dam began. At that time, the residents decided gambling should be kept out of their community. To this day, gambling is not allowed within the city limits.

against modern technology. It is a love affair that has never waned, with 45 percent of all gamblers now hooked on video poker.

I caught up with Dwight Crevelt at International Game Technology, where he is manager of technical support for IGT's Las Vegas engineering department. Crevelt has a list of credits a mile long. He co-authored the book "Slot Machine Mania," helped design and engineer the slot player tracking system, developed the Memory Comparator to verify slot payouts, and has worked for over 20 years with such slot manufacturers as EDT, Gamex and Mills-Jennings.

When I asked Crevelt why IGT's stock had gone through the roof ($58 a share as this was written), he said, "There is a giant boom in the gaming market. We've got casino gambling on Indian reservations, with 40 or 50 tribes that have signed to build casinos. There's riverboat gambling, with ten boats authorized in Illinois, and three or four more pending in Iowa. Riverboat gambling has just been legalized in Missouri. Mississippi has six or seven operating and another half dozen pending, and Louisiana has twelve boats authorized. Every one of those is 400 to 500 machines, and IGT is getting up to 90 percent of that market.

"Worldwide, we've just opened an office in Europe. We've got a manufacturing facility in Canada for both gaming machines and video lottery. There are three quarters of a million slot machines in Japan, and that country expects to add another 250,000 in the next two years. Compare that to the United States, where there are only 300,000 slot machines in the entire country. So Japan is a huge market," Crevelt said. "There is also Australia, Europe, Russia, Africa, South America. And they all want machines."

In Crevelt's opinion, slot machines have become popular because they are less intimidating than table games, and in many ways are more entertaining. "The picture tube in front of you is like a TV tube, and you just get mesmerized," he said. As a result, most resorts generate at least 60 percent of their revenue from slot machines, with half of that coming from quarter machines. Hence, the average number of slot machines in each casino has mushroomed from 500 to nearly 3,000 in the last ten years. In other words, as Crevelt explained, "What the casinos are doing is gearing themselves toward the middle income customers. They get a little bit from everybody, and make it up in volume."

That doesn't mean that table games are being phased out in Las Vegas. "There will always be table games," Crevelt said. "It's the traditional form of gambling, and in the United States that will continue. It's that atmosphere and involvement in the live game that people like. Slot machines are less social, more of a one-on-one situation, and they're popular in their own right. But table games are here to stay."

Yet it is the slot machine that is revolutionizing the casino industry, and it is video poker that is revolutionizing the slot machine. The main reason for this, according to Crevelt, is because video poker machines give a player the ability to choose the best payback percentage. "When you walk up to a video poker machine, you know the payback percentage by looking at the award glass. It's the only machine that gives you that information."

The payback percentage can vary, but the smart player will find the machine with a 6-9 payback—which means the machine pays six coins (per coin played) for a flush and nine coins for a full house.

Even though only 38 percent of all players insert the maximum number of coins, Crevelt insists it is the only way to play. "You should always play the maximum number of coins because there is a bonus when you win, and on a slot machine that bonus can be up to five percent of the payback on that machine. If you're not playing the maximum number of coins, you're giving five percent of your money right back to the casino." Crevelt admitted that video poker machines are going to hold within two to three percent of what they are programmed to hold, but said, "If you play an intelligent game, using optimum strategy, you can get closer to that theoretical payback." On a $1 video poker machine, the jackpot can be $4,000 and more.

Strategy is the key ingredient in winning at video poker, and in his book Crevelt offers three different strategies. The first is the royal strategy, where the player will discard jacks or better or two pair in order to try for a royal flush. The second is the conservative strategy, where the player will keep winning hands and try to draw to them. The third is the optimum strategy, recommended by Crevelt as getting the maximum return for money invested, where the player will discard jacks or better but keep two pair.

Crevelt dispelled a lot of myths about slot machines, and added impetus to another. "One of the things you find," he said, "is that machines run in streaks. They do have hot streaks and cold streaks." But in his book *Video Poker Mania*, Crevelt debunked the following myth conceptions:

A machine is never ready to hit; each play is independent of every other play.

The change person cannot tell you when a machine is due to hit; no one in the casino knows any more than you do.

Just because a machine hits right after you walk away from it doesn't mean you would have won; this is controlled by the random number generator inside the machine (which chooses a new hand every 1,000th of a second) and the machine's microprocessor (which controls the machine's timing).

Some other tips from Crevelt's book:

Set time limits when you play; set cash limits and stick to them; cash out your credits frequently; keep records of wins and losses for tax purposes (winnings of $1,200 or more are reported to the IRS by the casino); and—most importantly—quit while you're ahead.

This is easier said than done, and maybe that is what makes video poker so addicting. In fact, video poker was described in *USA Today* as "the crack cocaine of the gaming industry." Statistically, Crevelt writes that 95.5 percent of women gamblers treated at one institution played only video poker. A survey taken among 52 women members of Gamblers Anonymous showed that 47 were addicted to video poker machines. Over 50 percent of male members were also video poker addicts.

So it is no surprise that Crevelt ends his book by writing:

"Video poker, like any other game of chance, should not be

(Left) For many, video poker is the most captivating game in the casino. Many persons from all walks of life have been motivated to research and analyze the game in an effort to obtain maximum odds while playing. Pictured above is one of the world's authorities on video poker in one of his favorite casinos—the Gold Coast, where the machines have been statistically friendly over the years. Philosophically stated, some nights the casino wins, and some nights the player wins. But statistically, it is the long haul that really matters. A forthcoming book by Robert N. Geddes will address winning strategies for video poker players.

construed as a golden road to the land of wealth and happiness. Treat it as a game or expensive hobby. For every player who attains royal status, there are hundreds of thousands who are never touched by that magic wand."

Signs

FINDING A GOOD RESTAURANT or a place to spend the night must have been a genuine nightmare back in biblical times. "Go past the parting of the sea, veer to the right when you get to the burning bush and take the first turn-off after you come to the lion's den. You can't miss it."

Then came electricity and the discovery of neon. For Las Vegas, the future was as rosy as a 50,000 watt light bulb. The first electrical giant was Vegas Vic, the lanky cowboy tipping his hat at the old downtown Pioneer Club. Unfortunately, he was also bawling, "Howdy Partner" every 15 seconds. Finally, a disgruntled actor trying to sleep in a nearby hotel room could stand it no longer, and started taking pot shots at old Vic with his Winchester. Vic still tips his hat from time to time, but he quit talking shortly after his run-in with Lee Marvin.

Maybe Vegas Vic is just mad because he has so much competition these days. At Circus Circus, there is Lucky the Clown, a 13-story monstrosity that makes Vic look like a pip-squeak. Personally, I like Lucky, but more for sentimental reasons than anything else. He reminds me of how my uncle used to dress on Saturday nights.

The Stardust built a neon sign that was so magnificent it could be seen from three miles away. Seven thousand feet of neon tubing and 11,000 light bulbs were required just to spell out the word "STARDUST." Later the sign was rebuilt, using 30 tons of paint, steel and concrete. Eighteen stories tall and dotted by 40,000 light bulbs, the sign is said to use enough electricity to light up a city of 30,000 people. And to think, I used to get bawled out for leaving the porch light on.

Another sign with a lot of light bulbs is at the Las Vegas Hilton, and I decided to count them one night after consuming

(Left) The most famous sign in Las Vegas is Vegas Vic, who waves "Howdy Partner" from above the Pioneer Casino in downtown Las Vegas. One day Vic broke his waving arm. "Too bad," management said. "Medical treatment is too expensive." Residents and tourists cried out loudly, and in 1993 management reluctantly sent for the medics. Vegas Vic's arm was repaired, and now he happily waves again.

four margaritas in a nearby Mexican restaurant. "One thousand, three hundred and twelve—one thousand, three hundred and thirteen—one thousand, three hundred and . . ." "Barney, who do you like in the play-offs this year?" Damn. "One—two—three—four . . ."

The 125-foot high marquee at the Rio has 12,930 feet of neon tubing and 5,460 light bulbs, and in a recent survey was voted the best neon sign in Las Vegas. For one thing, it features a couple of gigantic maracas that shake constantly, nestled among a colorful cluster of huge sheet metal leaves and Fiberglas strands of confetti. The only problem is that everyone is so busy looking at the sign that nobody goes inside the casino.

My favorite sign was the one in front of the Dunes Hotel. It was shaped like a great big ace of spades, with orange and red lights rippling up the sides like a gentle electrical breeze. Suddenly the colors softly merged together into an almost ethereal glow, and then the lights blinked off as the melody began anew.

Just down the Strip is the Flamingo, with a sign out front that is almost like watching a movie on the Playboy channel. Colors rippling upward—merging—shudder, shudder, shudder. Poor Bugsy, what would he think of it all?

The sign in front of Caesars Palace is computerized, and is more like an electronic scoreboard than a Las Vegas marquee. BE A - blink - MILLION DOLLAR - blink - BABY ON - blink - CAESARS - blink - PALACE - blink - MILLION DOLLAR - blink - SLOT MACHINES - blink - AT - blink - CAESARS - blink - PALACE - blink. No wonder Nero started playing the fiddle when Rome burned; he went blinking crazy!

I used to like the sign at the Sands. It was about the size of a Volvo, and never did look like it was finished. "SANDS" was scrawled in longhand across the top, and "A Place In The Sun" was down at the bottom. The marquee was more like a telegram than a billboard, but it told you what you needed to know.

★ ★ ★ ★ ★ ★ ★ ★ ★ ★ ★

Jack Entratter
Presents
DEAN MARTIN
Maybe Frank Maybe Sammy

★ ★ ★ ★ ★ ★ ★ ★ ★ ★ ★

It's a sign-builder's dream come true; it's what the fabulous Las Vegas Strip looked like in 1977.

Have you driven down the Las Vegas Strip recently? Try reading the marquee at Bally's some night while weaving through slow-moving traffic and jaywalking pedestrians:

Bally's Celebrity Room—Dean Martin
Musical Director Ken Lane, The Golddiggers
Catch A Rising Star, Comedy Music Club
Margaret Smith, Dwayne Cunningham, Gary Lazer
Musical Director Steve Beyer
Nightly Except Wednesday, 7:30 P.M., 11 P.M.
Don Arden's JUBILEE
Color, Motion & Music—Over 100 Performers
Pro Boxing, Two-Time Heavyweight Champion
Tim Weatherspoon VS. Larry Alexander
$10,000 Top Pay on 97% $1 Slots
Free Daily Slot Tournament—$1,000 In Cash
Double Deck 21

Nobody reads all that stuff. Why, just the other day I was driving past Palace Station, and this was on their marquee in five-foot high letters:

"$1,000,000 IN CASH GIVEN AWAY FREE!"

I was the only person who slammed on his brakes.

Slide Show

GLAD YOU COULD STOP over, Bob. We nearly gave up on you, but come in, come in. You're just in time to see the vacation slides we took last month. Wilma, you want to get the lights?

Here's my father-in-law, standing next to this Indian fellow we met at the Nevada state line. We got to talking with him after we bought pretty near two hundred dollars worth of jewelry, and come to find out he is the direct descendant of the Paiute chief who founded Las Vegas back in 1500, or at least so he said. That was about the year Wilma's mother was born. Just kidding, honey, is the coffee ready yet?

CLICK. This one shows the Colorado River, sort of the lifeline of the whole Southwest. That's Wilma in the two-piece there. Hey Bob, knock off them woof whistles, or did you want a knuckle sandwich with that coffee?

CLICK. Here's the Grand Canyon, discovered back in 15-something, according to the tour guide. Funny thing is, some bird named Coronado discovered most of this stuff—the Colorado River, the Grand Canyon, the Mohave Desert. And the only thing that ever got named for him was some shopping center down near San Diego.

CLICK. That's Hoover Dam, and there's our station wagon next to the railing. The picture would've come out a whole lot better if I'd used a flashbulb, but you can still make out most of it.

CLICK. Here's one of them cat houses up in Pahrump. Whoops, how did that get in there? Ha, ha, Wilma, check on that coffee real quick, will you? I think I hear it boiling.

CLICK. Now here we're coming into Las Vegas. That's part of Caesars Palace over there on the left, and behind it is part of the Mirage. On the right is Bally's, which is supposed to be about the biggest hotel in the world. Is that right, honey, or did the man tell us it was the Hilton? Well, we've got the Hilton in the other batch, so you can decide for yourself.

CLICK. This is the inside of the Flamingo. We had no idea you weren't supposed to take pictures inside these places, and that big face you see here belongs to one of the security guards. He got downright hostile, like we was trying to steal something, for crying out loud. Nearly scared the kids senseless, and then we come to find out they weren't supposed to be in there either. Seems to me they ought to give you some kind of rule book when you get to Las Vegas, so you don't look like a blasted idiot every time you turn around.

CLICK. You recognize these fellows? The one frowning is Dean Martin and the one shaking his fist is Frank Sinatra. That's me in the middle. We just happened to spot 'em in the restaurant, and hell, they're people just like you and me. I gave the camera to Wilma, and she took the picture just as I sneaked up behind them. I would've got their autographs but they was both holding silverware at the time.

CLICK. Here's our station wagon in front of the Desert Inn. I jumped out of the car at a red light to take this picture, and accidentally locked my keys inside. Yeah, Bob, well it ain't that funny. Wilma and the kids was trapped in there for almost an hour.

CLICK. This is the swimming pool at the Tropicana. I had Wilma get up on the high diving board to take this shot, and that's me in the red shorts over there by the concession stand. I wasn't waving at the camera, I was just trying to get her closer to the edge so she could get a better picture.

CLICK. This is the swimming pool at the Tropicana from underwater. Wilma got just a little too close to the edge of the diving board, bless her heart.

CLICK. That's me at Circus Circus. They had some peckerwood in there guessing your occupation for five dollars. He said I was a farmer, and when I told him I was in the insurance business he give us this set of plastic coasters. So I give him another five, and had him try to guess my father-in-law's occupation. He said farmer again, and we got some more coast-ers. It's a wonder them people can stay in business.

CLICK. Here's a sort of aerial shot of downtown Las Vegas, what they call Gritty Gulch, or something like that. The reason it's a little blurry is because I was holding Wilma out the hotel window to take the picture, and my darned foot slipped. Everything turned out all right, though. It was just a sprain.

CLICK. Here's one you'll like, Bob. Bob? Hey, you ain't leaving already, are you? Well, all right, but we've got aspirin in the medicine cabinet. I understand, I get 'em myself, but come back soon. You haven't even seen Reno yet.

CLICK.

Tourist Beware

A FEW YEARS AGO, there was a seafood restaurant in Las Vegas that advertised fresh lobster on its menu for only $4.95. Tourists would line up at the door for this sensational bargain, only to discover when the bill came that the lobster was $4.95 an ounce! Complaints by the hundreds were dutifully filed with the Better Business Bureau, but as Bureau Director Paul Nutter explained, "The price was right there on the menu. Of course, you needed a flashlight and a magnifying glass to read it, but the price was there in small print."

The restaurant burned to the ground shortly afterwards, but the owners are getting the last laugh. They built an even larger restaurant, where the price of their lobster dinners isn't even listed. The more prudent diners will ask the waiter how much the lobster is, and then learn there is a three-pound per person minimum—at $18.95 a pound. It may not be a rip-off, but it is enough to send a tourist home with a bad taste in his mouth.

Or how about the Las Vegas resort that recently advertised a lounge show called "The Great Pretenders." On the marquee in bold black letters was the price: $12.95 per person. The marquee neglected to add there was also a two-drink minimum, which nudged the cost per person up to $23.25—or almost twice the advertised price.

Before commercial air service made Las Vegas easily accessible to tourists, Californians had to drive into Nevada over 4,731-foot Halloran Pass. Paul Nutter explains what would happen. "The engines would overheat and a tow truck would haul you 72 miles to a gangster garage that would tear down your engine. You had a huge towing bill, your engine was laying in pieces in some strange garage, and so you went to the Better Business Bureau. These places used to slash tires, slice

Covered with kisses, this is Cheetah's Topless Lounge in Las Vegas. Although prostitution is legal in most rural counties of Nevada, it is strictly prohibited in Las Vegas (Clark County). So don't de duped by promises of sexual fantasy. The girls are there—but for the eyes only!

fan belts—especially cars with out-of-state license plates or women drivers. But thankfully those days are gone."

Nutter chuckled as he recalled how tourists were at the mercy of cab drivers once they finally made it to Las Vegas. "They'd go on some of the damnedest taxi rides you've ever seen in your life. And I haven't got enough fingers on my hands to count the number of people who used to ask me to point out a gangster to them. But the morals of this country have changed, and things in Las Vegas are pretty well under control now."

Or are they? According to Lieutenant Bill Young, head of Metro's Vice Section, at least 50 complaints a week are still being filed against local sex tease clubs that promise naughty girls and private ecstasies. Unsuspecting male tourists, many of whom think prostitution is legal in Las Vegas, pay up to $40 to get inside such iniquitous places as Nasty's, Chaser's and the Black Garter—with half of that money being kicked back to the cab driver that brought them there.

"The girls are nude, the music is loud, the room is dark. And the girls lay this song and dance on you about how they'd like to sell you this bottle of non-alcoholic wine, telling you that if you buy it you'll get to party in another room with the girl of your choice. They start the price out on this bottle of wine at three or four thousand dollars, then they work their way down until the price is only two or three hundred. A lot of guys succumb to the pressure and buy a bottle. Then the girls take you to the back room, and they start bull shitting with you for a little while. Fifteen minutes later they say, 'Oh, our time's up. You need to buy another bottle of wine.'"

By now the hook is in place. If the customer balks, in come the warm towels, the lotions, the condoms. "The girls flat-out tell you," Young says, "that they're going to do whatever you want, and you think you're going to have this great sexual orgy. But as soon as your money runs out, two big bouncers come in and say, 'The party's over.' And out the door you go."

These sex clubs have been hard to regulate, since they don't offer gambling, liquor, or anything else for that matter. Recent regulations, however, will make it harder for these clubs to stay in business, since extensive background checks on all applicants are now required. As one county commissioner put it, "I don't think we can stomp out all the cockroaches in this community, but I think we ought to be able to turn on the lights so they all run for cover."

Still, it is hard to get past a street corner downtown without passing a rack of sleazy magazines. There's everything inside them from *Body Snatchers* to *Girls From Hell*, and personal ads that would make a sailor blush. Even the Centel yellow pages are not immune, with one recent issue sporting 47 pages (at up to $2,500 per month per page) of nude dancers, exotic strippers, belly dancers and bachelorette strip-o-grams.

It brings back memories of a time when Las Vegas was Sin City U.S.A. "Years ago, that was the image Vegas wanted to project," admits Bill Young of Metro. "But now they're trying to make it more of a family-oriented tourist destination, and this just isn't good for business."

Even so, Las Vegas remains one of ten cities in the country considered to be the hub of the prostitution circuit. "The trouble with these prostitutes," Young says, "is that they're not local girls, so they don't have anything to lose. Generally, they would rather steal than make money at prostitution."

Here's how one of them works. She injects ground-up sleeping pills mixed with water into an empty Visine bottle. Then she looks for a man who fits the criteria of a high roller: expensive jewelry, nice clothes, etc. "That's the kind of guy she wants to hook up with," Young says. "And in some instances, the girl won't even appear to be a prostitute. She'll strike up a conversation with a guy who's by himself and maybe had a few drinks. He doesn't think anything of it, because the girl hasn't mentioned sex. She tells him she's a schoolteacher in Las Vegas on vacation, and kind of bored. They have a few drinks together, and of course later in the evening he asks her if she would like to go up to his room and get a back massage, or watch TV, or whatever line he uses."

Once they are in the room, the girl waits for an opportune moment to squirt the sleeping pill solution into the man's drink. "And the guy is out. When he comes to, 16 or 20 hours later, everything's gone. All his money, credit cards, whatever she can take. And the subject of prostitution never even came up. This," says Young, "is the most serious and dangerous thing going on in Las Vegas today."

All in all, between three and four hundred hookers are arrested each month in Las Vegas, and the scariest part of it is that one in 20 of those has the AIDS virus. "Most of those," Young concedes, "are the real low-life downtown hookers, who would rather have a piece of rock cocaine than a $20 bill."

There are a dozen topless clubs in Las Vegas, most of which cater to conventioneers. Since 88 percent of all convention people are males, there is usually standing room only at such places as the Palomino Club, Olympic Garden, the Pussycat and the Can-Can Room. A $20 bill will get you inside most of these jiggle-joints, but beware of private "mini-shows" that can cost another $40 to $90.

When a large convention hits Las Vegas, more than 200 out-of-state prostitutes will converge on the city. Metro can deal with that. But a major sporting event, such as a championship boxing match, is another story. "It's unbelievable the scum that comes to town just to rip the fight fans off," Young says. Up to 5,000 thieves, prostitutes and professional pickpockets hit town, and their target is anybody with cash.

So what can you do to protect yourself? "Don't carry large sums of money," advises Bill Young. Paul Nutter of the Better Business Bureau gives the same advice. "Don't leave valuables in your hotel room," he admonishes. "If you do, you're out of luck."

A Las Vegas casino executive suggests that you establish a line of credit at the hotel where you are staying. It only takes a few moments while the hotel verifies your credit with your hometown bank. Then when you want money to gamble, simply take a marker at the table. This way you don't have to carry a wallet full of cash, and it also helps you qualify for such casino perks as free meals and discounted room rates.

The rest of it "all comes down to expectations," Nutter says. "Bob Stupak's literature and wide-angle photos show Vegas World next to the Sahara Hotel. When Mr. and Mrs. Iowa see the beautiful brochure, then come to Las Vegas . . ." Well, they're in for a shock. It's the same for chartered tours that ferry passengers to such scenic wonders as the Grand Canyon and man-made Lake Mead.

"We had a tourist complain about the Grand Canyon," Nutter laughs. "I don't know what he was expecting to see, but he said it was nothing but a big hole in the ground."

Barflies

IF YOU WANT TO LEARN to shoot craps, or if you are just nosing around for a good story, the best time to haunt a casino is late at night or mid-afternoon. The grinders are ground down by then, and it's still too early for the dinner crowd. Paste a smile on your face, and dress casually. For some reason, casino people don't trust strangers wearing dark suits and wingtips.

Bartenders are a great source of material. Spend one sleepy afternoon with a good bartender and you've got enough juicy stuff to write a bestseller. The one I met went by the name of Dan, but he didn't start talking until a $20 bill hit the counter. "Well, we had a fellow in here about a month ago," he started, "who didn't have a face."

"What do you mean, he didn't have a face?"

"Just what I said. No nose, no eyebrows, no jaw, one ear completely gone, and you couldn't tell about his hair because he was wearing a baseball cap. He'd been in a mine explosion, but the funny thing was that nobody even blinked when they saw him. In fact, every woman who walked by would stop and ask him what happened. You know, like it was something they saw every day of the week."

"Hmm, interesting. Hey, Dan, put a head on this beer, will you?"

Dan filled my glass and slid a clean ashtray in front of me. "Then there was the time a customer came in here and ordered a martini and a pack of cigarettes. 'And make it snappy,' he tells me. 'I've got to be at the health club in 15 minutes.'"

"That's a good one," I acknowledged, reaching into a pocket for my notebook. Dan left to mix something on a blender, while a heavy-set man two seats over leaned in my direction.

"I've got a story for you," he said, his voice barely audible over the racket. "But don't use my name." I nodded impatiently, trying to figure out how I was supposed to know his name in the first place. He popped a couple of peanuts in his mouth, and I fought the urge to dive for cover as he started to talk.

Want to know what's happening in Las Vegas? Talk to a bartender. This cocktail lounge is at the Stardust.

"I used to be casino manager at a place downtown, and at the time we had the best Chinese food on Fremont. Well, one night this fella takes it on the duffy after eating the lobster Cantonese, which was the most expensive thing on the menu. The security guard grabbed him, whacked him, and brought him to my office.

"The fella says, 'Mister, you're not going to throw me in jail, are you?' I said, 'Well, why shouldn't I?' And he says, 'Because I lost $600 tonight.' I said, 'Six hundred dollars? Where'd you lose $600?' And he says, 'Across the street at the Lucky Club.' I said, 'Well, why didn't you eat over there?' And he says, 'Because the food is better here.'"

This brought guffaws from a red-faced gentleman immediately to my left, who had been staring intently at a blank television screen for the past half hour. "Food's better here," he repeated, accentuating the punch line with a loud snort. "Only thing he ever bought's probably the four and ten."

I gave Red Face a grin, as if I knew what the devil he was talking about, and he answered with another snort. By this time Dan was back, wiping a clean glass with a dirty towel. I dug out a ten and put it on the counter next to where my twenty used to be. "Another round for these gentlemen," I said, and the casino manager suddenly graduated from beer to brandy. "Thank you, sir," he said in a gentle voice. "It does get mighty cold at night." Then he studied his glass, as though he were looking into a crystal ball, and maybe he was at that.

Meanwhile, Red Face had ordered two Buds, one for each mitt, and he was glued to the TV screen again. I swiveled my stool around and checked out two girls at the dice table. Probably airline stewardesses, I guessed, because the dealers' eyes were circling for a landing all over their trim gray uniforms. Someone could have parked a Mack truck on the pass line and gotten away with it.

A porter limped down the aisle with a crooked broom and a long dustpan, scouting the carpet for loose change. He appeared almost fragile, as though he might shatter into a thousand pieces if someone stuck a fresh vegetable in front of him.

Suddenly a man screamed, and the stewardesses followed

the crowd toward the slot machines. The porter went, too, although his eyes never got up past trouser legs and kneecaps. I looked around for Dan, but the only person behind the bar now was a black-haired man with a tangled gray mustache.

"Where's Dan?" I asked him.

"Over at the slot machines," he replied. "Some jerk gave him a $20 tip this afternoon, and as soon as he got his break he took off for the machines with it. Last pull, and he lined up three sevens for $15,000. You'll probably read about it in the papers tomorrow."

I pushed my beer glass away, and barely heard his last words. "It's just too bad there wasn't a reporter around when he did it. Boy, what a story that would have made."

Death Of A Sultan

FOR MOST OF US, it was just a blurb in the newspaper. A casino in Las Vegas folds, a couple of thousand people are out of work. Big deal. They'll get other jobs, and the rest of the joints will divvy up a few extra gamblers. Nobody really gets hurt except the guy who ended up holding the mortgage, and it was his fault for mismanaging the property in the first place.

Well, I don't buy it, because this hotel was special, and the people who worked there were special. This was the Dunes Hotel and Country Club, and when it threw aside its network of scaffolding in 1955, it stood as the most magical, mystical, marvelous place on the Las Vegas Strip. The memories of the Dunes will linger for a while, like a nice sunset or a good wine going down easy, but time has a way of killing everything—even memories.

So maybe it is time to write about it now, while the pain is still fresh, and before the bulldozers move in. You see, I was there. I was there in the glory years of Major Riddle and Sid Wyman, and I was there in the gory years of Morris Shenker and Masao Nangaku.

It was 1969, and I was a young hot-shot dealer getting his first big break: a job on the Strip. I knocked around for two years downtown, breaking in at the Pioneer Club, moving to the Mint, moving to the Landmark. In those days, though, it was juice that got you the good jobs.

A friend of mine knew a floorman at the Dunes; they went to school together, or something like that. It turned out that the floorman had a gambling problem, so I lent him 400 bucks, and that landed me an introduction to somebody else at the Dunes. Two weeks later, I got the job. I never did get the $400 back.

You've got to remember that in 1969 the Dunes was at the top of the heap. Working there was like following DiMaggio in the Yankee line-up, and I couldn't afford to strike out. Business was booming, with junkets arriving every Wednesday and Sunday, a thousand new faces with a thousand big credit lines, and every night was like New Year's Eve.

As luck would have it, I started on a Saturday night at the busiest craps table in the place. The dice rolled one time, and a player threw in a handful of chips. "Give me five thousand across," he growled. I turned to the boxman, my voice climbing several octaves, and said, "This man wants five thousand across." The boxman never raised an eyebrow. "Put him up," he said. Put him up? Hell, I didn't even know what it was!

By the end of the night, I was a seasoned veteran. I had dealt $500 chips for the first time in my life, and I couldn't believe they were the same size as regular old $100 chips. I learned that you didn't push the dice to a player on the number seven. He would throw them all right; he would throw them across the room. Still, it was fun, in a reckless almost dangerous way, and when the shift ended that night the other dealers invited me to join them at the Village Pub for a few brews. Just like that, I was one of the guys.

Sid Wyman ran the Dunes in those days. Wyman was a big, affable, lovable lug, and every dealer and cocktail waitress who worked for him would have walked across burning coals if it meant gaining his friendship, or just getting him to remember your name. Then if you had a problem, you saw Sid, and he took care of it. If you were short on the rent money, Sid would peel off a few bills to tide you over. If you needed some time off, Sid would make a phone call, and your job was waiting for you when you got back. If one of the crews blanked, Sid would take a couple of chips off the table and toss them to the stickman. You always went home with something.

One of the dealers married a cocktail waitress. They both worked there, and that created a problem. The policy was that married couples could not work at the same casino. So George Duckworth, a major stockholder in the company, got the two together. "Which one of you is leaving?" he asked. Neither said a word for several minutes, then the dealer shrugged. His wife had been there longer. "I'll go," he said.

Duckworth nodded. "We're not going to just throw you out in the street," he said. "I'll help you find another job." That was fine with the dealer, so Duckworth began listing the various casinos where he could put him to work. "How about the

(Left) The Dunes Hotel and Country Club opened in 1955 and was billed as the "Miracle of the Desert," with a ten-foot-high sultan as its mascot. In its heyday, it was a favorite hangout for highrollers, junketeers, sports figures, movie stars and mobsters. Along with Caesars Palace, Bally's and the Flamingo, the Dunes was an integral part of "the corner," the most popular and congested intersection on the Las Vegas Strip. Over the years it had a half-dozen owners and as many expansions.

Hilton?" he asked the dealer.

"It's too big," the dealer replied.

"How about the Flamingo?"

"It's too small."

Duckworth was getting impatient. "Well, decide what you want to do, and let me know."

The dealer's new wife made the decision. She went to Sid Wyman and explained the situation. They were in love, they wanted to be together, but one of them was being forced to find another job because of an obsolete rule that married couples couldn't work together. "Who made up that rule?" Wyman grumbled.

"You did," she answered.

Wyman shrugged. "Aww, forget it," he said. "You can both stay."

Maybe Wyman was sentimental. Maybe he was smart. He knew that if you were nice to the workers in the trenches, they would be nice to the customers, and the customers were the casino's bread and butter. He treated his people like family, and the result was a happy work force that stood loyally by him until the day he died.

The pit bosses and floor people were another story. In those days, little was known about civil rights, women's rights, or worker's rights. If you offended the wrong supervisor, you were out of a job. Simple as that. Forget about law suits. The casinos owned Las Vegas, and you would have been laughed out of court.

One dealer, who was new on the job, got his initiation to life at the Dunes the hard way. Someone at the table made a bet for him, and he announced in a loud voice, "The dealers are on eleven!" Here came the pit boss.

"Hey," he bellowed. "We don't have any dealers working here. When someone makes a bet for you, all I want to hear is the word 'two-way.' I don't want to hear the word 'dealer' again."

The dealer ducked his head. "Yes, sir," he whispered. The hand ended five minutes later, and a player pushed in fifty dollars. "This is for the dealers," he said.

The dealer turned to the pit boss, who was still glaring at him. "This money is for the—uh—this is a—uh—TWO-WAY HAND IN!" The pit boss got so mad he punched the dealer on the arm, but he must have been in a good mood that day. At least, he didn't fire him.

New dealer. Same pit boss. The old man watched the dealer work for several minutes, then sidled up to him. "Did they assign you a locker yet?" he asked him.

"No, sir," the dealer replied brightly. "Who should I talk to about getting one?"

"Don't bother," the pit boss barked. "You won't be here that long!"

I saw dealers fired for calling in sick, hustling with their eyes, smiling, having goofy messages on their answer machines, and refusing to work on their days off because of such lame excuses as a doctor's appointment or a wife in the hospital. This was before corporations took over, so it wasn't as bad as it sounded. There were plenty of other jobs in town, and back then you didn't need a presidential pardon or congressional investigation to get on somebody else's payroll.

I saw players kicked out of the Dunes for not betting enough money, betting too much money, smoking pipes, using systems, counting cards, getting drunk, and not throwing the dice all the way to the end of the table. I'm surprised one of them didn't take matters into his own hands, because in those days even the gamblers at the Dunes were a rough and tumble breed of people. Many made their money illegally, and their idea of staying within the law was not getting caught. One player got so excited during a hot hand at the dice table that when he signed a marker he suddenly cried, "Hey, wait a minute. Bring that back!" He had accidentally signed the marker with his real name.

Another customer, we'll call him Mr. G, was always the perfect gentleman. He dressed conservatively, never raised his voice, had a smile on his face at all times, and—most importantly—toked the dealers every time he played, win or lose. What a shock when he was found in a wheat field outside of St. Louis . . . tied up, strangled, and burned beyond recognition.

On the evening of October 27, 1993, following a spectacular fireworks display, the Dunes slid into oblivion in a blazing implosion—opposite of an explosion. Much to the delight of its new owner and visitors which came from all over the country to witness the event, 400 pounds of dynamite reduced the north tower and main sign to rubble in less than a minute. A movie starring new owner Steve Wynn created even more mileage from the nationally-televised event. The event was timed with the opening of Wynn's newest property, Treasure Island. Less than nine months later, on July 20, 1994, the south tower met a similar fate, at 4:03 A.M., without the fireworks, and unannounced.

Mr. G, it turned out, was a mob boss, and somewhere along the way he crossed the wrong people.

But this story is not about the players who turned the Dunes into an Arabian desert oasis. It is not a tribute to Sid Wyman, or his successors, or the chaotic tailspin the Dunes took after Wyman's death. It is a tribute to the people who worked there. When a hotel closes, the newspaper doesn't name the maids, bartenders, secretaries, dealers, carpenters, musicians, waiters, bellhops, valet attendants, doormen, pit clerks, cashiers, change persons, slot mechanics, porters, security guards, and all the others who make up a casino operation. It doesn't tell you about their hopes and dreams, and the families that looked to them for protection and support. Although they are all gone now, hopefully to better jobs and brighter futures, their memorial is that we remember. To do that, we have to go back to the beginning.

The Dunes Hotel opened May 23, 1955, on the southern-most tip of the Las Vegas Strip. Beyond it were wide open spaces, a small airport called McCarran Field, and a narrow highway jutting in from California. (The Hacienda would not open until a year later, and the Tropicana was two years away from reality.)

Built at a cost of $4 million, the Dunes started out with 200 rooms, a "Magic Carpet Revue" featuring Vera-Ellen, and a 30-foot Sultan—arms on hips and staring proudly into a some-what-cloudy future. If he could have seen exactly what kind of future lay in store, he would have probably sprinted back to Arabia as fast as his giant Fiberglas legs could take him.

First of all, there was a national recession going on. Sec-ondly, the group that built the Dunes had no gambling experi-ence. Between the two, and the fact that a dwindling number of tourists could choose from nine other hotels on the Strip, the Dunes got off to a very shaky start.

Then came Chicago oil-man Major Riddle, who took over the hotel in 1957. The eccentric and flamboyant Riddle, a highstakes gambler himself, put his whole bankroll on the pass line, and rolled a winner seven. By the time Riddle formed a new partnership in 1962, the Dunes was riding high. Three years later it would have over 1,000 rooms, a 24-story high-rise, and 16,000 people a week watching "Minsky's Follies," bare bosoms and all.

Riddle could usually be found in the casino poker room, where he banged heads with the likes of Johnny Moss and Puggy Pearson. Unfortunately, Moss and Pearson were professional poker players, and Riddle wasn't. In an interview with me, Pearson remembered those times in one short sentence. "I had my own little strawberry patch," he said.

Not only was Riddle losing at the poker tables, but the win percentage in the casino was starting to drop. Riddle retaliated, in some rather bizarre and unorthodox ways. If a slot machine paid a jackpot, he disconnected it. If the stickman on a dice game called too many winners, he replaced him with a dealer from another game. On one occasion, Riddle was alleged to have chopped a dice table to pieces with a fire ax after a losing day. So it was no surprise that when Sid Wyman, Charlie Rich and George Duckworth came to the Dunes under the auspices of the M&R Investment Company, they immediately barred Riddle from entering the casino.

Wyman, who had once been investigated by the Kefauver Crime Commission, was a colorful character in his own right. The St. Louis gambler moved to Las Vegas to take charge of the ailing Riviera Hotel, and now he was ready to turn the Dunes around in the same personable manner. One of his first moves was to hire New York junketeer Julie Weintraub to bring in high rollers from the East Coast. Soon the Dunes was the trendiest spot in town, where star performers like Wally Cox and Billie Holiday made their only Las Vegas appearances.

Four years later, the Dunes was on the front page of every newspaper in the country. The owners had transferred $59 million worth of stock to the Continental Connector Corporation, which was headed by some of the same people who owned stock in M&R Investment Company. The Securities and Exchange Commission charged the Dunes with defrauding stockholders.

In 1974, the Dunes was back in the headlines. This time the Nevada Gaming Control Board brought charges against the hotel for catering to one of the original eleven members of Nevada's Black Book of convicted felons. The Dunes was fined $10,000 for issuing complimentary services to the Kansas City mobster, which included providing him with a three-room suite during his stay in Las Vegas.

The greatest tragedy that ever befell the Dunes, however, was not its teetering inability to walk the tightrope of legality. As one former Dunes executive put it, "The Dunes died when Sid Wyman died." The 68-year-old Wyman died June 26, 1978, and St. Louis attorney Morris Shenker, who had bought controlling interest in the Dunes three years earlier, halted gambling at the resort for two minutes in memory of his long-time friend.

Shenker's troubles started almost immediately after Wyman's death. A $140 million lawsuit against the Teamsters Union for backing out of a construction loan was tossed out of court. Eight members of a New York crime family were discovered staying in complimentary rooms at the Dunes. Seven employees, including Shenker's director of Far East operations, were suspended after "irregularities" in management practices.

In December of 1982, an embittered Shenker sold the Dunes to former Caesars Palace owners Stuart and Clifford Perlman, but the $185 million deal collapsed the following year. The Perlmans, who advanced Shenker over $30 million, then tried to strike a bargain with the Dunes owner that would give them 46 percent of the company in exchange for the debt, but that deal also fell through.

There were more storm clouds on the horizon. A federal jury ordered Shenker to repay a $34 million loan to the Culinary Union. The Internal Revenue Service billed Shenker $66 million for unpaid taxes stretching back 20 years. Shenker filed for personal bankruptcy citing assets of $72 million and liabilities of $197 million, then borrowed $68 million from Valley Bank of Nevada in a frantic debt-restructuring move.

In May of 1984, Shenker sold a controlling interest in the Dunes to Maxim casino owner John Anderson. Anderson signed a $25 million note paying off the Perlman brothers, then a year later placed his extensive California land holdings under the protection of Chapter 11 in bankruptcy court. By the time the smoke cleared, lawsuits against Anderson by California creditors totaled $76 million.

Meanwhile, after waiting nearly two years for its money, Valley Bank moved ahead with legal steps required for a foreclosure sale of the Dunes. Almost at the same time, federal marshals began seizing cash from the casino cage to pay a $2.7 million judgment obtained by the Culinary and Bartenders unions because of non-payment of union benefits. In November of 1985, the Dunes filed for reorganization under Chapter 11.

Employee morale was at an all-time low. Workers were asked to delay cashing their paychecks, and some doctors would not accept Dunes insurance forms. One employee drew a cartoon of Shenker accepting insurance premiums from workers while an airplane waited in the background to carry Shenker and the money to Switzerland. The cartoon was circulated throughout the hotel, and when Shenker saw it he called all employees to a mandatory meeting. While business ground to a halt throughout the hotel, he demanded to know who drew the cartoon. No one came forth, and the meeting ended abruptly.

August 5, 1987 . . . Masao Nangaku strolled confidently into the Dunes Hotel and surveyed his newest business venture. Purchased at a cost of $155 million, Nangaku said his main concern was doing what was best for both the employees of the Dunes and the community. Since Nangaku did not have a gaming license, he took on Clark Management Company, headed by Dennis Gomes, to oversee the casino operation.

No one knew whether they had a job or not until they were interviewed by Gomes' management team. In the middle of one of Nevada's hottest summers on record, workers lined up at the time office to receive sealed envelopes notifying them of their future with the company. Either way, the news was not good. With their termination notices from M&R Investment Company, employees saw their seniority, vacation time and insurance benefits disappear into thin air like so many campaign promises. Even if they were re-hired, they would have to start all over again, and some were nearing retirement age.

Before Nangaku sold the Dunes to Steve Wynn in 1992, the

work force had dwindled from 2,000 to less than 1,300. By this time, the floundering property was losing up to $2 million a month, and Nangaku was forced by his bankers to unload it for $75 million, or less than half what he paid for it. Wynn's plan for the property was to turn it into a training center for his Treasure Island project, and then to bulldoze it for yet another theme resort.

The glory days of the Dunes will slowly fade into history. Never to return will be such unique Las Vegas creatures as the "Miracle Mile" golf course, the exquisite "Vive Les Girls" revue, Arturo Romero's Magical Violins, Frederic Apcar's "Casino de Paris," the Sultan's Table, the Dome of the Sea, the Savoy Room, the Oasis, the quaint bungalows overlooking three different swimming pools.

No more shall we see such moments of nostalgia as Lionel Hampton's band parading through the Dunes casino, serenading gamblers with Dixieland jazz. Or Billie Holiday, standing frail and alone on an empty stage, haunting a hushed audience with her raspy blues. Or a turban-clad Frank Sinatra drumming up business by riding a camel to the hotel's front entrance. And inside, the dealers lined up at their tables like soldiers in pillboxes, waiting for the enemy to land.

They are all gone now, and all that is left are the memories of another time, and another era. Dunes Hotel. Born May 23, 1955. Died January 26, 1993.

A Night At Palace Court

IT IS A SMALL CASINO, roughly 1200 square feet in size. There is no sign that says "Palace Court Casino," and no band beating out hard rock. In fact, there is a gentle hush about this place, as if speaking loudly would be almost sacrilegious.

You get there by climbing a curving brass staircase deep inside Caesars Palace, and looping past a brace of windows overlooking tropical gardens. Flowers grow with lush abandon, and the swimming pool, patterned after the one at Hearst Castle, reflects a lazy blue glow off the buildings standing over it.

Gazing quietly at the manicured scenery, you feel a sense of immortality. For one teasing moment all those images of nuclear warheads and strange diseases seem nothing more than some horrible nagging dream. You are back in Rome. Bring on the concubines. Let the wine flow. Hail Caesar.

Past an iron gate, a turn to the left, and the Palace Court Casino looms before you. Overhead is a crystal chandelier, almost the size of the room itself, and muted light sprinkles down like autumn rain. You feel the eyes of a dozen Roman emperors, whose faces stare from gilded frames. Julius Caesar, Augustus Caesar, and . . . all the rest.

Seven tables are in the room—a baccarat table on either side of the arching doorway, three blackjack tables positioned just so, and two roulette wheels. You stand there, drinking it all in, and visualize some maharajah or such betting a hundred thousand on one flip of the cards. Oh, the tales these silent sentries could tell.

Yet this is not the Las Vegas you saved your money to see. This is more like Monte Carlo, or one of those stucco casinos outside Paris, where a slot machine would be shot on sight. In-

Some gamblers don't like crowds. Those who wish to gamble in private at Caesars Palace can request to play in Palace Court, a small casino hidden away near the gourmet restaurant. An unlimited bank account will get you right in.

deed, even a dice table would seem out of place here. It would be too unsophisticated, too gauche, too American.

Then you remember. There was a dice table here once. You heard the story from a friend, and slowly it starts to come back, like a movie from long ago . . .

Dealers dressed in black tuxedos, static tension in the air as a man of great wealth strides into the room. Even the president of the hotel is waiting, and he presents a gift to the wealthy gambler. It is a pair of golden dice, the numbers of which are set in icy diamonds and red-fired rubies.

Idle conversation as the gambler's guests order cocktails and slowly gather around the table. The dealers stand woodenly at attention, eyes staring blankly ahead. Then, as though by silent command, the talk stops. The moment has come.

The player, a Mid-east potentate, scatters his wagers almost carelessly: $20,000 here, $40,000 there, $3,000 on a proposition bet. Then he takes the jewel-encrusted dice and tosses them down the table. The game is underway. Before it ends, an hour later, he has lost nearly half a million dollars. With a flourish of his pen, he signs a marker, pockets the pair of $10,000 dice, and casually walks away.

Your guide has been quiet all this time. And really, what could he say? That this exclusive little casino is now open only by special request? That it is strictly for that special casino player, to whom a couple of million dollars is like pocket change?

It is imagination that sets Palace Court Casino apart from all the rest. Time stands still—and the past, present and future merge into one magnificent fireball. You are rocketed into space, standing atop Mount Ararat, and sailing the bounding main. You are friend to all, seer of great truths, confidante of kings.

"Not every high roller comes up here," your guide says suddenly, and you turn with a start at the sound of a human voice. "Many would rather be down where the action is, where the people are." Abruptly you are back in the twentieth century, with a telephone buzzing somewhere, and the steady rumble of a crowd of people on the loose.

Descending the brass staircase, footsteps muffled on inch-deep carpet, and suddenly you are out of the clouds. The light grows brighter. You are back on earth. The noise gets louder. You are mortal again.

I Drove Through Las Vegas – And Lived!

I **FASTENED MY SEAT BELT** securely, adjusted the rear-view mirror, then pulled slowly into traffic. Ahead loomed one of the most congested streets in Las Vegas, but Spring Mountain Road was more than that. To local residents, it was the Bermuda Triangle, the Indianapolis Speedway, and Arlington Cemetery—all rolled into one.

Spring Mountain Road branched unceremoniously off the Las Vegas Strip next to the Fashion Show Mall, proceeding west past a sleepy trailer court and the side entrance of the Mirage. In the early sixties it was called D-4-C Road, and it dead-ended at a sprawling iron works in front of the railroad tracks.

If you took a left at the iron works, you bumped along a gravel road to the D-4-C Ranch, which was owned by former movie star Hoot Gibson and his wife Dorothy. According to a long-time bartender, Gibson's favorite drink was Old Grand Dad on the rocks, a beverage which more or less personified Gibson himself. His movie career was on the rocks, and he looked like a grand dad, with snow-white hair and a smile as bright as a Nevada sunrise.

I braked to a stop at the intersection of Spring Mountain and Industrial, waiting for the light to turn green. There was a bank across the street, but years ago a mobile home park occupied that very spot called "My Blue Heaven." It was owned by singer Gene Austin, and *My Blue Heaven* was the name of his biggest hit record.

Meanwhile, cars were now stacking up behind me, most of the drivers watching uneasily as a tattered man shuffled alongside the road with a shopping cart full of aluminum containers.

What was he going to do—beat someone to death with an empty Pepsi can? I had the urge to roll my window down and give the guy a few bucks. A couple of wrong turns, and my life could have wound up like that. But instead I sat there, watching uneasily along with everyone else, my mind going back to the old D-4-C.

The ranch was built in 1946, and soon became a popular local hangout. There was square dancing there every Friday and Saturday night, and a stable full of horses for riding through the open desert. At the time Hoot still knew a lot of Hollywood stars, and chances were that one or two of them would be at the ranch every weekend.

One thing I admired about the man was his sense of humor. If you said the word "D-4-C" out loud, it came out "Divorcee," and I guess he was hoping that all the divorcees who flocked to Las Vegas would keep the place jumping.

The D-4-C was part of history now, and alas, so was Hoot. D-4-C Road became Spring Mountain Road, and the only thing that stayed the same were those blasted railroad tracks. Apparently, Union Pacific signed some kind of secret pact with the city of Las Vegas to keep the tracks open—as long as the trains were at least 60 cars in length and only ran during rush-hour traffic.

As I approached the tracks, I glanced at my dashboard clock. It was 5:40 p.m. Sure enough, bells began to chime and wooden gates slowly wobbled down on both sides of the tracks, stifling the flow of traffic in all directions.

I suppose no one ever thought Las Vegas would get this big, or that Spring Mountain Road would become one of the city's main arteries. Land prices on the western edge of town were dirt cheap until a few years ago, when housing developments suddenly began popping up along mysterious avenues like Rainbow and Jones. Today, the only way people could get from there to the Strip was via Flamingo, Tropicana (formerly Bond Road), Sahara (formerly San Francisco Street)—and Spring Mountain Road.

The 62-car train rumbled on down the tracks, and the gates lurched up again. I raced my engine, and took off with a squeal. Maybe I could make it home by nightfall if I caught the next six traffic lights.

I got past Highland, the Interstate 15 Freeway Entrance, Polaris and Procyon. Then the three lanes of traffic heading west became two lanes of traffic heading west, as the extreme right lane suddenly ended. Naturally, all of the cars in this lane started moving into the next lane, which caused all the drivers in that lane to either try to get into the left-hand lane or to slam on their brakes. Not me. I hit my horn and kept on going. Didn't any of these people read street signs?

There was a huge cement truck in front of me, blanketing everything in its path with black smoke and punching another hole in the ozone. All I could see was another traffic light, which was changing from green to amber. I gunned the accelerator and sped through the intersection, leaving the truck in my exhaust. Take that, I chuckled, while off in the distance I thought I heard a siren.

One thing I never understood was where Las Vegas got the names for its streets. Sahara and Flamingo Avenues made sense. They were named for hotels that graced those boulevards, and you knew if you turned east on Tropicana that you would run into the Tropicana Hotel sooner or later.

But Procyon? I looked it up in the dictionary, and found that it meant "before-dog, a star of the first magnitude in the constellation Canis Minor, which rises before the Dog Star." Well, I shouldn't complain. They could have named it Dog Street.

Things were different where I grew up. All the streets were in alphabetical order in my home town, and they were all named after trees. There was Ash, Beech, Cedar, Date Palm, Ebony, Fir, Gumwood, Hackberry, Ivy and Jasmine. I left before the town got big enough to finish the alphabet, but I always wondered what they did when they got to X.

Nothing in Las Vegas, however, seemed to be in alphabetical order, and that was especially true of the streets. After Procyon came Valley View, which should mean just what the name implies. Well, once upon a time maybe there was a view of the valley here, but now the view was of Ted Wiens Firestone,

Blystone Rental Company, Pet Food Supermart, Green Valley Grocery, the Blue Ox West, Earl Scheib Auto Painting and approximately 40 billboards. If there were mountains standing guard over Las Vegas, you had to take somebody's word for it.

Here came Arville Street, and another traffic light. It was red. I braked my car and skidded to a stop, then heard the sound of a car horn in my ear. There was a cop in the next lane. He motioned for me to roll down my window.

"Yes, officer?"

"You stopped at this red light," he said. "How come you didn't stop at the last one?"

I could have told him that my foot accidentally slipped off the brake pedal and onto the gas pedal, resulting in one of those split-second decisions that a man has to make sometimes. Instead, I gave him a lame smile.

"Just be careful," he said as the light turned green. I watched him start down Spring Mountain Road, then turned right on Arville, narrowly missing two teen-agers on bicycles. Thank God I was almost home. There were a lot of idiots on the road tonight.

High Plains Grifter

I MET BENNY BINION when I was writing a book about Las Vegas, and the result was a chapter on the Texas gambler's life. My publisher suggested the idea. He wanted me to interview Benny about his family-run Horseshoe Club, and find out why he was so different from all the other casino operators in town. I was reluctant to do it, because I had just spent a week trying to reach the proprietor of a resort on the Las Vegas Strip—and never did find out who owned the place.

I called Benny on the telephone, and to my surprise he told me to come on down. In fact, his exact words were, "Come on down and have some dinner." That seemed a little strange because it was 11 o'clock in the morning, but I soon learned that to Benny, people ate dinner at lunchtime and supper at night.

The waitress hovered over Benny like a mother hawk while I studied the man out of the corner of my eye. A white Stetson was shoved back on his head, and the lines that branded his face were washed out at the jaw line by three days of stubble. My tape recorder rolling, I fired a few questions at him. His answers came out in a gruff whiskey voice.

"I never did plan nothin'," he said when I asked how he got into the gambling business. "I jest let it come."

He credited his success with something called "grift," or living by one's wits. "There's more grifters in Las Vegas than anywhere else," he explained. "Hell, I'm still a grifter." Call it grift, or fortitude, or whatever, but in 1951 Benny took his life savings and bought a run-down grind joint called the Apache Hotel. Now the block-long Horseshoe Club, it is one of the sleekest operations in town—even though it has no lounge, no showroom, and until a few years ago hardly any slot machines.

"The reason I never went fer the shows," Benny grumbled, "is because I don't know nothin' about it. I like the shows, and they're necessary, but I don't need 'em."

When asked to describe the Horseshoe, Benny's answer was short and simple. "Treat people with courtesy. Feed 'em good. And give 'em a good gamble. That's all there is to it, son."

The day spun by and then Benny went upstairs for a nap. I wandered across the street to the Golden Nugget, where a poker tournament had brought out some of the country's top card players. One of them was Johnny Moss." Benny Binion called me from Dallas one time to come play Nick the Greek," he told me. "We was playing stud, five card stud. Well, we played and played, and I beat him at every game. I was the best draw poker player there was, best deuce to seven player, the top stud player. He said, 'How about that new game of hold 'em?' I said I never heard of it, and I was the best there ever was playing *it*."

The game between Moss and Nick Dandolos lasted five months, and when it was over Binion's Horseshoe Club was on the map. People loved the high-stakes action, and they also liked getting their picture taken next to a million dollars in cash.

Casino executive Earl Junker: "If you go in the Horseshoe Club, you're going to see a horseshoe with one hundred $10,000 bills on it. Everybody in Nevada is under the impression that Binion put that horseshoe there. He did not.

"Joe W. Brown (who sold the Apache Club to Binion) put it there. He won the money in New Orleans from a man who had a habit of taking a bill on one end and rolling it until it was eight to ten inches long . . . and he would bet it at the dice table." On one particular night the gambler lost ten of these rolled-up bills before winning a bet.

"I've got to pay it," said Junker, who was the dealer. "So I picked up the bill and opened it to see what it was, and it was a $10,000 bill! It was not only the first one I had ever held, it was the first one I had ever seen. I didn't know if I should throw it to the boss, or fold it up and put it in my pocket. I didn't know what to do with it. Then I found out that all those

Benny Binion came to Las Vegas from Texas in a beat-up old car with a couple of suitcases full of money. In August of 1951, he bought and opened a place at 128 East Fremont Street. He called it Binion's Horseshoe Club; it's still in operation—much enlarged.

bills we beat him out of were $10,000 bills.

"And that's how Joe W. came to have one million dollars in $10,000 bills."

Another story that bears repeating is the time a young man began work at the Horseshoe as a craps dealer. The son of a famous musician, he found to his dismay that the big money was being made on the Las Vegas Strip and not downtown. One afternoon he sat dejectedly on the stairs leading to the dealer's room when an elderly man tried to get past him.

The young dealer slowly moved out of the way, but the older man could see that he was not happy. "What's the matter, son?" the man asked.

"Oh, I'm not making any money," the dealer answered sadly. "I've got to get me a blankety blank job on the blankety blank Strip."

The old man gave him a fatherly smile. "Well, hang in there," he said. "Your day'll come."

As the man disappeared down the stairs, one of the young dealer's friends came running up to him. "Hey," he said. "What were you and Benny Binion talking about?"

On another occasion, Binion and a friend were walking through the casino when Benny spotted an acquaintance waiting to see him. "I'll show you how to save ninety dollars," Benny whispered to his friend. He approached the other man and wrote him out a ticket for a complimentary meal in Binion's famous steak house.

As the man disappeared into the restaurant, Benny's friend said to him, "That meal's bound to cost you ten dollars. How in the world did you save $90?"

Benny smiled sagely. "Because he was gettin' ready to borrow a *hundred!*"

Another man down on his luck once offered to sell Benny an ornate western belt buckle he was wearing. "How much do you want fer it?" Benny squinted.

"Thirty-two dollars," the man replied.

"I'll give you twenty-five."

As the two men continued to argue over the price, the pit boss suddenly appeared. "Benny, there's a big player at the dice table and he's got us stuck $40,000."

"Not now," Benny exploded. "Can't you see I'm busy?"

Benny spent most of his time at the Binion ranch outside of Las Vegas, where he raised horses and cattle. One of the horses was so mean and ornery that Benny kept it in a corral by itself, with a long-standing offer of $100 to any man who could ride him.

One morning Benny was roused from a sound sleep to see one of his new cowhands sitting casually atop the wild horse. In disbelief, Benny gave the man a hundred dollars, then asked him how he managed to do it.

"It was easy," the man replied. "I just hit him between the eyes with a two-by-four."

A few months after my interview with Benny, the book was released. With a shiny autographed copy in hand, I called him again on the telephone. "Come on down," he said, barking instructions on how to find his suite at the Horseshoe.

"Well, okay," I hesitated. "But my wife's with me."

"That's fine."

"And her mother."

"All right."

"And my wife's girlfriend."

"Bring 'em on down."

I knocked on the door and Benny let us in. He was wearing a rumpled bathrobe over rumpled pajamas, and scarcely looked at the book when I presented it to him. "Help yerself to some fresh apricots," he growled, gesturing to a bowl of fruit on the table. "Got 'em from Texas this mornin'."

My stomach gave a drum roll, as I had my sights set on a juicy T-bone and not some shriveled-up Texas produce. Besides, there was the distinct possibility I could wind up with apricot juice all over my brand new book. "Turn to the chapter called 'Last Of A Breed,'" I insisted. "It's all about you and the Horseshoe Club."

Benny never gave the book another glance. "You know, son," he began in a confidential tone, "I ain't got much education.

(Left) You can always tell a serious slot machine player; she wears a glove on her handle-pulling hand. This woman is playing a nickel Mills GOLDEN FALLS, which had an eight-dollar jackpot. The arch behind the machine at the Horse-shoe Club is Binion's famous display of a hundred $10,000 bills—or one million dollars in cold cash. Although the casino loses about $220 a day in interest on the money, the Binions say the money that gawking tourists spend more than makes up for the loss.

Never did go to school. Would you mind readin' it to me?"

"Hell, Benny," I sputtered. "It's a whole chapter!"

"Then jest read me the good stuff."

So I did. Granted, it wasn't a Shakespearean sonnet, but it had some good down-to-earth quotes from the man who was sitting right across the table from me. When I read a part that he liked, he let out a deep chuckle and then told the story all over again. When I read anything flowery, he screwed up his face impatiently and waited for the punch line. Then he got his book, and I got my steak. A year later, on Christmas Day, Benny Binion closed his eyes for the last time.

There is an old western song called *The Streets Of Laredo*. It's about a dying cowboy and it makes me think about Benny. Someday I'll saddle up my horse for the last time and mosey down that same road—and when I do, maybe I'll see him again. I just hope they don't have apricots in heaven.

Breaking In

BREAKING IN, verb: *learning to deal—getting a job dealing without prior dealing experience.*

"When I hit Las Vegas," the first dealer said, "I had $117 on me. I was sleeping on the couch at my cousin's apartment, and after a couple of days I decided to look for a job. The first place I went was the Stardust. I asked for the casino manager, and it happened to be Al Sachs. I introduced myself and said, 'Mr. Sachs, I'm looking for a job.'

"'What kind of job are you looking for?' Sachs asked me.

"'I want to be a dealer.'

"'How long have you been dealing?'

"'Well, I've never dealt.'

"Sachs chuckled. 'You've got to start downtown,' he said. 'Come back and see me in a couple of years.'"

The dealer laughed as he recalled the story. "I didn't know that you had to break in," he explained. "I thought they showed you how to do it, and you just did it. Little did I realize the complications involved in becoming a dice dealer."

The second dealer nodded his head in agreement. "I remember when I got a job breaking in at the Fremont Hotel. This was back in the late sixties. I was making nine dollars a day, which came to about $1.12 an hour. I worked from eight o'clock at night until four in the morning, and then at ten in the morning I had to be back for two hours of school. The

---

(Next Pages) This is what "Glitter Gulch" looked like in 1948. The big guys on the street were the Golden Nugget, the Frontier Club, the Pioneer, the Boulder Club and the Eldorado Club. Student dealers learned their trade from seasoned veterans. They worked long hours for little pay—for a chance someday at the big time.

school lasted six weeks, and cost $20 a week. So at the end of each week, I had about $20 left. Party time for me was going to the Lady Luck on payday and having a 15¢ beer.

"After the first four weeks of school, the Fremont would give each of us an apron and tie which we kept in our back pockets. Then when the action on one of the dice tables got a little slow, they would let one of us go in and work the stick for ten or 15 minutes. We'd be standing about ten feet from the game, watching and waiting. One of the guys said, 'When I get in there, I'm going to make such an impression that they'll put me on a regular crew right away.' Sure enough, the pit boss calls him and tells him to go in on the stick. He puts on his apron and tie, takes the stick, looks at both ends of the table, and the first thing out of his mouth is, 'Okay, folks, how much on that two-way eleven?' (A bet on eleven for the player and dealers.) The pit boss screamed, 'Get that kid out of there!'"

"I broke in at the Carousel Club on graveyard," the next dealer said. "We didn't have too much business around four o'clock in the morning, so they would close the table for half an hour to clean it. That gave us time to go across the street to the Nevada Club and grab a beer. In those days, they didn't care if you drank on your breaks or not, just as long as you did your job. Well, one of the dealers named Buddy got back to work after a couple of beers, looked around the table, then said to the boxman, 'This doesn't look like the Carousel Club.'

"The boxman, who saw people audition for dealing jobs all the time, said, 'It isn't the Carousel Club. This is the Golden Gate.'

"'Excuse me,' Buddy said, putting down the stick. 'I'm in the wrong place.'"

The first dealer leaned forward. "I think the funniest thing I ever saw was at the Las Vegas Club. There was this kid named George from Minnesota who was breaking in, and on his very

---

(Right) If you want to be a dealer nowadays, you have to go to school. In this 1981 photograph, MGM casino manager Morris Jaeger talks to a group of student dealers at Clark County Community College. Today dealer and slot machine technician schools are common in Las Vegas and Reno.

first night with a regular crew he got into an argument with a player. By the time a security guard got there, George and the player were going at it with their fists. The guard broke up the fight and threw the player out, but five minutes later the player came back inside, sneaked up behind George and hit him again. Again the security guard threw the player out, standing by the front door to make sure he didn't come back in. Well, this time the player came in through the back door, and by the time the guard knew what was happening George and the player were fighting right on the dice table.

"The guard grabbed the player and hauled him off to the office, while George stood there with a torn shirt and bloody nose. He said, 'That's it, I'm going back to Minnesota. Any-

body who stays in this racket is crazy.' He threw his tie and apron on the table, walked out, and nobody ever saw him again."

This is what it was like breaking in as a dealer in the old days. I can vouch for it myself, coming to Las Vegas in 1967 and paying my dues at such establishments as the Pioneer Club and Del Webb's Mint Hotel. I was paid a whopping $11 a day at the Pioneer, but I did get to deal occasionally; and on my breaks I could drink free cokes at the concession stand. Unfortunately, somebody hit a keno ticket for $1,500, and that was the end of the free cokes. I guess they had to make up the money somewhere.

Then I graduated to the Mint, where my salary skyrocketed to $14 a day. Aside from being treated like an android, it was a fun place to work, and many of the regular customers were genuine characters out of a Damon Runyan story. There was Irish, rumored to be an ex-hitman for the mob, who once said to a dealer after a dispute on a crowded 25¢ craps game, "How would you like to wind up floating in Lake Mead?" The weary dealer replied, "Frankly, I could use the rest." There was Yum Yum, a frail bespectacled Oriental whose favorite expression was, "No shootie, no tokey." There was Tyrone, who used to roller-skate down the casino aisles, and there was Mugsy. Mugsy was a degenerate gambler who was consequently broke most of the time. After a bad run at the tables, he would approach one of the dealers and ask him what size shirt he wore. The dealer would rattle off the information, and Mugsy would disappear for an hour or so, returning with a brand new shirt still in the wrapper. Mugsy was back in action again.

Mugsy liked to make proposition bets at the dice table, one of which was $5 on high-low (or aces and twelve). This was about the time I mustered up the courage to ask the shift boss for a raise, because you were never really considered a full-fledged dealer until you were making $25 a day. The shift boss was watching Mugsy play at the table, and he said, "Okay, kid, I'll give you a raise if you can tell me what $5 on high-low pays."

I hesitated. "Well, what rolled—aces or twelve?"

Needless to say, I didn't get my raise. However, I did make some lasting friendships, as break-in dealers seemed to band together in those days. One of these was a dealer named Rick who had actually worked on the Strip, but was back downtown because he couldn't make it to work half the time. It was a different story downtown. If you lost one job, there was another waiting somewhere else on Fremont Street.

I remember one night when Rick called in sick at the Horseshoe. His part of the conversation went like this: "Hi, this is Rick. I'm calling in sick. I don't? You will? Thanks."

"What was that all about?" I asked him when he hung up the phone.

"Oh, they told me I don't work at the Horseshoe anymore. I work at the Fremont. But it's okay. They're going to call them for me."

Rick and another dealer named Jim Sinay were on a dice game at the Mint one day when a blind man came to the table. They knew him, as he spent most of his time selling pencils in front of the Horseshoe. Occasionally, he would amass enough money to buy a few chips at the dice table, and in this instance came up with a wrinkled $10 bill.

"Young man, I cannot see," he told Jim. "Would you please put my 25¢ chips in the front row, and the $1 chips in the back row?"

"Sure," Jim replied.

"Now I want to bet all the hard ways for 25¢ each," the blind man said to the stickman. "But I want them off on the come-out roll."

At that moment, a new stickman came on the game. The next roll was a winner seven, and without saying a word the new stickman took down the blind man's hard way bets.

"Hey!" the blind man hollered. "I just told you guys that my hard ways were off!"

Nicknames

WHEN I WAS GROWING UP in Texas, very few of us had nicknames. Oh, there was a blonde-haired kid everyone called Whitey, and a runt down the street named Shorty, but that was about it . . . except for Four Eyes, who had the misfortune of wearing glasses, and Lefty, whose right arm was about four inches shorter than the other, and Spots, who had freckles, and Atlas, who had asthma.

Then I moved to Las Vegas, where everybody either had a nickname or was trying to get hold of one. "Hi, my name's Arnold, but you can call me Spider." Or: Frenchie, Sterno, Squatty, Blinky, Starvin' Marvin, California Red, Amarillo Slim, Minnesota Fats, Mississippi Mud. Why, if a man didn't have a nickname, he just wasn't a member of Las Vegas society.

These were not just nicknames, they were tidy little phrases that summed up in a word or two everything one needed to know about a person. Take California Red, for instance. Just by his nickname you knew he was from California and he had red hair, or a red complexion, or a red nose, or all three. Starvin' Marvin got his nickname because he was broke all the time. His nickname should have been Dumbo, because he tried to rob a bank one day on his lunch hour and forgot to take his name tag off. (True story.)

Some nicknames are poetic masterpieces that catch the public's fancy and live forever in the annals of mankind. Charles Lindbergh is a good example. His nickname, the Lone Eagle, is all it takes to picture him in that tiny plane, stuttering across the Atlantic, his wings scarce feet from the angry sea. At least, that's the way it was in the movie with Jimmy Stewart, who is one of those actors who should have had a nickname and never did.

For some strange reason, a woman generally doesn't have a nickname, unless it's something like Angel or Dumpling or Peaches, or Trish. The only female I ever met with a nickname was Big Dotty, a cocktail waitress at one of the local casinos. Big Dotty's gone now. She left town with Fast Eddie after breaking up with The Claw.

The Claw was a craps dealer, and not a very good one at that. He was on the same crew with Shaky Bill, Tony the Flea and Hose Nose. I've never learned why dice dealers have such vile reprehensible nicknames, while blackjack dealers get pegged with nice distinguished monikers like Professor, Doc and Deacon. Baccarat dealers have nicknames that hardly even make noise when you say them. Cruise, Willow, Biff, Cloud.

Bosses rarely have nicknames, or at least none that they know about. The boss is treated with respect and dignity, with reserve, distinction and importance—until he leaves for the day, that is. Then he becomes:

Hands, High Pockets, Scrooge, Chrome Dome, Skin Flint, Birdbrain, Marble Head, Fatso, Leather Legs, Toad Face, Fish Mouth, Wart Hog, Big Foot, etc.

I was lucky. I never had a nickname. In school I tried calling myself B.V. for a while, but then some joker tacked a "D" on the end of it. It was probably just as well. I might live to be 80, and for a man that far up in years, Beevie Vinson doesn't sound right.

That's another thing. What's going to happen to all these people with nicknames when they reach retirement age? Do you want to play checkers with some senior citizen named Bubba, or car-pool down to the medical center with Pee Pie, Hambone or Dink? Nicknames were meant for the young. I don't know about you, but I think there is something deeply disturbing about a middle-aged man introducing himself to everyone as The Beaver.

Of course, a good nickname can mean money in the bank, especially in the brassy arenas of professional sports. William Perry was an unknown lineman for the Chicago Bears until somebody dubbed him The Refrigerator. Who can ever forget Grantland Rice's immortal tribute to the fighting Irish of Notre

Dame and "the four horsemen of the Apocalypse"—Pestilence, Famine, Death, and the other one. Then there are all those prize fighters who do battle for fame, glory and lots of little pictures of dead presidents. Iron Mike, Sugar Ray, Bonecrusher, Hit Man, Macho, Boom Boom.

I suppose as long as men roam the earth, some of them will give nicknames to the other ones. That's the way it has always been, ever since caveman days when one grunt meant "Harold" and two grunts meant "Dinosaur Breath." I'm just surprised that when Las Vegas was being laid out in the mid-1940s, no one gave Bugsy Siegel a nickname.

Bugsy

BUGSY SIEGEL was no saint. He was a gangster, but he was a gangster in an era when breaking the law was on the same par with cleanliness and godliness. Big government was shoving so many rules and regulations down our throats that when someone stood up for his rights (even when they were misguided) he became almost a folk hero.

His real name was Benjamin Siegel. Those who knew him called him Ben, and those who didn't called him Bugsy. The nickname, which he detested, was given to him when he was a boy. The story goes that he went "bughouse" when anyone crossed him. This was in the 1920s, when anyone who worked in an insane asylum was referred to as a "bughouser."

He would join Murder Incorporated a decade later. A boyhood pal of Meyer Lansky, Siegel catapulted to a top position in the deadly organization. Then in 1942 he came to Las Vegas. Vegas was a small ranch town, better known for its magnesium production and aviator training than for its booze and gambling. After all, there was a war going on, and it wasn't with Reno and Atlantic City.

Siegel's job was to set up the Trans-America wire service, which would become a lifeline for bookies across the country. Once that was done, he saw the possibilities of a new enterprise guaranteed to give him the respect he desperately wanted.

Siegel would build the largest and most luxurious casino in the world, and he would build it in the desert outside Las Vegas. Lansky was against it, and so was Siegel's confederate, Mod Sedway. "For heaven's sake, Ben," Sedway told Siegel. "It's seven miles out of town, not a tree in sight, and there's nothing but bugs, coyotes and heat."

Siegel just laughed. "That's the whole point. Wine and dine

'em, and let 'em spend their money. There's nothing else to do out there, except gamble."

In fact, he would later brag, "I've got thirty acres here, and I picked it up for nickels and dimes in the only state where gambling is legal. I put my blood in this place, and the beauty of it is that I've got the law on my side—for a change."

Siegel figured it would cost $1 million to build his casino, and he borrowed the money from Lansky and mob boss Lucky Luciano. He wanted to call his casino the Desert Flower, but then he thought of a better name. When he would go to the horse races at Hialeah Park, he always saw pink birds outside the track. They were flamingos. That's what he would name his casino.

Construction began in early 1946, which turned out to be bad timing on Siegel's part. The war had ended, and building materials were at such a premium that he was forced to pay top dollar for everything, including labor. Then when something was done, it wasn't done right. The air conditioners kept breaking down. The curtains were flammable. The boiler room was too small, and had to be rebuilt at a cost of $115,000. The kitchen needed $30,000 in alterations. Siegel's dream was becoming a nightmare.

By the time the Flamingo was finished eight months later, building costs had soared to an unprecedented $6 million. Lansky had financed the whole thing, and he was starting to worry about Siegel's lofty goals. Siegel, however, wouldn't budge. After all, the money would roll in when the casino opened.

But Siegel's bad luck continued. The night of the Flamingo's grand opening was set for December 26, 1946. Invitations were sent to Hollywood's top celebrities, and a private plane was hired to fly them to Vegas. Then a sudden storm broke out in Los Angeles, grounding the plane. It was an omen of things to come.

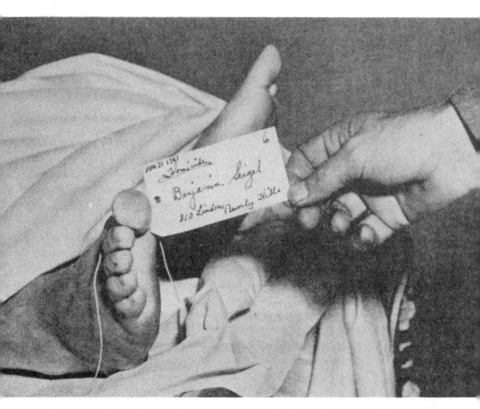

Benjamin "Bugsy" Siegel's I.D. morgue tag lists his address as 810 Linden, Beverly Hills, California. Actually, Siegel was living in Las Vegas and was assassinated while visiting his girlfriend—who was absent at the time. People knowledgeable about such things say Siegel was overspent with his "associates" and that his goals were much too grandiose. Moe Sedway and Meyer Lansky walked into the Flamingo the following day and announced: "We are the new owners." Nobody objected. The Beverly Hills police department has never closed the case; when time permits, they still drag out the old files and pursue the matter.

The night after Christmas, Siegel stood at the front door in a black tuxedo, watching grimly as a sparse crowd entered his half-finished hotel. Even a brave speech to the press did little to help. "What you see here is nothing," he said. "More and more people are moving to California every day, and they love to gamble. In ten years, this'll be the biggest gambling center in the world."

Siegel was right, of course, but ten years was a long way down the road. In the meantime, each of his 92 rooms at the Flamingo needed $3,500 worth of furniture, and he couldn't use any of the casino's profits because there weren't any. The casino was $300,000 in the red from the first two weeks of operations. There were either some very good gamblers in Las Vegas, or some very unscrupulous casino employees.

Siegel closed the Flamingo to furnish the rooms, opening again three months later. The casino lost another $400,000, but then slowly the Flamingo began to show a modest profit. Unfortunately, it was too little too late.

A hit on Siegel had already been ordered by mob boss Lucky Luciano. "If you don't have the heart to do it," Luciano told Lansky, "then I will have to order the execution myself."

It was the summer of 1947. The House Un-American Activities Committee was holding hearings in Washington. Joe Louis was defending his heavyweight title for the 24th time. Clark Gable was wowing crowds at the box office in *The Hucksters*. The number one song in the country was Arthur Godfrey's *Too Fat Polka*.

In Las Vegas, the Club Bingo (later the Sahara) opened across the road from the El Rancho. The Las Vegas Press Club was organized, and United Airlines inaugurated service to Las Vegas. At the Flamingo, singer Lena Horne made her debut, as did dancer Bill "Bojangles" Robinson. Siegel's hotel was becoming the hottest place in town.

On June 20, Ben Siegel let himself into girl-friend Virginia Hill's Los Angeles home for a weekend of rest and relaxation. For some never-explained reason, Virginia was out of the country at the time.

That night Siegel went out to dinner with a group of friends, and upon his return to the house he sniffed the air. "There's a strong smell of flowers in here," he said to Virginia's brother Chick.

"I don't smell anything," Chick replied. "There's not a flower in the house."

Siegel shrugged. Everyone said good night, leaving Siegel and friend Al Smiley alone in the living room. Siegel sat down on the sofa with a copy of the *Los Angeles Times*, not bothering to draw the drapes. It was a fatal mistake. An unidentified gunman fired nine rounds from a .30-30 carbine through the window, five of the shots hitting Siegel.

When Virginia Hill was told of Siegel's death, her first comment to authorities was, "It looks so bad to have a thing like that happen in your house." As for the Flamingo, it went on to show a profit of $4 million by the end of the year. Today, half a century later, it is still one of the Las Vegas Strip's most dazzling resorts.

If Siegel's luck hadn't been so bad, maybe he would have seen it all happen. He would have witnessed other things, too. An American astronaut would walk on the moon, and a punk with a $20 rifle would change the course of history in a town called Dallas. And someday his Flamingo would be owned by a hotel chain, with slot machines blinking and oinking from one end of the casino to the other.

Of course, no one ever figured that gambling would become a respectable pastime, and that owning a casino would be a respectable profession. Even so, things could have turned out a lot differently, if not for a guy named Bugsy.

Phyllis's Pad

HEY, BOB, how's it going? Make yourself at home while I throw a shirt on. I see you found that last beer in the ice box. Naw, go ahead and drink it, I'll get some more on payday.

You know, Bob, if I had it to do over again, I think I would be a singer. You pop into a recording studio every six months, knock out a couple of songs and the money just rolls in. Well, look at Wayne Newton. He did something in German called *Donkey Shine*, and now he's got a ranch bigger than Woolworth's. I'd take you by to see it, but my gas tank's on empty. Tell you what we could do, though. We could drive over to Rancho Circle, it's right down the road, and I'll show you where Phyllis McGuire lives. Who's Phyllis McGuire? Haven't you ever heard of the McGuire Sisters? Well, they're about one of the most famous singing groups to ever come down the turnpike. They did that song *Sincerely* and a whole bunch of other hits.

I'll hum it for you and see if it stirs up the old memory strings. Still doesn't ring a bell? Well, maybe I was off-key a little bit. Back when I was going with Rose Mary, they used to play it on the radio all the time. You remember Rose Mary, don't you? Bob, you're getting *old*.

That's one of the nice things about living in Las Vegas, though. You've got movie stars living all over the place. This friend of mine was working for a car rental agency, and he had to deliver a car one day. So he knocked on this door, and guess who opened it? Why, none other than Mister Johnny Carson. He said Johnny Carson was just as nice as they come, invited him in and everything. Then another time my friend was going to buy a house, and the real estate agent showed him this big

mansion that used to belong to Engelbert Humperdinck. It had an indoor swimming pool, and a barber shop, and a tennis court—and it was only $78,000. Turned out, though, that the real estate agent had his fact sheets mixed up. It was $78,000 *down.*

Okay, we're almost to Rancho Circle, Bob. It's right past this guard house. Kind of a nice touch, keeps out the riff-raff. Oh, don't worry about the guard. He's just waving hello. Everybody's real friendly here in Las Vegas.

There she is, Bob—the big place on the left. That's Phyllis McGuire's house, buddy. All 26,000 square feet, give or take a mile. Why, she could put your pickup truck inside and use it for a coffee table.

You want to do something crazy? Let's go up there and ring the doorbell, just to see the look on her face. I read the other day, or maybe it was on TV, that Phyllis McGuire moved here back in the late fifties and liked it so much she never left. Hmm, the doorbell doesn't seem to be working, or she could be off doing a show somewhere. Well, she probably wouldn't mind if we just let ourselves in. After all, I've got practically every one of her albums.

Hey, that was a neat trick, Bob—poking that bobby pin in the door lock. Opened her up just as pretty as you please. How about those hand-carved oak doors, pal? Does that say class or what? And look at that replica of the Archey Triumph. It's the same as the one in Paris, only bigger. I wouldn't advise sticking your chewing gum on there, Bob. It might set off some kind of alarm.

I'll tell you one thing, partner. That Phyllis McGuire must be half-French, or something. Look here in the living room. That's the Eiffel Tower, or I've got scrambled eggs all over my face. You'd best get off that thing, Bob. It might not be as sturdy as it looks.

Come on, let's take this circular staircase upstairs to the sec-

---

(Left) Phyllis McGuire is said to have visited Las Vegas in the 1950s, fell in love with it and never left. Today she owns one of the city's most lavish homes.

ond floor. What a view, huh? Those matching chandeliers on the ceiling used to be owned by the maharajah of one of those countries over in India. Sure, that's real crystal. Listen to it ring when I tap it with my car keys.

Have you ever seen such flimsy-looking furniture in your whole life? Those curvy little legs look nice enough, but I bet they wouldn't take your weight, Bob. See, what'd I tell you? You better stick to Barcaloungers. Either that, or lose about 75 pounds.

Take a gander at that shiny table there. How'd you like to be eatin' supper on something like that? Why, you'd have to put newspapers under your plate just to keep the thing from sliding off on the floor. Hold on a minute, there seems to be some kind of writing on top. Let me see if I can make it out . . .

BoB wAS hErE.

Bob? Come on, put that pocketknife away before you get us *both* in trouble

Table 21

THIS IS a true story.

Back in the days when the Dunes Hotel was one of the glory spots on the Las Vegas Strip, there was always a line of well-dressed and well-heeled people waiting to get inside the hotel's most famous restaurant. Oh, the coffee shop was fine, and the Dome of the Sea was very nice, but the Sultan's Table was the town's number one in-spot.

This restaurant was the brainchild of Dunes owner Major Riddle, who had the room specially-built in 1961 for Arturo Romero and his Magical Violins. As each diner passed the maître d's desk, he was greeted by name and then whisked to a nearby table. The room was dark except for candles on the tables and a row of spotlights strategically located in the ceiling. These were set for a certain number of violinists, and each stood under his own light, serenading the diners with haunting Strauss waltzes.

The tables were individually numbered inside this elegant restaurant, and the table directly across the room from the maître d's desk was known simply as Table 21. It was no different from all the rest, save one terrifying fact. Sometimes, when a diner stopped there for a meal, he was never seen again. Not by mortal men, for sure. It's true, my friends, for even thunder and lightnin' cannot be as frightenin' as Table 21.

The first to face its cold embrace
was a local man of fame.

His power grew, but we all knew that nothing
stays the same.

He stopped to dine and taste the wine,
to have himself some fun.

The music played, he over-stayed at Table 21.

When he would leave that fateful eve,
no more his foes he'd shun.

His bones were found beneath the ground
before a week was done.

The victim in question was Las Vegas Culinary Union leader Al Bramlett. He had allegedly hired a local man and his son to torch a Las Vegas bar that wasn't unionized, but neglected to pay them for their work. They drove him to the desert, gave him a drink of whiskey, then shot him to death. Unfortunately, he was not the last victim of Table 21.

Another gent, whose power went across this
spacious land,

became the next within our text to feel
the Reaper's hand.

He took a chair, he lingered there,
at Table 21.

He ate his fill, he paid his bill,
he said he had to run.

He went his way, and to this day
he's never seen the sun.

Again we see the mystery of Table 21.

Victim number two was former Teamsters boss Jimmy Hoffa. Hoffa had spent his hours at the Sultan's Table huddled with his lawyer and other cronies, presumably discussing Hoffa's return to the union after serving a prison sentence. He took a plane back to his home town, where he disappeared several days later. His body was never found.

Soon after that, a gangster sat with others
    at this table.

As victim he was number three to circumvent
    our fable.

While laughter boomed around the room,
    an evil web was spun.

For lurking near, intentions clear,
    was someone with a gun.

Outside of town the hood was found,
    his life on earth quite done.

Few things are worse than this old curse
    of Table 21.

Las Vegas crime boss Tony Spilotro had left the city for a gangland meeting in Chicago when he and his brother were abducted at gunpoint and taken for their last ride. On a farm outside Chicago, they were both bludgeoned to death and buried in a makeshift grave.

Perhaps the fact that Spilotro, Hoffa and Bramlett all dined at Table 21 shortly before their deaths was purely coincidental. Then again, who can say? After all, the Sultan's Table is gone now, and Table 21 is just another relic of a time gone by. Someday, however, the furniture from the Sultan's Table may be moved to another restaurant in Las Vegas. The violins will begin to play again. At the desk will be a smiling maître d', and in the background you may see a candle-lit table with a fresh red rose at its center.

So if some day you come this way, and pardon
    please the pun,

you fail to see the maître d' get something
    when he's done.

Don't tarry if he tells you less your blood
    begins to run:

"This table's just the one for you.
    It's Table 21."

The Double Whammy

BACK IN THE EARLY DAYS of the big money poker tournaments, a table-load of wizened card sharks sat at Binion's Horseshoe Club, waiting for the first hand to get underway.

The dealer shuffled the cards noiselessly, burned one, then proceeded to give five cards to each player. The game was stud poker, no limit, each player starting with a $10,000 bankroll.

Peeking at his hand, the first player couldn't believe his eyes. Ace of clubs, ace of diamonds, ace of hearts, king of clubs, king of hearts. Full house, aces high. Heart thumping wildly, he pushed all his chips toward the middle of the table.

"Fold," the next player said, shaking his head. "Fold," said the next. "I'm out," sighed another. The last player picked up his cards, studied them calmly, and shoved his $10,000 into the pot.

Then he turned his cards over, one at a time. Ten, jack, queen, king, ace. All spades. Read 'em and weep.

The upshot of this true story is that the player with the full house got hit by fate with a double whammy: some unbelievably good luck followed immediately by some unbelievably bad luck.

The stories go on and on. There was the 37-year-old Boston cook who hit the Massachusetts lottery for $3.6 million. He bought only one thing with his first $180,722 installment: a Dalmatian puppy for his two young children. Two weeks after hitting the jackpot—and on his first day back at work—he died of a sudden heart attack. Doctors said it was brought on by stress, but it was also the old double whammy: good luck followed by bad.

A Texas teen-ager got caught stealing stamps, but the good

news was that charges against him were dropped after he paid for the stolen stamps. The bad news was that he did it with a forged check for $9,700. Now he faces charges on both counts.

A Michigan couple won $10 million when a hamburger chain drew their ticket during a nationwide contest. "It just hasn't sunk in yet," the couple said at a press conference—which was just as well, because the next day the couple was disqualified. It seems their daughter was working part-time as a hamburger helper in one of the company's outlets. The couple was so upset they wouldn't even take the company's consolation offer: an all-expenses-paid weekend at a Michigan hotel.

In a Las Vegas casino, a man playing a quarter slot machine suddenly had to go to the bathroom. "Keep playing this machine," the man told his wife. "I'll be right back."

This particular machine was part of a slot arcade called "QuarterMania," where the jackpot with two quarters invested was much more than what it would be if only one quarter was invested. Well, you can guess what happened next.

The man exited the bathroom to see a large crowd gathered around his wife's slot machine. Yes, she hit the jackpot, but being a very conservative gambler she put only one quarter in the machine. So instead of winning the progressive jackpot of $360,817.38, she and her husband got a paltry $1,250.

This set off the biggest altercation since the second Ali/Frazier fight. A right to the chin and the wife was down; a jab to the midsection and the husband was down. Security guards called Metro for reinforcements, but as one policeman later told reporters, "There isn't a judge in the world who would convict the guy of assault."

An even sadder story concerns an Arkansas family who tried something called the "million dollar baby" slot machines at a fancy Las Vegas casino. The father didn't have any luck, the mother didn't have any luck, but the son lined up a row of 7's for a million-dollar payoff. Yet the casino refused to pay him because he was only nineteen years old.

He was old enough to vote, and old enough to go to war, but not old enough to gamble—even though he had been do-

but not old enough to gamble—even though he had been doing so up until the moment he hit that jackpot. The casino
wound up in a no-win situation of its own. Pay the teen, cause
a scene. Stiff the youth, look uncouth. It opted for the latter.

In the Philippines, the government lottery had few takers
because of rumors that it was rigged, so President Aquino came
up with a novel idea. She appointed Brigadier General Alfredo
Lim to investigate alleged irregularities, then televised the
weekly drawing to show the whole thing was on the up and
up. The winner of the $200,000 top prize was—Brigadier
General Alfredo Lim.

Then there was the man who won the lottery in Washington. I won't bother giving his name or age because the police
already have that information. Anyway, according to a story in
the newspaper this fellow was getting $40,000 a year as a re-
sult of hitting the lottery, but couldn't survive on it and wound
up knocking off a grocery store.

The story caught my eye a lot quicker than one I had
stumbled across a few weeks earlier about a retired millionaire
who won a new car and gave it to charity. Personally, I cannot
relate with someone who doesn't have to work for a living, but
I do have a certain rapport with: (A) anyone who makes
$40,000 a year or less; and (B) anyone who spends $40,000 a
year or more. Besides, grocery stores have been robbing us
blind for years, so what's wrong with one half-skinned lottery
winner trying to get even?

The sports world has had its share of double whammies.
Andy Hawkins of the New York Yankees pitched a no-hitter
against the Chicago White Sox one summer, only to lose the
game 4-0. How did it happen? In the bottom of the eighth,
with two out and the score tied 0-0, four consecutive batters
scored after errors by Yankee fielders. That's almost as bad as
the golfer who gave up two strokes after losing his ball. He
found it soon afterwards while playing another ball on the
same hole. It had landed in the cup for a hole-in-one.

Losers! Give us your poor, your homeless, your downtrod-
den, your losers. Most of us, who have never won a World Series pool, who have never even found a good parking place,

are the stories that inspire great novels, beautiful music, priceless paintings.

Schubert's *Unfinished Symphony* will always be everyone's favorite, simply because he died before he finished it. Vincent Van Gogh never sold a painting until he chopped off an ear, and then he was the talk of the art world.

The point is that we really don't mind when other people have bad luck because we've all had our share of it, and it's nice to spread it around. In fact, the only time we seem to be troubled by news of bad luck affecting others is when it happens to one of our animals. A race horse breaks its leg and the sports commentator practically cries as he reads the story. If someone finds a dinosaur bone it rates 25 pages in *National Geographic*, but the tomb of an ancient pharaoh is only important if it is filled with gold and precious stones. Then it is newsworthy.

For some reason, we seem to breathe a little easier when we hear about someone else's misfortune. Maybe the reason for this is that our own problems seem so inconsequential in comparison. After all, how can a busted sprinkler pipe or a tax audit compare with the following true story. A millionaire gambler died after a long illness. In his will, he left instructions that his long-neglected wife fly to Las Vegas and place a $5,000 bet in his memory at the dice table.

She flew to Las Vegas. She made the bet. She lost. Now *that's* a double whammy.

The Heist

(As told to the author)

IT WAS MY IDEA. Well, maybe it was Paulie's idea, but my parole came through and his didn't. Of course, I wouldn't have done anything until he got out—what with honor among thieves and all that—but then he tried to climb an electric fence during a rainstorm, and that was the end of Paulie.

He was quite a guy, though, when he was alive. At lockup everybody else would be mooching one last cigarette, and there was Paulie, standing at attention in front of his cell, his hair parted in the middle and wearing those thick horn-rimmed glasses. It drove the other cons crazy, but that's just the way Paulie was.

I guess I should tell you that Paulie was a computer nerd, which is what got him in the joint in the first place. I don't know the technical term for it, but he was patching in on government secrets, then selling the info to the Russkies . . . and here I thought the only thing you could do on a computer was play *Pac Man.*

We'd been sharing the same cell for seven years, and if you've ever been in prison I don't have to tell you what it's like. Once you've gone through the new *Playboy,* there ain't a heck of a lot to do for the rest of the month except talk. So one night we're in our bunks, shooting the breeze, and Paulie comes up with this great idea.

We drive to Vegas, Paulie gets a job running a computer in one of those swanky casinos until he finds out how much cash is laying around, then I come in on a busy night and grab it all. It sounded good the way Paulie put it, and it was another year before I figured out I was getting the short end of the stick. If the coppers started blasting, they wouldn't be aiming at some guy on a computer. They'd be aiming at me.

Anyway, that's when I got my parole and without even thinking about it I hitched a ride to Vegas. I'm figuring maybe I'll go to computer school myself, but then I hear you have to know how to type and that let me out right there. The only training I had was making license plates and scraping trays in the prison lunchroom, although there was one bright spot: I could fill out a job application in about 15 seconds.

I was staying in some flophouse downtown when I got word that Paulie fried himself, and it hit me real hard. The story was buried on the back page of an old newspaper, and I wouldn't have even seen it if I hadn't been scrounging through a garbage can looking for free meal coupons.

There was another story in the same newspaper. Some Vegas big shot was being interviewed, and he said the average casino kept a million dollars in cash on hand in case they had to pay any big winners. I stood there in the alley with tears running down my face. It was like Paulie was speaking to me from the grave.

I had enough cash salted away to hit the local pawn shop, but the only thing I could find in my price range was a chrome-plated starter pistol. It was for shooting blanks, but I didn't care. I wasn't out to ace-deuce anybody; I just wanted that million dollars.

The next day was a Saturday, and I spent the afternoon casing this big joint on the Strip. I didn't see any coppers, just a few security guards carrying flashlights and nightsticks. The place was crawling with tourists, and they all looked like bums. For once in my life, I felt like I belonged.

Night fell, and I made my move. I walked right up to a blonde cashier and said in my gruffest voice, "Give me all the

(Right) Not all executive jobs in the casino are glamorous. This surveillance man at the Union Plaza used binoculars to zero in on the action below in this mid-1970s photograph. When the Union Plaza opened in mid-1971, at the site of the former Union Station railroad depot, it was the world's largest casino.

big stuff." Without a word she started dropping packets of bills into a cloth bag, and 30 seconds later I was beating a hasty exit out the side door.

I holed up in my room for the rest of the weekend with a bottle of Jack Daniels and the sack of money. It wasn't a million dollars, but it was close enough: $86,505. Then the local news came on TV and my caper was the leadoff story. To my amazement the announcer described me as a "smooth-talking well-dressed businessman," and said I got away with half a million dollars.

Well, it didn't take an Alfred Einstein to put two and two together. These guys were jacking up the take to get a bigger payoff from the insurance company, and with the description they gave nobody would ever find me. How's that for fate? I was finally at the top of the heap, somewhere I'd tried to get all my life, and I was still the fall guy.

Of course, I still had eighty-six grand in my kick, so I wasn't about to holler to the feds. Instead, I hiked over to a used car lot and bought myself some wheels, and three days later I was sipping tequila in some burg in the middle of Mexico.

I had just motioned to the señorita for another bottle when two big bruisers walked in. The bar was full of empty tables, but they headed straight for mine. "How you doing, pal?" one of them said, dropping into a chair next to me.

"No hobble Engles," I stumbled, my heart thumping out the Mexican Hat Dance.

"Sure you do," he smiled.

"Okay, you got me. So what do we do now?"

What we did was walk over to my room at the Buenas Noches and collect the rest of the cash. The next thing I knew we were in a big Chrysler on our way back to the states. It turned out the two goons weren't even coppers, but a couple of hired guns working for the casino I knocked off. They deposited me in the owner's office, and he counted the money while I stood there wondering if I was gonna see Paulie again real soon.

That was three years ago. For some reason the owner took a

shine to me and put me to work in the casino's surveillance department. Maybe he figured that since I was a crook I wouldn't have any trouble spotting other crooks before they got cute.

Now I've got a big office up on the second floor, and a secretary named Goldie who does all my typing for me. There's also a row of TV monitors on the wall, which helps me keep track of what's going on down on the casino floor. So if you're ever out in Vegas, and you're thinking about putting something over on one of the casinos, you'd better think again. I might be the one watching you. Never mind my name, or where I work. Just think of me as—Paulie's friend.

Las Vegas In Blue Jeans

IN 1931, two incidents of note occurred in Nevada. One was the advent of legalized gambling, introduced in the state assembly as Bill Number 98 by freshman legislator Phil Tobin. Tobin, who didn't even like gambling, admitted receiving three bottles of Scotch for introducing the bill, but promptly gave them away. Tobin didn't like to drink, either. He also didn't like politics and he didn't like Carson City, so he moved to a ranch near Tonopah. Then he found that he didn't like cows and he didn't like horses, so he died.

The other event that forever changed the face of Nevada was the construction of Hoover Dam. Originally known as Boulder Dam, it was renamed in honor of Herbert Hoover in 1947. According to one historian, Hoover—who was living out the twilight of his years—felt sorry for himself because nothing was named after him. Somebody brought this to President Truman's attention, and he reportedly said, "That damn Hoover." to which the reply was, "Good idea, Mister President."

The dam was built for $49 million, which is peanuts by today's standards. In fact, it did not even rate front page news at the time. Everyone was too busy reading about other shattering events: the unrest in Europe, the civil strife in China, the Las Vegas wedding of big time movie stars Rex Bell and Clara Bow.

In 1935 the dam was opened, and tons of water from the Colorado River instantly formed Lake Mead, making it the largest man-made body of water in the country. Fishermen loved the vast expanse of shimmering blue water, thrashing with a dozen varieties of fish, while on shore wives waited with eager anticipation.

"Look, hon, I caught a bluegill."

"That's nice, dear."

The same year that President Roosevelt dedicated the dam, the local Elks Club inaugurated a yearly celebration to honor the town's western heritage. It was also a publicity stunt to attract more tourists, so the Elks had to come up with a snappy slogan.

"What do you think of Western Week?" proposed one.

"Hell, no," grumbled another.

"How about Eldorado Time?"

"Hell, no."

"Well, hell, you think of something."

"Hell, that's it! Hell, it's perfect. Hell, let's call it Helldorado Days!!"

Meanwhile, the fabled Las Vegas Strip was established when the Pair-O-Dice Club reopened as the 91 Club on the future site of the Last Frontier, which would later be rebuilt and renamed the New Frontier, which would later be rebuilt and renamed the Plain Old Frontier.

In 1947, United Airlines started up service in Las Vegas. Unfortunately, McCarran Air Field would not be completed for another year, so passengers either had to parachute onto a dry lake bed behind the Strip or land in Los Angeles and hitchhike to Barstow where a bus took them to Reno where the train depot was located.

The year 1951 opened with a bang when the Atomic Energy Commission exploded the first atomic bomb at the Nevada Test Site. Local electricity sales dropped dramatically, because for some reason everybody in Las Vegas began to glow in the dark.

Big time movie star Jane Russell arrived in town to film the movie *The Las Vegas Story*. The picture was originally called *A Place In The Sun*, but producers changed the title at the last minute because they thought it was too corny.

The Sands Hotel became the seventh major resort on the Strip when it opened in 1952. Its motto said it all: "A Place In The Sun."

In 1954, big time movie star Ronald Reagan headlined a va-

Although Benjamin "Bugsy" Siegel's Flamingo was not the first resort on the Strip, it is credited as being the most plush. Nobody knew it at the time, but the Flamingo was destined to shape the future of Las Vegas.

---

riety show at the Last Frontier, and cracked up the audience with:

"I don't know why everybuddy's mad at President Truman. He hasn't done anything."

When reminded that Dwight Eisenhower is now president, Reagan retorted with:

"Well, that's a coincidence. There used to be an army general with that very same name."

The Nevada Tax Commission met in 1955 and created the Gaming Control Board. The three members of the board—affectionately known as Moe, Curly and Larry—vowed to rid the state of crime, corruption and anything else that started with a "C."

In 1957, the first permanent building was erected on the

University of Nevada Las Vegas campus. It was a basketball gymnasium.

Nine-year-old Liza Minnelli made her Las Vegas nightclub debut, but canceled after one show because of "Vegas throat." She was replaced by six-year-old Jay Leno.

The Nevada Legislature met in 1959 and created the Nevada Gaming Commission. The five members of the commission immediately challenged the Gaming Control Board to a pie fight.

Big time movie star Frank Sinatra brought his clan to the Sands Hotel in 1960. By the time his first engagement ended, he had belted 267 songs, 88 jokes, two security guards, a pit boss and three photographers.

Oran Gragson began his 27th term as Mayor of Las Vegas by hosting a celebration party at his home on Gragson Road just off the Oran Gragson Freeway.

In 1966 Howard Hughes took up residence at the Desert Inn, making local headlines when he put $546 million in the hotel's safety deposit box.

Caesars Palace, built at a cost exceeding Hoover Dam, opened on the Las Vegas Strip. Builder Jay Sarno called it the eighth wonder of the world.

In 1967, Elvis Presley married Priscilla Beaulieu at the Aladdin. Elvis jokingly suggested that the resort be renamed Heartbreak Hotel, and was immediately hit in the face with a pie by the members of the Gaming Control Board.

Circus Circus opened on the Las Vegas Strip, and was billed as the first family-style casino in town. Builder Jay Sarno called it the eighth wonder of the world.

In 1969, a rugged cross-desert race named the Mint 400 was instituted by hotel owner Del Webb. The race, which was picketed by desert tortoises and other wildlife, ended in near tragedy when Webb's Jaguar sideswiped two Mazerattis and a Ferrari.

Eight years after being built, the Landmark Hotel finally opened amid roars of approval from both tourists and creditors. Jay Sarno called it the eighth blunder of the world.

Frank Sinatra left the Sands and went to Caesars Palace.

The MGM Grand Hotel, built at a cost exceeding the national defense budget, opened on the Las Vegas Strip in 1973. Jai alai was introduced to the city's gaming public, and although no one at the MGM was exactly sure what jai alai was, people were assured they could bet on it.

The Culinary Union went on strike in 1976, but the walkout ended three weeks later because people stayed too sober to gamble.

Leon Spinks won the world heavyweight championship at the Las Vegas Hilton in 1978, dethroning Muhammad Ali. This established Las Vegas as the boxing capital of the world and made promoter Don King a very rich man.

Frank Sinatra left Caesars Palace and went to the Golden Nugget.

Siegfried and Roy began their animal magic show "Beyond Belief" at the Frontier Hotel. When told how much the tickets cost, customers exclaimed, "This is beyond belief!" Frank Sinatra left the Golden Nugget and went to the Riviera.

In 1981, the Imperial Palace opened its display of antique automobiles. At the same time, police headquarters was flooded with calls from irate casino workers whose cars had been stolen.

Larry Holmes retained his heavyweight crown at Caesars Palace against challenger Gerry Cooney. Cooney was unable to answer the bell for the eighth round after choking on a pepperoni pizza.

Frank Sinatra left the Riviera and went to Bally's, which used to be the MGM but was sold so the owner could buy the Desert Inn and the Sands, already having sold the International to the Hilton which then bought the Flamingo. Any questions?

It has been almost 60 years since President Roosevelt threw the switch that got the dam to humming. Circle around it on your way to Arizona, fingers drumming on the steering wheel, and you lose sight of the fact that if it weren't for the dam none of this would really be here today. The lake, the cities, the casinos, the tourists.

(Left) Three-time winner Kirk Kerkorian stands at the construction site of the 1,568-room International Hotel in 1969. In 1970, he sold it to the Hilton Corporation. In 1973 he was back again and built the 2,100-room MGM Grand. In 1986, he sold it to the Bally Corporation. His final endeavor was in 1993, when he built and opened the 5,000-room MGM Grand Hotel and Theme Park. As this is written, he still owns it. Each property was heralded as the world's largest at the time of its construction. Kerkorian, a self-made billionaire, has also played a major role in the entertainment industry; He has owned controlling interest of Metro-Goldwyn-Mayer studios since 1969, and purchased United Artists in 1981.

That all stands for water—precious, scarcest water. Without that dam, none of this (fact or fiction) could have happened.

Seizer's Palace

DWARFED AMID THE SHADOWS of the Mirage Hotel, there is still something almost magical about Caesars Palace in Las Vegas. At night it resembles a giant iridescent birthday cake, with bluish-green lights filtering through lacy white stone. Thirty thousand tourists a day file onto the moving walk-way at Caesars, then are disgorged inside the casino like so many pounds of potatoes coming off a conveyer belt. Cameras at the ready, they prowl every corner—searching for a movie star, a seat at the bar, a slot machine with a free play on it.

They will take pictures of the statue of David, which came from the same quarry as the original by Michelangelo. They will take pictures of the $3 million swimming pool, and wonder if it is filled with water or Dom Perignon. They will take anything else that is not nailed down. "Look what I got at Caesars Palace . . . a foil-imprinted drinking glass bag from the room where Anthony Quinn's ex-wife stayed!" Caesars Palace will go through 600,000 of them a year, along with 12,000 ashtrays and half a million dinner napkins.

Nearly 200,000 drinking glasses vanish each year, and more than 100,000 ball-point pens wind up in the wrong pocket—simply because the name of the hotel is written on them. I was fortunate to grab a dozen myself before some greedy tourist beat me to them.

Here are some more annual usage figures from Caesars Palace, what someone in the hotel's marketing department calls its "Gee Whiz" statistics. Perhaps after reading them you will not feel too badly the next time you blow half your paycheck at the grocery store.

The electric bill at Caesars for one year is three million dol-

Caesars Palace is without question the most opulent resort in Las Vegas. Statuary and fountains adorn the grounds, and it's even nicer inside. Oh, oh . . . what happened to the head on this statue?

lars. Is that shocking, or what? Over 240,000 gallons of water will be used in the same twelve-month period, not to mention 249,600 rolls of toilet paper, and 11,700,000 Kleenex tissues.

Half a million glasses of milk are served each year, compared with a whopping 744,000 bottles of beer. Tomato juice out-sells orange juice 2,152,000 ounces to 1,105,920. Coffee: 156,000 pounds. Vodka: 594,000 shots.

For some strange reason, pork loin is about ten times more popular at Caesars than beef tenderloin. People eat over

200,000 pounds of pork loin a year in the different restaurants, compared to only 26,400 pounds of tenderloin. Being from Texas, I didn't even know what pork loin was until I got to Las Vegas. The only thing I ever got to eat at home was bacon and pork chops, and that was on special occasions—like when my uncle had a job.

Caesars believes in buttering up its customers—with 2,492,880 pats consumed each year. What I am beginning to wonder is who counts all this stuff? Does Caesars Palace have someone in its employ whose official title is something like "butter pat tabulator?" I would hate to be having breakfast in their elegant coffee shop when a voice came bellowing over the loudspeaker, "You there in the Caesars Palace sweatshirt and the Caesars Palace baseball cap! How many butter patties did you just put on your raisin toast?" Or even worse:

"Drop that butter knife and spread 'em!"

Then there is the matter of those little red maraschino cherries. These are always found at the bottom of one's drink, usually under two or three half-melted ice cubes, and almost impossible to retrieve with the little plastic stir stick that says "Caesars Palace" on it. Nonetheless, some 2,080,000 maraschino cherries go to their depths at Caesars each year. I never did find out how many sticky stir sticks got stolen.

To me a salad is not a salad without a couple of slices of cool crispy cucumber. In fact, at Caesars no vegetable outnumbers cucumbers. Caesars Palace peels 93,600 of them a year, compared to only 74,880 heads of iceberg lettuce rolling onto the butcher's block. Lettuce pray.

These "Gee Whiz" statistics would not be complete without talking eggs. Whether they wind up scrambled, poached, boiled or fried, diners at Caesars wade through 2,808,000 eggs a year. And if you do not find the eggs at Caesars all they are cracked up to be, there is always Heinz catsup to smother the taste—1,310,400 ounces of it a year, to be exact.

It is hard to believe that just a hundred years ago this whole chunk of Nevada was nothing but desert. Heck, a good meal back then would have probably been rattlesnake and wagon ruts. But thanks to the culinary artists at Caesars Palace and all the other fancy places, and to the advent of grocery store chains and jet aircraft, the average tourist can now eat himself silly during his stay in Las Vegas. Never mind that his luggage rattles all the way to the airport. (Even the room towels will not stop an occasional ashtray from sliding around in a suitcase.)

The casino usually winds up with the last laugh, however. After the average tourist spends $58 on a room, $46 for a show, $46 on food and drinks, $59 in miscellaneous expenses, and $77 for gambling each day, that ashtray turns out to be a pretty expensive souvenir.

Ben

I USED TO HAVE a boss named Ben. He was average-looking as far as pit bosses go, except for the fact that he had a glass eye. At least, so the rumors went. "Which eye is it?" I finally asked a friend.

"It's the one with the glint of human kindness in it," he replied.

Well, that described Ben. For instance, a dealer once asked him for a week off. His grandmother had died, he told Ben, and he wanted to go home for the funeral. Ben gave the dealer a long cold stare and then said, "Son, were you really *that* close to your grandmother?"

Another man who worked for Ben got an emergency phone call from his wife that their house was on fire. He rushed to Ben and said he had to leave. "What can you do?" Ben replied. "You're no fireman."

Then there was the time the hotel moved the employee parking lot right next to a cyclone fence, which separated the grounds from the golf course. Sure enough, one of the dealers walking into the hotel got hit by a wayward golf ball. He limped up to Ben and explained what happened, holding out the golf ball as evidence of his injury. "Tell me," Ben said to the dealer. "Did he holler 'fore?'"

Ben spent the rest of the day chuckling over that one.

One thing I remember about Ben was that he never got excited. Maybe it was because he had seen it all in his 40 years of casino work, or maybe it was because he was half-gassed by the middle of the day. He would perch on a stool in the middle of the dice pit, and every afternoon at exactly 2:30 he ordered a cup of "coffee" from the cocktail waitress. The fumes, almost visible to the naked eye, were enough to bow the knees of anyone within ten yards.

Surprisingly, Ben ran a tight ship. No pun intended. So it was a surprise to all when Ben was fired one day. He didn't meet his end for some off-the-wall reason like "change in personnel" or "reduction in staff." Ben went out in a blaze of glory. The owner of the hotel, who made Jesse James look like a choirboy, was convinced that everyone in the place was out to rob him blind. He spent a fortune on sophisticated surveillance equipment, and even hooked up microphones to the dice tables so he could listen in on the dealers' conversations. Appearing before a group of stockholders, he once bragged that he was the lowest-paid casino owner on the Strip. He neglected to add that the salaries of his wife and son, who were also officers of the company, raised his income to over a million dollars a year.

So it had to happen. The hotel owner kept harping about crooks and thieves until Ben could stand it no longer. He looked the owner dead in the eye and said, "You know, my granddaddy used to say that any man who worried about people stealing from him was usually a thief himself."

That was the end of Ben. It was also the end of an era. The hotel went into bankruptcy shortly after that. Then the owner left town, and all the good help gradually moved on to greener pastures.

And Ben? I saw him one last time. It was a spring morning, and I stopped at a convenience store. When I walked inside, the clerk asked if I had a coat hanger. An elderly man had locked his keys in his car, she explained. I looked around and there was Ben, perched on a stool next to the magazine rack.

I had always seen Ben when he was wearing a dark suit and a starched white shirt, so I didn't recognize him at first. He didn't look like my Ben, the hard-as-nails pit boss who had barreled into my nightmares on many a queasy night.

This man was old and thin, and so frail I might have killed him if I slapped him on the back. "How are you, Ben?" I asked, standing in front of him as I did so many times before.

Ben mumbled something back, all the while staring blankly past my face. We walked outside, and I fished a coat hanger inside his window, finally hooking it onto the door button and springing the thing open. Before I had a chance to say another word, Ben eased into the driver's seat and cranked the engine to life. He nodded, then slowly backed out of the parking lot. Without another look in my direction he was gone.

Five days later Ben died in his sleep.

Oh, I won't say that his death had a profound effect upon me. Still, when I heard the news I felt a little twinge inside. Someone I knew was gone from the world for good, and the truth is he really wasn't that bad. I may have gone home a few times with a lump in my throat, or a flush on my face, but the next day I was right back at work again.

And so I miss Ben. I miss him in this age of corporate razzmatazz, when experience and ability mean everything—as long as you're under 40 years old. I miss him when I see workers losing seniority and vacation benefits because a new management team comes to power. I miss him when I drive through a local suburb and see a massive casino doing business where a neighborhood shopping center used to be. I miss him when I bounce over outdated streets, and when I see artificial lakes and waterfalls that blatantly waste this state's most precious resource.

Yes, I miss Ben, and I wonder if somewhere in the heavens he isn't perched on a cloud this very minute, sipping nectar out of a coffee cup and giving the angels a hard time. I know I was scared to death the whole time I worked for him—but I would give anything to do it again.

The Awards Banquet

MAY I HAVE your attention, please?

Welcome to our first annual Casino Awards Banquet. We are extremely happy to have the . . . could I get you to hold it down, guys? Frank, you want to take that lamp shade off and have a seat?

Thank you. First of all, I think we should give a big round of applause to the kitchen staff. The mashed potatoes and peas were great, and the meatloaf was really tasty. We've got dessert coming later, too, so hold on to your plastic spoons.

I'd also like to thank the management of the hotel for allowing us to use this meeting room tonight. We have to be out of here by 7:30, so I'll make this as short as possible.

Our first trophy is what we call our Top Gun Award. It goes to the person who has done the most to make our jobs a little easier and a lot more fun. And our Top Gun Award this year goes to Casino Manager Don "Warning Slip" Ballinger. Come on up, Mr. Ballinger, and say a few words. What's that, he's not here? Oh, well, we'll get it to him somehow. He says the door to his office is always open, and now I know why. There's never anyone in it. Ha ha, just kidding, Mr. Ballinger—wherever you are.

Incidentally, I want to thank Ralph Ironsides of Security for these beautiful trophies. Ralph managed to get 'em wholesale through his brother-in-law, so you'll all be getting a little refund on your next paycheck.

And now our Dealer of the Year Award. As you no doubt remember, we had all 43 of the dealers vote last month for who they thought was the best dealer in the hotel. And believe it or not, this year we have a 43-way tie. Unfortunately, we only have one trophy, so each of you will get to keep it for one week and 13 hours.

Now I'd like to read something out of our dealer's manual, which I think exemplifies what we are all striving for in this crazy business.

"Casino customers spend more time with the dealers than any other employees. It is important that the dealers give the normal courtesies and customer services that let the customers enjoy themselves so they want to return to our hotel again and again."

With that thought in mind, we present our Most Courteous Dealer of the Year Award—and this year it goes to roulette dealer Freddy Rodriguez. Freddy? Hey, you didn't have to rip the damn thing out of my hand. I was going to give a little speech first. Yeah, same to you, pal.

We also have three Purple Heart Awards to present tonight. Our first one goes to Harvey Ferris, who has worked graveyard shift for nineteen straight days without once calling in sick. Way to go, Harv.

The next Purple Heart Award goes to cocktail waitress Shirley Killebrew. Shirley's kind of a mainstay in the keno lounge, where she has served cocktails for the last 17 years. I understand she is unable to be here tonight because of the bus strike, but maybe we can get a volunteer to run the trophy over to her at the trailer park.

Our third Purple Heart Award goes to blackjack dealer Joyce Markle. I think the caption on the bottom of her trophy says it all. "To Joyce Markle, for dealing to Jerry Lewis."

To Entertainment Director Pete Valentine, we would like to present our Service Excellence Award. Thanks, Pete, for making our showroom, "The Seven Drink Minimum", the talk of the Strip. And as a special treat I am pleased to announce that Pete has arranged a 4:30 A.M. show tomorrow for all casino employees. Featured will be Janet Stanton and her all-girl orchestra along with Elvis impersonator Steve Simmons. Sounds like a great line-up.

We also have a Special Achievement Award for Bo Whittenburg, who has done such a remarkable job this year of heading up the Dealer's Toke Committee. Unfortunately, Bo is still in Acapulco, but we're hoping to have him back in the near future—just as soon as we can arrange some kind of extradition proceedings with the Mexican government.

To Dean Brumley, our Golden Casino award. As you all know, Dean is in charge of making up the schedule. It certainly hasn't made Dean the most popular guy here tonight, but in our opinion he has done the best he could under the circumstances. No need for you to come all the way up here for your trophy, Dean. Here, catch.

Well, that's about it for tonight. On behalf of the owners of the hotel, who have just announced record profits for the third straight year, a special thank you for a job well done. And don't forget to pick up your certificate for a free turkey when you punch in at the time office on Christmas morning.

Hey, wait a minute, everybody, where are you going? Don't leave yet. We've got Jell-O coming!

Stardancer

THE HEAVY SHIP churned through the blue Pacific, leaving a frothy wake nearly half a mile wide. I stood at the railing and searched for sea life, but all I saw was another gorgeous sunset. Every day it was the same. The sun would hang in the sky like a flaming orange ball, then suddenly drop below the horizon in the wink of an eye.

They say this is a special moment, and that if you watch closely you will see a green flash at the very instant of sunset. I thought I saw it once, but staring into a dying sun I could not be sure. Perhaps it was my imagination, or maybe it was just scar tissue forming on my corneas.

I felt my way inside the ship, almost shocked to find other people moving about. Like it or not, we were in this together, each of us fused with the rest. You see, this was one of the last voyages of the great *M.V. Stardancer*, flagship of the Admiral Lines. It would go into dry-dock soon, then steam under a new flag with a new name——*Viking Serenade*.

What a mighty vessel she was, eleven stories tall and complete with health club, library, hospital, movie theater, beauty salon and disco. When not in line for meals, however, the thousand passengers aboard seemed either to be at the ping-pong table or wedged inside the ship's casino.

The casino was small by Las Vegas standards, but big enough to hurt you. In sight were 95 slot machines, a two-dealer craps table, three blackjack games, a roulette wheel and a Caribbean Stud table. Most of the dealers talked with clipped British accents, and I soon learned why. If an English dealer stayed away for a year, he paid no taxes. Americans, of course, were afforded no such luxury, since the ship docked in Long Beach once a week.

Still, it sounded like a glamorous way to make a living. Then I met dealer Fiona Stephen (English), supervisor Mark Davies (English), and dealer Sharon Scott (American). "We sign a nine-month contract," Mark said. "At the end of it, we get a return flight home."In the meantime, casino personnel work six days a week, and put in eight to nine hours a day. "We're like flight attendants," Sharon added. "We make the same run every week and we're around the same people all the time." While at sea, dealers eat all meals in a staff dining room, and sleep two to a room that measures ten by 20 feet. (On this particular cruise, there were only eight rooms available for casino personnel—thus the staff consisted of nine dealers, three supervisors, two slot technicians and two cashiers.)

"We make $400 a month in salary," Fiona said. "But with the tips, it's still a good job." Exotic ports of call, free room and board, tips that aboard the *Stardancer* averaged $300 a week— it all sounded wonderful to me. Then again, I would have probably spent all my money on Dramamine. And there were sharks in the water, I learned, one being an Austrian company that paid its dealers $1,000 a month in wages—and in return kept 95 percent of their tips!

The biggest complaint of those who gamble on cruise ships is the dissimilarity between the games in Las Vegas and those on the high seas. At blackjack, for instance, the maximum bet on the *Stardancer* was $100; a player could only double down on 9, 10 and 11; and he could only split pairs once. There were single odds at the dice table, a maximum bet of $50 on the pass line, no such thing as come bets, and most proposition bets paid $1 less than they do in Las Vegas. The slot machines were even worse, their paybacks set at around 83 percent. That compares with an average return in Las Vegas casinos of between 90 and 97 percent, depending upon what the competition is doing.

Yet there was something exhilarating about gambling on the *Stardancer*, or at least my wife thought so. She discovered a game called Caribbean Stud, and almost paid for the trip with her winnings. Others were not as fortunate, including one player who spent half his time at the table and the other half at the purser's desk cashing traveler's checks.

Basically, Caribbean Stud is a simple game, and I still have not figured out why it isn't popular in Las Vegas. Each player antes and receives five cards. Players who fold lose their ante, and those who stay must double their ante. The dealer then shows his cards. If he does not have a king and ace, or better, then the hand is over and the players win their original ante. Otherwise, the game continues on the same principle as regular stud poker, except no one gets any more cards. The other variation is the payoffs, which range from even money on a winning pair to 100 to 1 for a royal flush.

The atmosphere on board a cruise ship is relaxed and informal, and the views from the portholes are breathtaking. That is, if you like ocean, sea and water. It's old hat, though, to the dealers and other ship personnel, who no longer blink when they hear such questions as:

"Do you live on the ship?"

"Do these stairs go up?"

"What time is the midnight buffet?"

And so we steamed to Mexico. Open sea, a spot on the horizon that gradually became a peninsula, then the coastal villages of Cabo San Lucas, Mazatlan and Puerto Vallarta. Better known as the Mexican Riviera, these towns along the Pacific were as old as time—Cabo San Lucas, discovered in 1517 by Hernan Cortez; Mazatlan, discovered in 1519 by Francisco Fernandez de Cordoba; and Puerto Vallarta, discovered in 1964 by Elizabeth Taylor.

I loved it all, and spent my time in Puerto Vallarta at a rustic outdoor cafe called Chico's Paradise. Situated in the mountains outside of town, there were babbling brooks, rushing waterfalls and a delicious Mexican lunch for only 15,000 pesos. Four phrases in broken Spanish got me through the day in fine fashion. "Un cervesa pronto." "Otra cervesa, por favor." "Mas cervesa." And: "Donde esta el cuarto hombres?"

Back aboard the *Stardancer*, we started the long trek home. You would think that on a ship this size there would be little to do except count the passengers and then count the life boats, but not so. There was cash jackpot bingo (the pot up to

$4,000 by the end of the journey), video poker tournaments, skeet shooting, and swimming in a salt water pool. For the faint-hearted, there were trivia contests, walking on the deck (weather permitting), napkin folding, and guessing the ages of your dinner companions.

On the last night of the voyage a stack of empty envelopes and a small card mysteriously appeared in our cabin. The card read "Guidelines on Gratuities," and suddenly we found out why everyone had been so nice to us. From the cabin steward ($2.50 a day per passenger) to the busboy ($1.25 a day per passenger) to the head waiter (at your discretion).

The farewell dinner was a gloomy affair, even though the food was excellent. There were warm hugs for Pepito the waiter and Joseph the busboy, and envelopes changed hands as smoothly as clockwork. My wife cried as she said good bye. Pepito had always been there when she needed him. I am not ashamed to admit that I wept, too. After all, I would never see all those $20 bills again.

Counter

BARKELY CRUM, not his real name, is a card counter. I was to meet him at a secluded table in an anonymous restaurant on the outskirts of Las Vegas. Our eight o'clock appointment rolled past with no sign of Crum, so as I sat waiting for him I reviewed all I knew about card counters.

The card-counting theory was devised by computer expert Julian Braun, and its purpose was to help blackjack players win by keeping track of the cards. According to Braun, if there were a lot of small cards left in the deck, it was advantageous to the casino, and if there were a lot of big cards left, the player had the best of it. So all the card counter had to do was memorize which cards had been played, and make his bets accordingly.

To help the player do this, he used a plus and minus system. Every time a small card was played (2 through 6), the player added a point, and every time a big card was played (7 through Ace), he subtracted a point. When the pluses exceeded the minuses, the player upped his stakes. It was a good concept, and also a lot cheaper than marrying a blackjack dealer.

Suddenly I heard footsteps, and there was Barkely Crum. He wore a pair of large sunglasses, an ill-fitting wig, and a baggy plaid suit with a fake flower pinned to the lapel. "Sorry I'm late," he said, casting a furtive glance toward the front door. "But I had to make sure I wasn't being followed."

"Why would anyone be following you?"

"Why?" he repeated, dropping heavily into a chair. "Because I'm a card counter, that's why."

At that moment the waitress appeared before us, and Crum coldly inspected her while I browsed through the menu. "Give me a BLT, hold the mayo, and a side of fries," he said briskly. I

The player gives the dealer the eagle eye; the dealer stares down the player. Who knows what lurks in the minds of these two. It's the modern version of a wild West showdown: the player against the dealer.

ordered the same, then waited for Crum's next comment as the waitress disappeared.

"I wanted to make sure she was a real waitress," he confided. Then under his breath he added, "I *hate* bacon and tomato sandwiches."

"So how long have you been counting cards?" I asked, impatient to learn more about this man of the green cloth.

Crum looked off into space. "Let's see. This is 1993, and I got into card-counting in 1975 . . . uhh, that would be 23 years, right?"

"No, not if you started in 1975. That would be 18 years."

"Oh, okay, 18 years then. See, I was a math major in college, and we used to play cards in the dorm all the time. Then when I graduated, Las Vegas just seemed like the place to go."

"And that's when you started counting cards?"

"Yeah, and I was really good at it." He smiled wistfully as the waitress approached with our sandwiches, then immediately covered his with a paper napkin. "I used to get thrown out of casinos all the time."

"Well, maybe it had something to do with the way you dress."

He looked down at his baggy plaid suit. "You mean this?" he laughed. "No, this is just one of my disguises."

"Oh."

"I must have a hundred different disguises. That way I can count cards all day long without being recognized."

Is one of these people at Sam's Town Casino counting cards? Card counting by professional gamblers used to be of great concern to casinos. The practice of counting cards has been discouraged, however, by the use of multiple decks dealt from plastic boxes called shoes. Practically speaking, however, one mistake in a hundred plays by a counter reduced the player's edge back to the house.

"What are some of your other disguises?"

He counted them off on his fingers. "Priest, farmer, cowboy, construction worker, race car driver, astronaut, human cannonball. I even disguised myself as a woman once, but that didn't work out."

"Why? What happened?"

"Oh, some poker player made a pass at me. I guess I was wearing too much lipstick."

I dug into my pocket and brought out a deck of battered Bicycles. Crum wet his lips as I began to shuffle. Frrrip, frrrip, the old cards went—a sound to a gambler like no other in the world. "Let's play some blackjack," I said, pushing the deck over for him to cut.

"I left my money at home," he said woefully, and I swear I saw a tear running down his cheek.

"Not for money," I exclaimed. "I just want to see how good you are."

Well, we played that game till the sun came up. I'd shuffle and deal, he'd double-down or split. I'd shuffle and deal, he'd stand or hit. When it was all over, we walked out into the warm desert air and I gave him a ride back to town. He was afraid to drive his own car, he said, suspecting there might be a bomb hooked up to the ignition.

You're probably wondering who won the blackjack game, but Crum swore me to secrecy. I can tell you this much. The man is still out there counting cards and wearing his funny disguises. And I still see him quite a bit, now that we both have homes on the same golf course near the Las Vegas Strip. I even named my 40-foot sailboat after him, *The Barkely Crum II*. It isn't all peaches and cream, though. Especially when I'm getting ready for work, and my son looks up at me and says:

"Daddy, how come you're dressed like an Indian chief?"

Land O' Cotton

FRANCE TOOK HER in but didn't want her. Spain wooed her and couldn't afford her. The United States bought her, then didn't know what to do with her.

Situated on a steamy bog between Lake Ponchartrain and the great Mississippi, it is a wonder she found any suitors at all . . . but perhaps that is part of her charm.

She is New Orleans, Louisiana, and her name is whispered almost reverently by those who live here. Born out of wedlock in 1718, she is as old as the South, and a jambalaya of sight, sound, speech and smell.

Her heart is the French Quarter. Iron-tatted balconies looking down on narrow brick streets, Dixieland jazz and git-down blues wailing from murky saloons, the heady aroma of chicory coffee drifting from open courtyards, and every broken cobblestone etched with history.

Jean Lafitte walked these same streets when piracy was a respectable profession, and Andrew Jackson mapped his strategy here against the British. Jefferson Davis's wife died here of "mosquito fever," Carry Nation preached the gospel here, and Mark Twain dodged the draft here during the onset of the Civil War.

Alongside New Orleans churns the muddy Mississippi—too thick to drink, too thin to plow—which gives the whole area a feeling of timelessness. Yet trying to sum up the essence of New Orleans in a sentence or two is impossible. The best description I read was in a Triple A tour book: "A gentlewoman with a ready repertoire of spicy stories." Or how about this one from a Mississippi river cruise pamphlet?

"Let us take you back when cotton was king and life was as slow and graceful as the current on the Mississippi." That's worth $29.75 (Children $15) right there.

The chief crop of Louisiana is sugar, the state flower is the magnolia, the state holiday is Mardi Gras and the native drink is the Hurricane . . . a beguiling blend of rum and fruit juice invented at a French Quarter pub called Pat O'Brien's. After one of these, you're ready for just about anything, but beware of young locals who will approach you and say, "I bet I can tell you where you got your shoes."

Five bucks later you're a little wiser. The joke ain't that funny but what the hell, this is New Orleans. "You got those shoes on yo' feet on Bourbon Street!"

The French Quarter is similar to Las Vegas in many ways. There is 24-hour drinking here, with an economy braced on tourism and a devil-may-care spirit that makes New Orleans truly "the city that care forgot."

The only thing missing was casino gambling, but in 1992 even that changed when the Louisiana senate grudgingly voted to establish a single state-controlled casino in New Orleans. By a 69.2 percent margin, Louisiana residents also voted to remove the constitutional amendment against a state lottery, which had been in effect since the 19th century. So after all the wrinkles were ironed out, Louisiana became one of 35 states with its own lottery.

Religious groups fought it, as did lobbyists from state horse racing tracks, but a hundred years of near purity had come to an end. What made it so irresistible was the fact that Louisiana was in a financial tailspin, and anyone with any money was leaving it 79 miles away—in Mississippi.

One of the oldest towns in Mississippi, Biloxi stretches along the squeaky-clean beaches of the Gulf of Mexico. This is the deep South, where residents still commemorate Robert E. Lee's birthday and the battle of Vicksburg. Stately mansions sit back on shimmering green lawns, buffeted from the highway by moss-draped magnolia and oak trees—a gentle reminder of a time gone by.

Biloxi was founded in 1699, a hundred years before Missis-

No, it's not a scene from *Gone With The Wind* or *Showboat*. The south will rise again, or so say riverboat operators along the banks of the mighty Mississippi. The Hilton's *Queen of New Orleans* riverboat near New Orleans is one of the largest, and certainly one of the most ornate.

sippi became a territory. The capital of Louisiana during the French occupation, Biloxi was shuffled from government to government like an old deck of cards. She was French, Spanish, English, Confederate.

By the time the Civil War rumbled to a close, Mississippi was near ruin. Homes were burned, crops destroyed, livestock seized . . . and of all the gallant young men who marched off to battle, only a fourth of them came home.

At Biloxi, tourists by the thousands still file somberly through the Beauvoir home of Confederate President Jefferson Davis. Over 700 rebel soldiers and their wives are buried on these grounds, while behind the main house rests the Tomb of the Unknown Confederate Soldier.

The chief crop of Mississippi is cotton, the state flower is the magnolia, the state holiday is Confederate Memorial Day and the native drink is iced tea. Everybody in Mississippi drinks sweet iced tea, so if you don't want sugar in yours you'd better say so.

People here talk slow and deliberate, and families are close-knit. There is an air of dignity about Mississippi, where even the land is treated with respect. The state has over 17 million acres of forest, for instance, yet thousands of seedlings are planted each year to replace the trees that are harvested.

Aside from the scenery, however, there is little to entertain most visitors. Maybe that's why riverboat gambling was legalized by the Mississippi legislature. A company called LA Cruise is already in operation, billing itself as the largest Las Vegas style casino on the Mississippi coast. Its one big ship leaves Biloxi every day, and—thanks to a revised law—gambling gets going as soon as the floating casino leaves the dock.

More ships are headed for Mississippi in the future, because of a county option that allows for dockside gambling. The dockside gambling issue has already been approved in Biloxi, Gulfport and Natchez. This could have a domino effect on other port cities such as Vicksburg, Greenville and Rosedale.

Regardless of what happens, the winds of change are blowing down south. There may not be full-fledged gambling here before the turn of the century, but sooner or later it'll come. You can bet on it.

Mall Of The Roman Empire

REGARDLESS OF ALL the talk about gambling in Illinois, Louisiana, Connecticut, Mississippi, Iowa, Colorado, and on every Indian reservation in the country, Las Vegas doesn't seem to be worried. Oh, sure, there are a few casino operators in Nevada who want a piece of the pie elsewhere, but there isn't that feeling of utter panic which occurred when Atlantic City opened its first casino in 1978.

Part of the reason is that gambling in Las Vegas is slowly being shifted into the background, and the spotlight is now on theme resorts. It's as though the people who run these places are saying that you can gamble in Las Vegas if you want to, but there are lots of other fun things to do on the way to the tables and slot machines.

The Mirage has its volcano and its dolphins. The Excalibur has its royal Lipizzaner stallions and jousting contests. Circus Circus has its big top acts and carnival-like midway. The new MGM Grand has its own movie lot and indoor sports complex. Caesars Palace has the pomp and pageantry of old Rome and a new shopping mall almost as big as the original Coliseum.

Before building the mall, Caesars found itself in quite a dilemma. The resort owned a valuable piece of land next door to the Mirage, but wasn't sure what to do with it. Should they build more guest rooms on the property, make it into an exotic amusement park, or what? Then Caesars chairman Henry Gluck read a survey that showed 85 percent of all travel plans were made by women, and the idea of a glamorous shopping mall came to be.

The mall is known as the Forum Shops, and tail-ends off

Caesars' Olympic Casino. You would think that for almost
$200 million they could have come up with a better name for
it, but then again even Caesars Palace sounded kind of goofy
back when the hotel was built in 1966. And to show you how
much the American dollar has plummeted in the last quarter of
a century, the Forum Shops cost three times as much to build as
Caesars itself.

Of course, as I understand it, it isn't costing Caesars anything. In fact, Caesars can't lose. The resort is leasing the property to a private company, and all that foot traffic will undoubt-
edly wind up inside the Caesars casino—which is the name of
the game in the first place.

(Left) A hand-painted sky stretches over the Forum Shops at Caesars Palace. It's indoors; it's beautiful; and if you see a 2,000-year-old statue come to life, don't be too surprised . . . you're in the streets of ancient Rome!

Yet when I visited the Forum Shops shortly before its grand opening (along with 4,000 other employees and hangers-on), I must admit I wasn't too excited. After all, Las Vegas already had three big-time shopping malls, so what was the big deal about another one?

If you wanted to talk about great tourist attractions, there were three that I thought rated gold medals. One was Wet 'n Wild, another was the Lagoon Saloon at the Mirage which served up the best piña colada in the civilized world, and the third was Mount Charleston. Silver medals went to the Dunes "Miracle Mile" Golf Course, the Liberace Museum and the antique auto collection at the Imperial Palace. Purple hearts went to the Ethel M chocolate factory, the walk of stars sidewalk in front of the Fashion Show Mall and the "Believe It Or Not" Odditorium at the Four Queens.

Other attractions brought in tourists by the bus load: Hoover Dam, Lake Mead, Valley of Fire, Red Rock Canyon, Bonnie Springs Ranch, Death Valley. The sort of people who like to hike and swim, however, usually aren't the sort who like to throw dice and play blackjack.

The fact is that people are fickle, and what is popular today won't necessarily be popular tomorrow. Less than a decade ago, top local attractions included the Olde Tyme gambling museum at the Stardust, the Las Vegas Museum of Natural History featuring animated dinosaurs, a reconstructed Western fort called Old Vegas, and Bally's movie theater which had reclining seats and push-button drink service. They're all gone now, found only in old newspapers like the now-defunct *Las Vegas Bullet*.

So here I was, setting off to explore the new Caesars mall, and wondering how I would write about it. At the moment, I was employed by Caesars Palace, and if I said the wrong thing I could easily find myself in the company of Old Vegas and the *Bullet*. If I went overboard in my praise, I might come across as another casino yes-man—and the town had enough of those already.

I edged through the towering archway at the north wall of Caesars, almost skidding into a slot machine on the glassy marble floor. "What's so special about this?" I started to ask myself, and then suddenly a hundred different images battled for my attention. Bugs Bunny manned a chariot atop the Warner Brothers Studio Store, water splashed noisily in the nearby Fountain of the Gods, booming voices and eerie music came from another fountain further down the mall, while overhead fragile white clouds whispered across the sky. Was I outdoors? Was I indoors? For a moment I did not know.

I was walking down a cobble-stoned Roman street. It was twilight, dawn, then a picture-perfect Autumn afternoon. Later I would learn that the bullet-domed ceiling was painstakingly hand-painted, with lighting technology giving it the look of a soft Mediterranean sky.

Shops and restaurants on either side of the street beckoned silently: Spago, Victoria's Secret, Field of Dreams, Brookstone. A millionaire would be at home in this place, where $3,000 suits, $675 slacks and $75 neckties made nice stuffing for a Gucci suitcase. An ice cream shop was selling the stuff by the scoop for $1.95, and would later sell $6,000 worth of it in a single day's time. The Sweet Factory was hawking candy at $1.79 for a quarter of a pound, and people were shoveling it into plastic bags as fast as they could. Well, no wonder. After checking out the price on a man's suit, the candy was practically free!

Next to the second fountain was an antique shop, and I wandered inside. By the front door was a genuine 1940's jukebox, its glass bubblers lazily changing from purple to amber to green and churning back memories of Fats Domino and Little Willie John. Price: $7,495, including delivery anywhere in the continental United States.

In the show window was a completely rebuilt Whizzer bicycle, and again I was tromping down memory lane. When I was a kid, a Whizzer was the ultimate mode of transportation. It was actually a motorized kit that you hooked up to your bicycle, and when you got to peddling at a certain speed the motor would kick in. The kit sold for $97.50 in those days, which sounds cheap now but back then was more money than most adults made in a week. Now you could have a Whizzer for only $5,995, or if you opted for the one on a black Phantom frame the price was $6,750.

I never had a Whizzer. My childhood possessions amounted to a Columbia bike, a secret decoder ring that glowed in the dark, some comic books (or what we used to call funny books) and a Daisy air rifle with a wooden stock. Today all those things would be worth a small fortune, and here I was still working for a living.

Suddenly I heard booming voices again, and out by the fountain the crowd let out a collective gasp. Four ten-foot statues had come to life, talking and moving like real human beings. Lasers and lightning lashed across the domed ceiling, and music filled the air. I stood there awe-struck, seeing constellations in the sky that couldn't be real and yet in that magical instant they were as real as you and I.

Then the show was over. I was swept along with the crowd, and with a brief pang of regret I saw the exit up ahead. My visit to the Forum Shops was over. Caesars had pulled off the impossible. It made a believer out of me.

Same Old Stuff

I WAS BROWSING through some old periodicals at the public library recently when I came across a 1954 *Life Magazine*. The pictures inside stabbed at my heart briefly, because in 1954 I was raring to knock the world on its backside. The only thing stopping me was something called high school.

Now here I was, almost 40 years later, looking at three Michigan State co-eds on the cover of an old magazine. They were probably all grandmothers now, with their photographs shored away in forgotten scrapbooks.

I thumbed through the magazine, looking for memories of my own. Grainy photos in black and white depicted the way it was that week of 1954. Haiti was recovering from Hurricane Hazel. ("Four hundred known dead in the worst hurricane of the last decade.") The French were withdrawing from an obscure Vietnamese outpost. ("The French tricolor, which had flown for 68 years over Hanoi, was slowly pulled down.") Studebaker and Packard had teamed up to produce a new gleaming four-door. ("Here they are, America, packed with new power, sparkling with new beauty.") And baseball slugger Ted Williams was expounding the virtues of Lucky Strike cigarettes. ("Luckies give me what I'm looking for, and that's better taste.")

What really caught my attention, however, was a story called "Gambler's Paradise Lost," which turned out to be an eyewitness account of a reporter's visit to Reno. From the headline, you knew the story would be a put-down of the entire gaming industry, and sure enough the reporter proceeded to chip away at Nevada. First, he set the scene.

"The dull metal gleam of the slot machines with a grind-whir like a covey of golden quail as the handles were pulled; a

roulette wheel spinning slowly, with the ivory ball purring softly along the top; the wonderful green table with the big red dice hopping against the cushioned ends and the stickman chanting the lovely harmonies of seven, eleven and the hard-way eight."

Keep in mind that this story was written almost four decades ago, so back then "a grand-whir like a covey of golden quail" was probably damn good stuff. What the writer was trying to do, I suppose, was capture the flavor of a gambling town, but it was the same old rehash with a few new adjectives. Here's the way he wrote it.

"In the old days you could walk into a strange town and sit down at a strange bar almost anywhere and ask the bartender, 'What do you like today?' He knew you meant what horse— and within five minutes you had his theory of handicapping and a bet with his bookmaker.

"So when this Reno bartender poured my bourbon and soda, I was all expectancy. How had the dice been going? Any big killings? Anybody make a dozen passes in a row? Anybody tap out for the rent money?

"The bartender put my drink down, scooped up my five dollar bill, replaced it with some small change and four silver dollars, and walked away.

"Not a word."

The *Life Magazine* reporter left the bar and went to a blackjack table. The dealer, he wrote, was "a middle-aged woman with a double chin, severe rim-less glasses and flat feet."

Two men were playing, and the reporter sat between them, stacking his four silver dollars on the table. "The dealer was putting out the cards," he went on. "When she got to me, she asked, 'You in?' I nodded, shoved a dollar into the betting circle and found myself looking at two cards which totaled nine. Not knowing exactly how the game went, I asked, 'Can I

(Left) Cowboy Wolford exemplifies the rough, gruff and say-nothing stare of a professional poker player with his white stetson, bib overalls, string tie, and plenty of chips. The photograph was taken in 1989 at the Maxim's Texas Hold'em tournament.

get hit?'"

Later that night, the reporter was playing blackjack at another table. "Nobody said a word," he wrote. "Except for the dealer's hands as she distributed the cards, we hardly even moved. Once in a while I took a sip of my drink. Once in a while the dealer moved her wrists to glance at her watch, counting perhaps the minutes until she could sit down and rest her feet, or perhaps until her eight-hour day would end and she could go home with another $15 in pay." Then the reporter heard himself being paged. "Excuse me," he said automatically, rising to his feet. "The dealer and players looked at me," he wrote, "as if I were a man from Mars."

That's pretty much the way the story went. It ended with the reporter getting into a limousine and heading for the airport three days later. He summarized his visit by writing, "It was something like watching a long, sleepy and rather sad movie. I'll never go back."

In five short pages, this writer from *Life Magazine* had succeeded in denouncing Reno and everything it stood for. Meanwhile, he spent his time badgering a bartender with stupid questions, playing blackjack at a dollar a pop, and sizing up a woman dealer as being middle-aged with a double chin and flat feet. What did he expect—a parade down Virginia Street?

A more recent article on the silver state appeared in *GQ Magazine.* It was called "Lost Vegas," and the author had this to say:

"Vegas never had a chance, not in America, the land of moral cleansing. Once a prodigious sanctuary of greed, indulgence, materialism and victim-less crime, Vegas was doomed from the day Bugsy Siegel, who built the fabulous Flamingo, started bragging about what a good time everybody was going to have. A town like Vegas ends up becoming a family-destination resort or it dies." And the story ended: "Las Vegas has become a great city, a family town, as pristine as a Mormon picnic. It couldn't have turned out better. That's right, isn't it?"

The outsiders who write about Nevada never cease to amaze me. The good stories, like *The Green Felt Jungle* and Donn Knepp's *Las Vegas* pictorial, are few and far between. A well-known author made a fortune writing half-truths and down-right lies about Nevada, one of these being that Las Vegas casinos pump pure oxygen into the air to loosen gamblers' inhibitions. This, he said, caused the 1980 fire at the old MGM Grand to spread so quickly. Not true, and I am surprised that somebody at the hotel didn't file a lawsuit against the guy.

Personally, I like living in Nevada. If it were as bad here as all these writers make it out to be, why would 20 million people a year make a bee-line for Las Vegas on their vacations? Why would almost a million people live here, and why would so many other states turn into dull monotonous clones by instituting their own forms of legalized gambling?

If I could have one wish—well, make that two—one of them would be to have lived here back in 1954 when *Life Magazine* was so busy tearing the state to shreds. I would have been witness to some amazing things that could only have happened in Nevada. In 1954, future president Ronald Reagan was performing at the Last Frontier, cowboy star Rex Bell was elected lieutenant governor, and exciting construction was going on all over Las Vegas. In that one year, the Showboat opened on the Boulder Highway, the Dunes was almost completed, and a near-finished high-rise called the Riviera was poking into the clouds down the street from the Sands.

My other wish? That's easy. I wish I had bought some land back in 1954—where all those other hotels on the Strip are today.

Inside Las Vegas

NEARLY TWO MILLION people visit Las Vegas each month . . . and most don't get their money's worth. Reasons:

They are unaware of the many freebies and services that are available to casino customers.

They fail to use the game strategies—many of them simple and straightforward—that greatly increase their odds of winning in the casinos.

INSIDE INFORMATION ABOUT COMPS

Because of the economy, there aren't as many high rollers as there used to be in Las Vegas. Result: Casinos are luring people with comps—complimentary meals, free rooms, even free plane tickets.

To take advantage of this, you must be willing to gamble a reasonable amount of money for several hours a day during your stay.

Example: If you play for as little as an hour, betting between $10 and $25 per hand, you can get a free meal at most casinos. For bigger perks, you must gamble at least five hours a day.

$25 minimum bets can earn you a casino rate—usually about half-price—on your hotel room.

$75 minimum bets can earn you a free room.

$150 minimum bets can earn you a free room, food and beverages.

Bets that exceed $150 can earn you a free room, gourmet meals and possibly a round-trip plane ticket between your home and Las Vegas.

Before you start to play, register your name with the floor supervisor in charge of your table. He/she will monitor how long you play and the size of your bets. If you move to a different table, be sure to alert the new supervisor.

Another way to obtain comps is by establishing a $5,000 line of credit at a casino. To do so, you'll need either $5,000 in cash or in a pre-authorized checking account.

One type of casino comp is available to anyone who has the nerve to ask for it—even people who don't gamble at all. A line pass gets you into the nightly shows without having to wait in the long lines. If you have tickets to a casino's show, ask any floor supervisor to give you a line pass.

To get a good seat, when you get into the theater, tell the maître 'd that you want to sit ringside, and that you'll take care of the captain. Then tip the captain who seats you—but only after you're given a seat that you like.

INSIDE INFORMATION ABOUT TABLE GAMES

Baccarat: Many players are intimidated by the upper-class origins and elegant trappings of baccarat, but it is one of the best—and easiest—games to play.

The house advantage is only slightly more than 1%. What that means: If the average player sits down to play with $100 in his pocket, he can expect to leave with almost $99.

And there are no strategies to learn; you win or lose by pure chance. Your only decisions are whether to bet with the player or banker—an arbitrary choice—and how much to wager.

Bet to avoid: The tie—where you bet that the player's hand and the banker's hand will tie. The house advantage is far greater because this happens so rarely.

Blackjack: The house advantage on blackjack is 4% to 5%.

Best bet: Doubling your wager when your first two cards total 10 or 11, since chances are one in three your next card will be a 10.

Bet to avoid: Splitting 10's. If you're dealt two cards of equal value, you can split your hand and play both, doubling your bet in the process. But if you have two 10's, you already have a probable winning hand. Why throw away one good hand for two possibly bad ones?

Craps: The fastest game in town. The house advantage is slightly more than 1%—but only for the most favorable bets.

Best bet: The Pass Line. You bet that the shooter will win.

Bet with the highest odds (or multiples of the original pass line wager) you can get.

Bet to avoid: Proposition bets, such as Any Seven, where the house advantage can rise to 17%.

The roulette wheel is synonymous with Las Vegas. It can also be one of the casino's most beautiful gambling devices, as illustrated by this wheel at Arizona Charlie's. Even though the space age is here, roulette wheels are still handcrafted from rare and beautiful hardwoods.

Roulette: This is an unpopular game in Las Vegas, and for good reason. Roulette can be painfully slow, and the double-zero wheel—in contrast to the fairer single-zero wheel favored in Europe—gouges out a house advantage of more than 5%.

INSIDE INFORMATION ABOUT OTHER WAGERS

Slot machines: Very popular, but one of your least advantageous bets. Most nickel slots in Las Vegas return only 80% to 85%, quarter machines return 88% to 92%, and dollar machines return 90% to 97%.

Even the million dollar jackpots offer less than fair value. To win one, you must insert enough coins to light all the lines (it's the last coin that earns the biggest jackpot) and wind up with four sevens. If the machine paid out according to actual odds, your return would exceed $29 million. As this book goes to press, the biggest slot jackpot ever hit in Nevada was $9.3 million on a Megabucks machine at Harrah's Club in 1992.

Poker: Here you play against other players, not against the casino. But the house gets its money with a 5% rake of every pot in small games, or a flat chair-rental fee of $75 an hour in big games.

Best: The player's advantage is greater with the large-game rake.

Race and sports books: Betting on sports events is perfectly legal in Las Vegas—but the standard house advantage ranges from 2% on baseball to 5% on football.

Bets to avoid: Multi-game parlays. The odds against winning a 10-team parlay are more than 1,000 to one—and the payoff is only 600 to one.

Reprinted courtesy of *Bottom Line Personal Magazine*, Boulder, Colorado.

Favors

Rrring!
"Las Vegas Metropolitan Police Department."

"Robbery detail, please."

"One moment, I'll connect you."

"Robbery. This is Jenkins."

"Harry? Jack Fletcher here. How are you doing?"

"Great, Jack. How about you? Still running things over at the Wanderlust Casino?"

"I've still got the same job, if that's what you mean. But that's not what I'm calling about. I need a favor."

"Name it, buddy."

"Well, I got a speeding ticket this morning on my way to work. Stupid thing, really. I overslept, and I had a nine o'clock appointment . . ."

"Hey, you don't have to give me your life story, Jack. I'll take care of it. After all, what are friends for?"

"Thanks, Harry, I really appreciate this. The hotel has started a safe driving campaign, and it would look bad if the assistant casino manager got a speeding ticket."

"Forget it, buddy. By the way, I don't know if you ever met my kid brother Jeff, but he's getting married in a couple of days. And I was wondering if maybe you could put him and his new bride in your honeymoon suite next weekend."

"Oh, heck, I wish I had talked to you sooner. The hotel's filled up because of the Evander Holyfield-Floyd Patterson fight. Let me do some checking around, though. I'll call you back."

"Thanks, buddy."

Rrring!

"Ritz Hotel, Mary speaking."

"Bill Hankins, please."

"One moment."

"This is Hankins."

"Bill? Jack Fletcher."

"Hi, Jack."

"I wish you wouldn't always say 'Hi, Jack' like that. It makes me feel like I'm on an airplane or something."

"Ha ha, same old Jack. So what's new?"

"I need a favor. Some friends of mine are getting married next week and I promised them a nice room somewhere. Have you still got that honeymoon suite up on the tenth floor?"

"Yeah, but the new owner's living in it. I can get you a room down by the pool, though. It's a little small and the bathroom's out of order, but it's got a great view."

"Well, if that's all you've got."

"I'll put a hold on it right now. Say, while I've got you on the phone, do you have any extra tickets for the fight next week? My brother-in-law's been driving me crazy."

"I don't even have any for myself, Bill. But let me make a phone call and I'll see what I can do. I'll call you back."

"Thanks, Jack."

Rrring!

"Good morning. Pleasure Dome Hotel, Terri speaking."

"Tim Shindler, please."

"One moment."

"This is Tim."

"Tim? Hi, it's Jack Fletcher."

"Jack? How are you, pal?"

"Good, thanks. Say, I was wondering if you had any tickets left for the Holyfield fight. I need two if you've got them."

"Lotsa luck. About the only thing I've got is center row in the balcony at the convention center on closed-circuit TV. Will that do?"

"I guess it'll have to. Thanks, Tim."

"Don't mention it. By the way, do you have any juice at the Camelot? My wife and I are celebrating our anniversary on Wednesday, and she's been after me to take her to that fancy Chinese restaurant over there. If you could get me a comp, it would save me about a week's pay."

"Let me make a phone call. I'll get back to you."

"Thanks, Jack."

Rrring!

"Camelot, Carrie speaking."

"Walt Dingle's office, please."

"One moment."

"Walt Dingle."

"Walt? Hi, Jack Fletcher."

"Hello, Jack. What can I do for you?"

"I need a comp for two next Wednesday at your Chinese restaurant. It's for a friend of mine."

"Sure, but they'll have to share a table with the state spelling bee champion and his grandmother, if that's okay."

"I'm sure they won't mind. Thanks, Walt."

"My pleasure. Incidentally, do you know anybody at the Desert View? My folks are coming in from Sacramento Tuesday and they're dying to see Rich Little."

"Let me make a phone call, Walt, and I'll see what I can do."

Rrring!

"Desert View Hotel, Cherry speaking."

"Rod Brinkley's office, please."

"One moment."

"This is Rod."

"Rod? Jack Fletcher here. I need a favor. Do you have any seats available for the Rich Little show Tuesday night?"

"Sorry, Jack. Rich closes on Monday. Tuesday we've got Hank Snow and the Blue Ridge Mountain Boys. Will that be all right?"

"I don't know. I'll have to call you back, but thanks anyway."

"No problem. Say, while I've got you on the phone—do you have any connections over at the Shoreline?"

"Yeah, I know the groundskeeper. Why?"

"I need to get a foursome on the green at four o'clock . . . my boss and three junket guys from Chicago. If you could help me out, you'd really be getting me off the hook."

"I'll call you right back."

Rrring!

"Shoreline Golf Course, this is Moony."

"Moony? Jack Fletcher."

"Jack! I thought you'd died and gone to Reno! How the hell are you, buddy?"

"Great. Say, what's the chances of squeezing four people on the course around four o'clock this afternoon?"

Fine with me if they don't mind getting a little wet. That's when we run the sprinklers."

"Ouch."

"Tell you what we could do. We could put 'em on the back nine for four holes, move 'em to the front nine, then let 'em finish up the back nine. That way they ought to avoid most of the water anyway."

"I'll have to let you know, Moony. Thanks."

"By the way, Jack you wouldn't know anybody at Metro, would you?"

"Why?"

"Oh, I bought a new pickup last week, and I opened it up on the freeway just to see what it would do, and I got a damned speeding ticket. Jack? Jack, are you there? Hello? Jack? Jack?"

Tipping

TIPPING IS A CUSTOM based on the generosity of an appreciative customer, and fortunately for many of us is subject to no concrete rules. Actually, in some countries tipping is not even permitted. In New Zealand, for example, tipping is a no-no, but then salaries there are higher than they are in the U.S., which means prices for the customers are higher. So in a way the customer is still tipping, only in New Zealand he is tipping the people who own the various establishments so that they can pay their help.

But today we are only concerned with tipping in Las Vegas, and many of you coming here for the first time need to know this information. So if you are unsure of who to tip, how to tip, when to tip, and where to tip, here are a few suggestions based on my own observations from watching Las Vegas tourists in action.

Bartenders: The rule of thumb for bartenders varies. Bartenders I talked to suggested a tip of $10 a round, but that seemed a little steep. Seasoned drinkers have their own ideas of how much to tip—or, in many cases, how not to tip at all. The most coherent of these is pretending to watch a football game on the big-screen TV while the bartender counts out the change. Later, of course, there is the inevitable trip to the bathroom. "I'll be right back," you say to the bartender, and then it's a quick exit out the side door.

Dealers: Tips for dealers are called tokes (or tokens), and zukes (or zukens). Anyone who tips the dealers is called a George or a natural. Anyone who does not tip the dealers is called a &$%#* or a $@#+! Since it is a documented fact that players disliked by the dealers will automatically win huge sums of money, it is important to be as obnoxious as possible

(Left) They are not called tips in Nevada; they are called "tokes" . . . short for token of appreciation. If you are playing at a table, it is customary to toke with a gaming chip. This lucky cocktail waitress at the Gold Coast gets a $5 chip from this generous player. She will keep an eye on him and offer to freshen his drink when his glass runs low.

---

when playing at a table game in Las Vegas.

In order to do this, you should spill drinks on the dealer, step on his feet, glare at him, cough in his face, curse him loudly while losing, and blow cigar smoke at him. Men should be even more revolting.

When cashing in your chips, smile pleasantly and wait for the dealer to say something in a low voice like, "Don't forget the dealers."

Then reply sweetly, "Oh, I won't. I'm going to play on your table from now on."

Showroom maître d': To improve seating, like being wedged at a long table of 150 people instead of being wedged at a long table of 250 people, flash a $10 bill to the showroom maître d' with your left hand. In your right hand, of course, is a $1 bill folded so that no numbers show. Don't forget now— ten in the left hand, one in the right. Don't make a mistake, or you won't enjoy the show.

Showroom waiter: This is the person who does all the work while the maître d' practices his Italian accent. The waiter lugs in the drinks and lugs out the empties, and some- times even gets the orders right. When he presents the bill, usually during the only topless part of the show, simply give him someone else's room number, and add a nice 25% tip. If you get caught, say you were merely trying to repeat what the waiter said when he brought you the bill, and he must have misunderstood you because it's so damn noisy in here.

Keno runners: If you are playing for an extended period of time, say for instance while your wife is in the powder room, it doesn't hurt to give the keno runner something. But don't give her money! What you do is show her one of your keno tickets, and say, "I'm playing this ticket for you." (Just make sure the ticket is from a previous game and has been double-checked as a complete dud.)

Change persons: Tips for change persons vary. Technically, if you hit the Megabucks slot machine for $10 million, you should give the change person 2.5 percent, or $250,000. Of course, if you want to have some fun, count it out to her in quarters. By the time you're finished, it'll be just about time for your second annual payment of the winnings.

On the video poker machines, it is a different story. Since the odds of hitting a royal flush are 40,000 to one, and the payoff is $1,000, you simply divide the $1,000 into the 40,000, subtract the $2,000 you spent trying to win the $1,000, then subtract the number of hours it took to get change, and multiply the total by 2.05. By this time the change person should have finished her eight-hour shift and gone home.

Cocktail waitresses: These are the lithesome creatures that bring the drinks to your table and say such things as, "Who ordered the gin fizz?" and "Who ordered the Tom Collins?" and "Who ordered the J.D. straight up with the water back?" Getting a drink without tipping the cocktail waitress is almost impossible. You can try engaging in deep conversation with the person next to you, or you can try fainting. The latter has been known to work on occasion, but only in the fancier casinos.

Restaurant waiters: The standard 15 to 20 percent rule applies, except if there is something wrong with your food - like finding a bobby pin in the meatloaf. Bobby pins can be purchased at the hotel gift shop for around 35¢ for a pack of 50, which should get you through all your meals in Las Vegas.

Hotel maids: Let's face it. How much time do you spend in your hotel room? Have you ever seen a hotel maid? Does the hotel maid really exist? If the hotel maid were to get married tomorrow, would you be invited to her wedding? If the hotel maid were to graduate from high school, would you be invited to the ceremony? Enough said.

Pool attendants: These are the guys that charge you a buck to use a 50¢ towel, and then expect a tip. Of course, if you don't tip them you're treading in dangerous water (so to speak), because there is always a possibility you might drown and they won't come to your rescue. So what you say is, "I don't happen to have any money on me because I'm wearing a bathing suit, but I can give you our room number. José will vouch for us; he was our showroom waiter last night."

Taxicab drivers: If the driver gets you from the airport to your hotel in less than two hours, give him at least a $3 tip. If you don't, he will tell the other four cab drivers in Las Vegas, and you'll never get a ride back to the airport.

Bellhops: Bellhops know all the important things, like where your room is, and how to turn the lights on, and how to open the curtains. They should get a nice tip—providing they replace the burned-out light bulbs, fix the curtains so they close all the way, stop the faucet from dripping, get rid of that rattle in the air conditioner, fix the knob on the television set, turn down the volume on the telephone ringer, set the clock to the proper time of day and soundproof the room.

If all else fails, there is always that old standby that has been used by tightwad tourists through the ages:

"I'll catch you later."

The Day Eddie Went Crazy

IT ALL STARTED on an overcast September morning in 1939. Without warning, German panzers thundered into Poland, and suddenly the world was at war. Adolf Hitler, his goose-stepping generals looking on in moronic admiration, had charted his own bloody destiny, and that of fifty million other people.

One of them, in a roundabout way, was Eddie Grimes.

Eddie had dropped out of high school after three tries as a sophomore, and was pumping gas at his father's filling station the day the news came on the radio. When he told his dad he wanted to join the army and kill Nazis, his clutch got let out real fast.

"You're still wet behind the ears," his father growled as the other mechanics watched in amusement. "When that peach fuzz of yours turns to whiskers, we'll talk about it." Eddie slunk out to the soda cooler, the old man's words burning in his ears, and it took three R.C. Colas to bring him around again.

Eddie spent the next couple of years checking dipsticks and wiping windshields, while Hitler's forces knifed into France and the German Luftwaffe rained bombs on London. America didn't want any part of a war over in Europe, but I guess we all knew we would have to fight sooner or later. Eddie did, anyway, and the day after Pearl Harbor was bombed he was first in line at the army recruiting depot.

I'm not trying to say Eddie was a hero, or anything like that, because I would have done the same thing except for one embarrassing fact. I was still in grade school. All I remember about December 7th was being dragged to church by my grandmother and eating chicken and dumplings for the umpteenth Sunday in a row.

You would have thought that with Eddie's training the Army would assign him to the motor corps, but the U.S. Army works in mysterious ways. As soon as boot camp was over, Eddie shipped out as a combat engineer. I know that sounds pretty impressive, but what it meant was that if one of our army units happened on an enemy mine field the combat engineers went in and cleared it.

Eddie saw action all over the South Pacific—Guadalcanal, Iwo Jima, Saipan, the Marshall Islands. The horror stories he told me later were enough to give any man nightmares for a long time to come.

At Saipan he and his crew were clearing a mountain road when Eddie found himself staring into an enormous underground cave. Flame-throwers were called in, but before they unleashed their deadly napalm some two-star general showed up with an entourage of dignitaries and newspaper people. Eddie and his guys were hustled out of the way so the general could have the press all to himself, and when the flame-throwers blasted the cave the whole side of the mountain disappeared. The cave had been a Japanese ammunition dump. Then there was the time Eddie and the rest of his men were ferried to a navy ship offshore for some hot chow. One of the engineers, a hatchet-faced sergeant named Rudy, politely asked for a second helping of mashed potatoes. The cook refused, saying there was just so much food to go around, so Rudy pulled out his .45 and shot the guy. It was a senseless tragedy, but you've got to remember these men had stared death in the face for so many months that it was almost like an old friend.

When the war ended, Eddie had worked himself all the way up to corporal. He didn't want to stay in the army, but civilian life didn't look all that great, either. His old man had retired and sold the service station, so Eddie took his pay and started bumming around the country. He wound up in Las Vegas, down to his last double sawbuck, and landed a job as a break-in dice dealer at the Boulder Club.

That's where I met him.

I was young and eager to learn, and Eddie—who was an old

hand at the game by then—took me under his wing. Maybe I reminded him of Rudy, I don't know, but we became good friends, and that's when I got to hear all of Eddie's old war stories.

There wasn't much else to do at the Boulder Club. The dice table was stuck way over by the sandwich counter, and the smell of ammonia and onions every morning was enough to chase even the grinders away.

In 1955 Eddie and I finally hit the big time. The Riviera opened on the Las Vegas Strip, and both of us got hired in the dice pit. The Riv was the classiest joint in town, with a nine-story high-rise that towered over everything else in sight. The food was good, the tokes were good, and . . . well, life was good. It was, I should say, until one morning in 1959.

I pulled into the parking lot that day just in time to see Eddie getting out of his car. We started into the building together, but Eddie suddenly stopped and jumped to one side. "What's the matter?" I asked him, a smile on my face.

"Mines," he whispered, giving me a cold stare. "You've got to watch where you walk."

I didn't know whether he was serious or not, so I changed the subject. "I tried to call you last night on the phone, but I guess you weren't home."

"I was home," he said, jumping around another mine. "I don't answer the phone anymore."

"Why not?"

"It never stops ringing. That damn Eisenhower has been calling me day and night. I can't even get any *sleep*."

I knew then that something was terribly wrong, but what was I going to do? I couldn't take him by the arm and lead him back to his car, and tell him, "Go on home, Eddie. You're missing on a couple of cylinders today." I just followed him inside, watching him hop to the right and jump to the left.

We were approaching the dice table when I noticed a bulge in one of his pants pockets. "What is that?" I whispered to him.

Eddie looked up blankly. "Sandwich," he answered, and although I didn't ask for an explanation he added, "They're trying to poison me, so I brought my own food."

As the day progressed so did a wet spot down the leg of Eddie's pants, the tuna fish sandwich inside his pocket beginning to lose its battle with the elements. Along with the stain came the horrendous odor of bad fish, and it became apparent that if Eddie were ever to eat that sandwich he wouldn't have to worry about any more phone calls from President Eisenhower.

It was at this point that the whole world started taking a closer look at Eddie. The game had slowed for lack of customers, Eddie half-asleep with the stick in his hand, when the pit boss stopped at our table. "Make it sound like a crap game," he ordered. "The show's getting ready to break."

Eddie waved the stick high in the air and screamed, "YOU CAN'T LOSE YOUR FISHING POLE IF YOU DON'T GO FISHING."

All movement in the casino ground to a halt. It was like looking at an old photograph with everyone stopped in midstep. Dealers and gamblers alike, all frozen in their tracks and all gawking at a hollow-eyed stickman on a craps game at the Riviera Hotel who by now was making another startling announcement.

"WHEN THAT PEACH FUZZ TURNS TO WHISKERS WE'LL TALK ABOUT IT!"

I never saw Eddie again, although a couple of the guys told me he was in the dealer's room a few days later cleaning out his locker. They said he carried everything away in a little doll's suitcase, holding it against him for dear life and walking through the hotel like he had never seen it before.

Then the rumors started going around. He had been committed to a mental institution. His wife had sold their house and moved back east. One story had it that Eddie stuffed all the air conditioning vents full of bed sheets and towels the day he went mad, and nailed strips of wood to the bottoms of all the doors. Something about poison gas seeping in, he was supposed to have said.

Maybe he is still locked away, or maybe he never was. All I know for sure is that life goes on and there are months when I don't even think about Eddie anymore. Me? I'm still dealing craps, and still hoping for that big score so I can get out of here myself. Of course, if it ever happened I'd probably go running out to my car—and find out that Eddie was right about those land mines.

Money

NO MATTER what you play, the name of the game is money. Take it from Mike Tyson, who made $28.6 million the year after losing the heavyweight championship. Buster Douglas only got $26 million, which was still three times as much money as Evander Holyfield made . . . who beat Douglas . . . who beat Tyson.

Other athletes, rated among the richest by *Forbes Magazine*, include race car driver Ayrton Senna at $10 million a year, golfer Jack Nicklaus - $8.6 million, basketball star Michael Jordan - $8.5 million, tennis ace Boris Becker - $7.2 million and football's Joe Montana - $4.4 million.

My first job was washing dishes in a Walgreen's drug store for 25¢ an hour—and I was happy. Of course, I was only 16 years old and in those days gasoline was cheaper than bottled water. That's all I needed. Give me my dad's car on a Saturday night and a tank full of gas, and I had found my heaven on earth.

That was 35 years ago. Today the only things you can do with a quarter are buy a pack of gum, play one song on a jukebox, make a phone call, or use it as a tool to unscrew that little whatchacallit on a digital watch when you need a new battery.

When I was young, Clark Gable got $5,000 a week making movies, which seemed like enough money to *buy* Walgreen's. Today a baseball player gets that much for signing autographs, or did you read where José Canseco signed a five-year contract for $23 million? Meanwhile, Don Mattingly of the Yankees is getting $19.6 million for the next five years and San Francisco's Will Clark is taking home $15 million for the next four years. And to think I used to play baseball for free!

In the world of big business, America's highest-paid executive (according to Business Week magazine) made $54 million in one year, compared to the average working stiff's take-home pay of $22,567. Two others with the same company, McCaw Cellular Communications, also made the top ten list although the company itself lost $289 million during the same year! It makes you wonder what their paychecks might have been if they had showed a profit.

Physicians get a pretty good piece of change, if these figures from the American Medical Association are accurate. The average orthopedic surgeon makes $217,000 a year, gynecologists and obstetricians - $163,200, anesthesiologists - $163,100 and general practitioners - $91,500. Psychiatrists earn $102,700 a year listening to patients with problems they probably wouldn't have if *they* were making $102,700 a year.

People who don't make a great deal of money spend their spare time watching television. Maybe that's why Bill Cosby makes $57.5 million a year, Oprah Winfrey - $34 million and Johnny Carson - $25 million. Those with more money go to the movies, and watch actors like Sylvester Stallone ($31.5 million a year), Arnold Schwarzenegger ($27.5 million), Jack Nicholson ($25 million) and Bruce Willis ($23 million). Those with the most money to burn prefer to do their homework while listening to compact discs: The New Kids On The Block ($39 million a year), Madonna ($31 million), Paul McCartney ($22.5 million) and the Grateful Dead ($15 million).

Every year *Parade Magazine* runs a story called "What People Earn," and it always amazes me that the people who earn the least are smiling the most. A bartender in Lincoln, Nebraska, said he was making $7,488 a year—which is what some people pay for car insurance—yet from his photograph you would have thought he just won the California state lottery. On the other hand, a utility company president in Sioux City, Iowa, said he was getting $295,000 a year, and he looked like he was waiting in line for a root canal. Another interesting fact was that computer systems analysts make $46,480 a year in Miami but only $34,680 a year in Nashville.

According to the National Education Association, the average schoolteacher makes $31,304 a year, or almost twice what everyone else in the country earns. Again, however, it depends upon the state. In South Dakota, for example, teachers only earn $21,300, whereas teachers in Alaska earn an average of $43,153—with three months off every year to spend it.

The chief of staff at the White House gets an annual salary of $96,600, or almost half what the president makes. Bill Clinton can't complain, though. He earned nearly seven times what Mikhail Gorbachev got as Soviet prime minister, but only one-fortieth of what Queen Elizabeth makes. I'm surprised this hasn't been reported on the CBS Evening News with Dan Rather, who makes $3 million a year talking about all those people.

For $6, the U.S. Department of Labor will send you a booklet called "White-Collar Pay," which is about as easy to decipher as a two-thousand-year-old Indian petroglyph. Still, I did learn the following:

Nursing assistants make $9,647 a year (remind me not to check into a hospital anytime in the near future) and everyone else makes more money the longer they stay at the same job.

This appears to be true everywhere except Las Vegas, where dealers start at whatever the minimum wage is, plus tips, and the only time they get a raise is when the minimum wage goes up. That could be why one Las Vegas casino asked its lounge band to stop playing the song "Take This Job And Shove It." All the dealers were singing along with it.

Some others in the tip industry fare just as badly. Change persons make $12,480 a year, doormen - $10,725, valet attendants - $11,128 and cocktail waitresses - $9,828. The tips, of course, make the jobs worthwhile. When Frank Sinatra was performing at the Sands, he told the audience how a $10 million remodeling project was being financed by the hotel. They borrowed $2 million from the bank, he said, and $8 million from the cocktail waitresses.

How do other jobs in Las Vegas stack up? Showgirls make $24,180 a year while topless dancers make $26,780. Casino floormen earn $40,000, hotel hosts make $60,000, casino managers average $100,000, and top gaming executives—such as corporation chairmen—make an average annual salary of $683,696. That comes to $13,148 a week, or $328.70 an hour.

It makes my 25¢ an hour at Walgreen's seem like chicken-feed.

Mr. X

IT TOOK ME six months to find him, and even then our meeting came about strictly by accident. I had gone to one of those mind-numbing gaming exhibitions, and there he was—parked in the corner of the room and surveying the scene with a look of near belligerence.

As I shouldered my way toward him, I thought back about countless interviews with Las Vegas casino people. His name always cropped up in our conversations. "If you want to talk about the problems in the casino industry," they would say, "then you really ought to talk to—." And then the same name would come up, over and over again.

The only trouble was that I couldn't find him. He wasn't in the telephone book, and no one knew where he worked. I was almost to the point of giving up on finding him, and now here he was, standing alone in a crowded room.

Interviews with guys like this were always an adventure. When you asked a question, you weren't sure whether you would get an answer, or a punch in the stomach. Still, if you wanted to find out why Las Vegas was changing so much, and why table games were going down the tubes, who better to interview than somebody who saw it all first hand?

I reached his side and introduced myself. He sized me up like an old gunslinger with the sun in his eyes, and then shrugged as if to say, "Make your move, kid."

First I asked him how long he had lived in Las Vegas.

"Thirty years," he said softly.

"Oh, you were here in the glory days," I remarked, remembering old photos of Sinatra at the Sands, when legendary movie stars were introduced from the audience every night.

"Yeah, it was a great town."

"So—what's changed?"

"Individuals in certain corporations."

He stopped, so I started thinking of another question. Then suddenly he went on again. "They don't know anything about the gambling business," he said. "They haven't studied it. They've surrounded themselves with high-priced and incompetent people to protect themselves and their positions."

"When did this start?"

"Oh, I'd say it started in the Howard Hughes era. Management became aloof and unfriendly. As a result, nobody knew where they stood. For instance, if you were of a certain nationality, you were viewed as a gangster. This bred a lot of contempt, which still exists in some of these casinos today."

"What else is causing all the dissension between the corporations and the workers?"

"Jealousy. An outstanding amount of professional jealousy."

"By whom?"

"By the people running these upper management teams. They look upon the seasoned casino worker as a man without a college education, and therefore he's not qualified to be earning the kind of money he's earning. But I've got news for them. Those CEOs that are making a million dollars a year aren't worth it, either. There's not a man on the face of this earth that's worth a million a dollars a year to run a casino. You can get the same results from casino veterans who have come up through the ranks as you can from somebody who's operating out of Memphis, Tennessee or Beverly Hills."

"What do you think about the theme parks that are popping up all over Las Vegas?"

He shrugged again. "I think that's the way to go."

"But is Las Vegas going to lose its reputation as a pure gambling town?" I asked.

"Well, in my opinion there are a few hotels that will still have that distinction. The town itself will become a family vacation spot. This used to be a town where a husband and wife came to be by themselves. But now you're going to find more and more blue-collar workers coming here because the children can be accommodated."

"What's this going to do to places in the medium-size range?"

"I think they'll die on the vine."

He spotted a friend and waved hello, while I reviewed a few statistics in my head. According to a recent study by the Las Vegas Convention and Visitors Authority, the average Las Vegas tourist gambled away $491 in 1991. This compared with almost $550 the year before, and to a whopping $1,068 in 1985. Slot machines were more popular than ever, accounting for over two-thirds of all play. Blackjack was the most popular table game (24 percent of the tourists played it), while craps, baccarat and roulette slugged it out for bottom place.

I asked Mr. X the reason for this, and he frowned. "I think it started when these hotels initiated around-the-clock toke distribution," he said, choosing his words carefully. "Dealers were not being as cordial to the customer. They wouldn't make eye contact with them, or say hello. Consequently, the customer felt unwanted and left the premises.

"Then when the casino did get a good player, and the player showed any speed, the floormen and pit supervisors were afraid to offer him any complimentaries for fear of being called on the carpet. 'What was this for? Why'd you comp this guy?' Hell, they were protecting their jobs. But as you can see, if you give a little, you get a lot. The people upstairs don't understand that. They don't realize that you've got to show respect to your customers by giving them something back, or you're going to lose a substantial amount of your table revenues."

"So what you're saying is . . ."

"I'm saying you can't staff a casino from the third floor," he interrupted gruffly. "What Las Vegas has to do is get some people in charge who know the customers and know how to get repeat business. If you don't comp a customer, the guy down the street will, and you'll lose that customer. But if you treat that customer right, acknowledge his action, and treat his wife nice, you'll get repeat business time and time again. And the word of mouth from that customer will repeat tenfold. He'll tell his relatives and his friends. It's a very simple procedure."

It was late, and the crowd was starting to thin out. Besides, Mr. X was getting fidgety, and I knew better than to push my luck. "One last question," I said. "Do you have any advice for someone who wants to get into the gambling business?"

"Become a lawyer," he laughed. Then his face grew serious. "I'll tell you something, though. I could step into a property right now and save the owner a million dollars a year, just by revamping the personnel and the work schedules. The rest of it would be easy."

That's how we left it. Mr. X went his way, and I went mine. Before we said good-bye, however, I did manage to get his local phone number. So if there are any casino owners out there who want to get back to basics, give me a call. I'll introduce you to a human dynamo named Mr. X. Who knows? I might just come along for the ride.

Bad Boys

IT SEEMS that every time you pick up a newspaper there's a story in it about Atlantic City, usually written in red ink if you catch my drift. The casinos there once did glorious battle with Las Vegas, I admit, and one year even racked up more profit than the big boys on the Strip. (1983: Atlantic City, $168.7 million; Las Vegas Strip, $120 million.)

Of course, that was a long time ago, and Las Vegas casino executives say it will never happen again. That's the good news. The bad news is that most of the Las Vegas casino executives are ex-Atlantic City executives hired to replace Las Vegas executives who outlined Atlantic City policy in the first place.

When gambling was approved in New Jersey, conditions were about the same as when Nevada legalized casinos in 1931. The only available talent was from somewhere else, and so Reno and Las Vegas immigrants were welcomed east with open arms. Then a problem arose. Las Vegas people had their own way of doing things. They were not familiar with corporate policy, and spent all their time worrying about something called the "bottom line." They were running Atlantic City like—heaven forbid—a Las Vegas outfit.

As a result, Atlantic City starting priming its own manpower, while most of the Las Vegas executives wandered back home or took jobs in the Bahamas. A good casino manager became someone who had been a good dealer and a good floorman, and who held the state licenses to prove it. It didn't matter if he was barely out of his teens; he had come up through the ranks. But summer was over in Atlantic City, and it was time for the fall. Casino profits skidded to an all-time low. Of eleven casinos on the Boardwalk, one had closed, another was operating under a conditional license and a third (Merv Griffin's Resorts International) lost $30 million in three months.

Take your pick as to what caused the problems: mismanagement, poor air service, market saturation, burgeoning expenses, snarling gaming restrictions, complicated closing hours, a shortage of rooms, the lack of non-casino attractions, the absence of convention facilities. The point was that the Boardwalk was beginning to creak. So in an effort to get things back on track, new programs were instituted which placed less emphasis on the high roller. Suddenly Atlantic City was a grinder's paradise with free bus rides, coupon giveaways and cheap meals. Meanwhile, over 50 casinos had cropped up in the Caribbean, and Las Vegas was recording its best years in history.

By this time the corporations were running Las Vegas, too, and freshly-scrubbed vice-presidents didn't like what they saw. These Las Vegas people were giving gamblers free rooms and free food, and there were days when the coffee shop hardly showed a profit. Never mind the win percentage at the tables. It was time to start making money in other departments. They would pare comps to the bone, and if a customer wanted a pack of smokes he would likely kick the habit by the time the paperwork was filled out. If he wanted a room, he would get one, but at a casino rate, and only if he gambled for six hours at ten dollars a hand. That was the only way to make money.

Las Vegas people didn't understand. All they did was walk around with their coats unbuttoned and get mad when the tables lost. Even worse, they were giving Alka-Seltzer or aspirin to anybody who asked for them. Didn't they know these were controlled substances? My gosh, think of the lawsuits.

There was only one thing to do, and that was to bring in some people who would follow orders. Atlantic City was a natural. Casino personnel there had been following orders most of their lives, and it was easy enough to find the right persons for the right jobs. A complete list was available from the New Jersey unemployment office.

The Atlantic City people brought new marketing programs with them, ones that placed less emphasis on the high roller. Suddenly Las Vegas was a grinder's paradise with discount room rates, coupon giveaways and cheap meals. Well, okay, maybe it didn't work in Atlantic City, but Las Vegas was— different.

The next step was to get Las Vegas underlings in line, and this was done with a barrage of memos that made the Library of Congress look like a mom and pop store. There were motivation meetings, courtesy symposiums, sexual harassment seminars, and leadership conferences. Work performances were evaluated, and five people doing the same job were making five different salaries.

Not surprisingly, table games began to lose popularity, and a high roller became someone who played the dollar slots instead of the quarter machines. Theme parks were built, and gambling was soft-pedaled as just another form of recreation. The idea behind this was that other areas of the country would surely legalize gaming, so Las Vegas had better start making itself known as a complete family resort.

Today there are big beautiful casinos all over Las Vegas, with a pyramid on one end of the Strip, a waterworks on the other and a movie studio in the middle. But one question remains. Have all these changes been good for Las Vegas, or did the corporations ruin the town's flavor somewhere along the way?

I decided to put the question to the first Las Vegas tourist I saw. His answer would stand for all of us. If my observations were correct, I would scream a warning from the roof-tops. If I were wrong, I would holler my apologies from the same precarious ledge. What could be fairer than that?

The first visitor I came across was a tall sunburned man named Gary who had just dropped $1,500 at the blackjack table. (One point in my favor.) Still, when I asked his opinion of present-day Las Vegas, the answer surprised me.

"I think Atlantic City is more of a business proposition, and Las Vegas is more of a tourist destination. Las Vegas is laid-back. It's a 24-hour town where you can go three or four days and wear yourself out. It's still a fun place."

It was obvious to me that the poor fellow was in a state of shock from losing so much money. Yet I had struck a bargain, and now I had to make good on it. Slowly I made my way to the hotel roof. No, I was not going to shout out an apology. I was going to jump off!

Adventures Out West

WE WAS FIVE MONTHS out of Kansas City when we come up on the great desert. As night was fast approaching, Mr. Hutchins give the order to make camp. Next thing, the wagons was formed in a ragged circle, and Riley the cook had a fire going in the middle.

I seen Shiny Pants standing off by hisself, smoking hand-rolled, and I joined up to him without saying a word. Shiny Pants was our scout, and only knowed about three words of English: me, hungry and whiskey. Consequently, when he was not scouting, he was in the pickles. Being Injun, however, he was hard-pressed to beat on a trip of such magnitude.

Shiny Pants never let on I was at his side, so when he offered me the terbacky I nearly fell into a ravine, I was so startled. Then he scratched a match on his leathers, and as I leaned forward to light my smoke I observed deep lines drawed around his eyes. He was as worrisome as me, and I took it as a compliment.

"Apache," he sniffed suddenly.

"Huh? Where?"

A grunt, and he pointed westward. I seen nothing, and heard less, but if Shiny Pants smelled Apache, by God they was out there. Still, they was not in rifle range, so we should be fine till morning. I would post sentry, though, just in case.

Shiny Pants stood there smelling his Apaches while I went back to camp, where white smoke was billowing off the fire like summer rain clouds. Riley was stirring something in the soup pot, and it brung water to my mouth, the first liquid I had tasted since morning. Mrs. Weatherbee clucked around like a year-old pullet, collecting tin plates and silverware. The two Taylor young ones was chasing each other by the fire, and it

In 1906, the main building on Block 16 was the Arizona Club; today it's the site of the California Hotel in downtown Las Vegas at the corner of Ogden and Main Streets. For many years, Block 16 was the city's red-light district.

would have been like a night at home if there was a roof over the place.

Then Lucy come out of her wagon, pretty as a picture in her blue calicoes. She had likewise done something to her hair, or maybe I was just used to seeing a bonnet on her head all day. "Ma'am," I said, as she got closer. She smiled shy like, and my heart took notice. I wanted to lead her by the arm past all them leering roustabouts, but if I touched her I was feared my legs would buckle—or at the very least my tongue tie up like a johnny knot.

For fact, I would not have made this mad journey if not for Lucy and her folks. Oh, I was never that friendly with none of them, and only seen them leaving church together on Sundays. Then, when Hutchins organized the trip to Californy, they was the first to sign on. Me, being at loose ends since the cattle drive, it seemed natural to go along. I was not gitting any younger, and Lucy was gone forever if I stayed behind.

So here I was, butt sore and hungry, with God's creation in back of me and nothing ahead but sand dunes and redskins. I took a plate from Mrs. Weatherbee, nodded a thank you kindly, and watched as Riley slopped in some beans. A cup of coffee, then I hunted a tree stump or other such contrivance. "Come," I heard a voice say, "and set here beside me."

It was Lucy for sure, with me turning a full circle to make

sure she was addressing such as myself. Sure enough, so I moved cautiously across to where her things was laid out.

I tried not to stare as I took my first fork-full, but it was hard work. She was brown as a cactus pear, with hands so flimsy they looked like flower petals at the break of morning. No more of her was visible underneath all them garments, but my eyes traversed her nonetheless. "Eat," she said directly, and so I gulped everything down like it was a direct order.

My plate clean, I give her another look, and here she was still on her first bite. Of course, that made me feel regrettable, even more so when she dabbed at my shirt with her kerchief. Apache or no, I was ready to take flight across the desert that very minute.

"What's your name?" she asked me then.

So I told her, gitting it out right on the third try.

"Where's home?"

Anywheres you are, I wanted to say, but instead I just give her a shrug. It wouldn't do to tell her my folks was dead, and I was facing things all alone.

She started in telling me her personal life, that her family was in the hardware business and had come on bad times. And she had done some school teaching, but wanted more than learning kids who was not even kin. I asked for her age, and she got shy again, which was when I mustered up nerve to grab ahold of her hand. Instead of a face slap, she come closer, smelling like fresh baked gingerbread, and the next thing I knowed we was touching lips.

Well sir, to make a long story short, me and Lucy never did git to Californy. Oh, it weren't the Injuns what scairt us off, but the fact that halfway across the desert we peeled off for Nevada. Lucy wanted to see it, she said, and that was good enough for me. We located in the south part of the state, and pumped up enough water out of some underground springs to git us a farm going. Other folks started settling in, and gambling come in '31. By then we had four daughters, all growed up now and married themselves.

They wanted no part of farming, however, but found city life more to their liking. Little Lucy, she got work serving cocktails at the Golden Nugget, Suzie hired on as a keno writer at the Flamingo, Glory heads up room reservations at the Frontier and Charity's over to the Desert Inn, dealing five-card stud, jacks or better to open.

Them kids, I swear. I only wish I knowed where they got their gumption.

The Martians Have Landed

FOR THOSE WHO LIVE in Las Vegas, it is a town like any other. There are churches and stores, and pot-holed streets choked with traffic. Kids mosey home from school, boys in one group, girls in the other. The twelve o'clock whistle cries in the hot stillness, just like it did when we were young . . . boys in one group, girls in the other.

The tourists who flock to Las Vegas fit right in. Kids again for a day or two, they look at this place not as a city of parks, schools, businesses and neighborhoods, but as a kind of escape valve from their own suburbs elsewhere. To them, Las Vegas is the world's biggest sandbox, the glittering mirror-ball over the dance floor, the eye of the hurricane, a frenzied and feverish state of mind.

So they pack their suitcases and board their pets and call their travel agents. Questions become accusations as the clock ticks down the minutes. No, there's no need for a rental car because once you get to Las Vegas all the hotels are within walking distance anyway. No, you don't need show reservations because if you slip the captain a twenty you can practically sit in the orchestra pit. No, you don't have to make room reservations because there's a hotel war going on in Las Vegas, or didn't you read the newspapers this morning?

So they check their suitcases and board their planes and buckle their seatbelts. Looking out their portholes, they watch the scenery change from green to gray, from velvet to marble. Dull mesas jut from monotonous terrain like commas on a page, and roads scratch across the desert at a thousand crazy angles.

"Where are we?" one passenger asks another.

"I think we're in Arizona," comes the answer. "That sure looks like the Grand Canyon down there at four o'clock."

"Nah, that's too small to be the Grand Canyon. I flew over it once in a helicopter and it's about ten times that size."

"This is your pilot, ladies and gentlemen. Those of you on the right side of the aircraft should be able to see the Grand Canyon right about now. Formed by geological faults in the earth's crust, this 217-mile fissure is one of the modern-day wonders of the world."

A man looks up from his magazine, and turns to a sleepy marine in the next seat. "It says here that Las Vegas gets eighteen million tourists a year."

The marine passes the story on to his sergeant across the aisle. "Eighteen million tourists in Las Vegas."

"Oh, no," the sergeant wails to the woman beside him. "And it ain't even a holiday!"

Conversation dries up for a few minutes, and then the plane starts a labored descent. "Hey, look at all that water down there. There must have been a flood, or something."

"Nah, that's Lake Mead. I ought to know . . . I flew over it once . . ."

"In a helicopter," somebody finishes, and nervous laughter breaks out in the crowded cabin.

Suddenly the landscape comes rushing up: houses, swimming pools, golf courses, shopping centers. Cluttered buildings crowd busy streets, and dots become cars and trucks and buses and RVs. With a shuddering thump the plane hits the runway. Bells chime, lights flash, engines roar in protest.

People smile wearily as they crowd the aisle, short friendships severed forever. There is a jumbled rush to the exit, and a lame smile for the stewardess at the door. Then they are through the gates, where the noise level goes up a dozen decibels. A handful of change disappears in a shiny chrome slot machine, and once again bells chime and lights flash.

Three days later the scenario is reversed. Harried and hur-

(Right) The interior of McCarran International Airport resembles a casino today. But, of course, it wasn't always that way. This photograph, shows the airport in 1947—with a record 12 flights arriving and departing daily. Is that . . . can it be . . . Elizabeth Taylor playing a slot machine?

ried, the people are back on the airplane, shopping bags crammed with souvenirs. Not yet airborne, some are already asleep, while others are telling new war stories to bleary-eyed seat-mates.

Somebody hit a hard 17 at the blackjack table and got a four, and the dealer busted. Somebody was down to his last chip at the dice table when a guy with a red beard threw 16 passes. Somebody made a pay telephone call after playing a slot machine all morning, and automatically put five quarters in it. Somebody met Jay Leno and got to go backstage after his show at Caesars, and here's his autograph if you don't believe it.

Other stories bring a tear to the eye, a lump to the throat. Somebody ate in a gourmet restaurant and the tab was four hundred bucks. Somebody played the same six keno numbers half the night but missed a game because he had to go to the bathroom, and of course all six numbers came up. Somebody was ahead $1,500 at the blackjack table, but they changed dealers and he left all his gravy on the table. Somebody didn't make hotel reservations, and wound up sleeping in the lobby at Vegas World.

The stewardess brings hot coffee and cold rolls, and although the food goes down hard everybody starts to feel a little better. Okay, so they didn't make the big score, and they've got to go back to the same old job and the same dumb boss for another eleven months and two weeks. So what? It was fun while it lasted.

And besides—there's always next time.

All Night Long

THE ONLY THING that stops in Las Vegas after 6:00 P.M. (8:00 P.M. in the summertime) is daylight. Casinos rock around the clock, and hospitals treat the sick and injured 24 hours a day. But any time, day or night, you can also:

✔ Watch TV (Channels 3, 5, 8, 13)
✔ Rent a movie (Major Video)
✔ Order a pizza (Eli & Wong's)
✔ Get gas (Holiday Texaco)
✔ Take an Alka-Seltzer (Village East Drugs)
✔ Fall in love (Marliza's Belly Dance School)
✔ Pick out a ring (Mordachi's Jewelers)
✔ Get a marriage license (Clark County Courthouse)
✔ Get married (Chapel of Love)
✔ Call the Pregnancy Counseling Service (Desert Springs Hospital)
✔ Get divorced (Clark County Courthouse)
✔ Hock your watch (Gold & Silver Coin and Jewelry)
✔ Shoot pool (Red Dawg Saloon)
✔ Get arrested (Las Vegas Metropolitan Police Department)
✔ Call a lawyer (Lillian J. Sondergoth)
✔ Post bond (Rusty's Bail Bonds)
✔ Take a lie detector test (Gary T. Robey & Associates)
✔ And have the tooth you lawth at the Red Dawg Thaloon replaythed. (Clark County Dental Society)

Anything Goes

IN THE EARLY DAYS, the only people who left Las Vegas as millionaires were the ones who came as billionaires. That was back before there were such things as Megabucks slot machines and million-dollar keno, and enough skyscrapers to make Las Vegas resemble an actual city.

During the mid-40s, the atmosphere was much different than it is today. Let somebody walk into a casino wearing blue jeans in 1945, and if he didn't have a hammer or saw in his hand he was in big trouble. That same year, the limit at the dice tables was $200; the top prize at keno was $10,000; and the biggest jackpot on a slot machine was $100.

Then in 1985 something happened in Las Vegas that surprised just about everyone. For the first time since gambling was legalized in 1931, slot machines surpassed table games in revenue. That was fine as far as the casinos were concerned. Slot machines did not need uniforms or meals, and they didn't complain when they worked overtime.

Yet the truth is that gamblers love the excitement and camaraderie of live table action. Besides, a night at the dice tables can log enough stories to get someone through a lifetime of cocktail parties. Take the craps shooter who plunked the last of his bankroll on the pass line and then threw the dice behind a stack of chips. "Loser seven," the stickman said, while the shooter craned his head to see the dice. "I hope you're cheating me," he roared. "I'd hate to think I was this unlucky."

Or how about the die-hard dice player who lost his last bet and then shuffled toward the door, his head down and his future a question mark. Suddenly, he felt in his pocket and withdrew one last lonely bill that had somehow been overlooked in his frantic grab at the brass ring of fortune. Will this be the solitary stake he desperately needs to climb back to self-respect and human decency? Of course not. The man walked back to the craps table, lifted the paddle from the money slot in the middle of the layout, and dropped the bill inside. "Here," he said bitterly. "You missed one."

The game of craps is winding down, though, and so are just about all the other table games. Maybe it is because the novice player feels intimidated, or because he was weaned on video games and therefore slot machines are right down his alley. That is what the experts say, anyway, and they must be right because they've been wrong every other time.

Without table games, however, Las Vegas would lose its special allure, that "anything goes" spirit which sets this place apart from all the other gambling towns. Consequently, a new host of live games has been introduced to the public. They stagger the senses, boggle the mind, captivate the heart—and some of them are even fun.

Red Dog: The dealer deals two cards face up, then each player bets that a third card will fall between the two cards showing. We played this game in Texas when I was a kid, and the biggest winner only lost $7.

Pai Gow: Each player gets four dominoes, divides them into two hands, and tries to beat the dealer. The player wins if both hands are higher, and loses if both hands are lower. All other hands are ties. Translated into English, Pai Gow means "Set Nine," which is the number of hours you set while waiting for the dominoes to be shuffled.

Pangingue: Also known as "Pan," the game is a blend of poker, gin rummy, pinochle and bridge—using eight decks of cards with all the eights, nines and tens removed. What's so great about that? A blackjack casino in northern Nevada did it for years!

Pan 90: Eight decks of cards are placed in a shoe, with all cards numbering 7 to 10 removed. Players are dealt three cards and the numbers of the cards are added together. They then try to beat the dealer's hand, getting a fourth card if they so desire. Or they can go play blackjack, the game that inspired this one in the first place.

Pai gow poker is played with dice, a bowl, a deck of cards, a "chung"—and plenty of chips! This game at the Gold Coast Casino could be easily mistaken for blackjack by a novice visitor.

Poker Bingo: This game combines poker, bingo and keno using ping pong balls marked with card symbols. The object is to make a winning poker hand, and the only drawback is figuring out what to holler when you finally win. "Bingo! Uh, Poker! Uh, Keno! Uh, Ping Pong!"

Aquarius: Similar to roulette, this game uses astrological symbols instead of regular numbers. During the game's trial run at a casino downtown, the ball landed on Taurus. It prompted one player to say in disgust, "This game is a lot of bull."

Pyramid Dice: This game combines various aspects of

craps and roulette, with a variety of one-roll bets. The top pay-off can be as much as $250,000, providing a shooter is playing alone and rolls all 21 dice combinations without repeating any. Since the odds of that happening are a zillion to one, chances are he will be playing alone most of the time.

Blackjack Tournaments: The ad reads: "Win Up To $1,000 (Based on 80 Entries), $35 Entrance Fee." Let's figure this out. Eighty times $35 equals $2,800, less $1,000 to the winner, for an $1,800 profit to your friend and mine: the casino owner.

Craps Tournaments: "Win Up To $1,200 (Based on 48 Entries), $50 Entrance Fee." I'm confused. Aren't you supposed to wear a mask when you rob somebody?

In other countries, the only casino games that have lasted through the centuries are baccarat and roulette. Europeans, for example, are not prone to change of any kind, and if roulette was good enough for their great-grandparents it's good enough for them.

Then again, perhaps the Australians have the right idea. Since a modern slot machine costs practically as much as a new car, the Aussies pinch pennies with a casino game called "Two-Up Ring." All that is needed are two coins, which the player flips in the air. If heads comes up three times in a row, he wins.

If tails comes up, he has to go to Tasmania.

The Life And Times Of Howard Hughes

AFTER MONTHS of painstaking research, including two trips clear across town to the library, I am able at last to chart the life of billionaire Howard Hughes. As one of those responsible for the glittering success of Las Vegas, his story is essential to any writer keen on tracking this oasis in the desert.

His full name was Howard Robard Hughes Jr., but he was called Little Howard because his father was bigger than he was. One time Big Howard refused to buy him a motorcycle, so Little Howard built his own and terrorized the neighborhood before being packed off to a private school in Houston. In fact, that is where we get his first signature—on a spelling test that earned Little Howard a big fat F.

Howerd Hughes

In 1924, Big Howard died, and the Hughes Tool Company was turned over to a son who was still in his teens. Of course, Howard didn't know a bit about drill bits, so he did what any red-blooded American youth would do. He went to Hollywood.

There he met an actress named Harlean Carpenter. He said to her, "Why don't you dye your hair platinum and change your name to Jean Harlow and I'll put you in a movie I'm gonna make called *Hell's Angels*."

"Oh, get off it, Howard," she said.

"I promise! I'll even sign you to a contract right now. Turn on the lights and give me your eyebrow pencil."

Howard Hughes

By the time he left Hollywood, Hughes owned one-fourth of RKO Pictures and three-fourths of Trans World Airlines. Aviation was already his great passion, as witnessed by a strange event that occurred ten years earlier. He had suddenly disappeared from sight, and in 1932 was found to be working as a co-pilot for another airline under the alias of Charles Howard.

Unfortunately, his signature in the pilot's log gave him away.

Charles *Howard Hughes*

Then World War II broke out, and Hughes was asked to build a cargo plane six times larger than any existing aircraft. When told the task was impossible, Hughes agreed to do it. As unconventional as ever, he decided to make the plane out of wood, hence its nickname "The Spruce Goose."

"It'll never fly," Henry Kaiser told him when he saw the giant flying boat. "There are knot holes in the fuselage."

"Of course there are not holes in the fuselage," Hughes replied impatiently.

"I know, so why are there knot holes in the fuselage?"

"Because if there were, this damned thing wouldn't fly!"

"Whatever you say," Kaiser sighed. "By the way, here's the contract from the government. Be sure to sign all 2,114 copies."

Howard Hughes

Shortly after the Spruce Goose was built, Hughes decided to test-fly his newly-developed XF-11 high-speed reconnaissance plane.

"Give me fifteen degrees flap," he barked to his co-pilot.

"Roger."

"Give me more throttle."

"Roger."

"Give me full reverse pitch."

"Roger."

"Give me a parachute!"

But it was too late. The plane crashed, and Hughes barely escaped with his life. From a custom-made hospital bed, he issued a news release stating that reliable, comfortable and safe air transportation was now a reality—and he signed it with a nurse's eyebrow pencil.

Howard Hughes

Under pressure from the government and other stockholders, Hughes sold TWA in 1966. His check, the largest in financial history, was for over $500 million, but that raised a problem. If he didn't reinvest it he might be forced to pay taxes. So he did what any red-blooded American millionaire would do. He went to Las Vegas.

"How much for a room?" he asked the desk clerk at the Desert Inn.

"Sixty dollars a night."

"How much for the entire floor?"

"Two thousand dollars a night."

"How much for the whole place?"

"Thirteen million."

"Okay, I'll take it. And throw in that joint across the street, the one with the big silver slipper up on top."

"Very well, sir. But you still have to sign the register."

Howard Hughes

By the time Hughes left Nevada, he had acquired another airline company, seven casinos, a television station, and all the

(Left) One of Howard Hughes' interests was aviation. Another was the movies. Still another was Las Vegas. When Hughes did things, he did them "big time." At one time he owned six Las Vegas casinos including the Sands and Desert Inn.

---

raw land and mining claims he could get his hands on. In the process, he had turned into a recluse guarded by a band of militant Mormons—who followed him from Las Vegas to Nassau to Nicaragua to Vancouver to London to the Bahamas to Acapulco.

In April of 1976, Howard Hughes died aboard a plane flying him back to Houston. A flurry of wills surfaced after his death, including one that left a big chunk of the Hughes estate to a Utah service station attendant.

The man claimed to have picked up Hughes while he was walking along the Tonopah Highway. "Kin I give you a lift?" the man reportedly asked Hughes.

"Thank you, sir. The Sands Hotel in Las Vegas, if you'll be so kind."

"You got it, hoss. By the way, my name's Melvin Dummar."

"You'll have to wrap that paw with Kleenex if you're shaking hands with me. I'm Howard Hughes."

"Not *the* Howard Hughes?"

"Yes, and here's a quarter for your troubles."

"Gee, thanks, mister."

"You'll get more when I'm gone, I promise. I'll even make out my last will right now. Do you have anything to write with?"

"No, sir. Nothing except—my wife's eyebrow pencil."

A Christmas Carol

'TWAS THE NIGHT before Christmas, and through each casino
 In Vegas and Laughlin and Tahoe and Reno

The stockings were hung by the lockers with cheer
 In hopes that a genuine saint would appear

Someone with a heart filled with kindness and such
 Who would tip all the dealers; it wouldn't take much

They stood at their tables, with heads almost bowed
 But no saints appeared, just the usual crowd

Why is it, they pondered, that things never change
 The players at Christmas seem almost deranged

It's as though their own families have cast them aside
 So they come to Nevada to spend their Yuletide

Alas, that is all that they usually spend
 And they wonder why no one regards them as friend

For example, all tables were open this night
 One player at each, and if that's not a fright

Their banter was corny and irksome and lame
 "Are you bored? Give me change, and I'll start up your game."

So each person waited, his thoughts far away
 For the long night to end and another new day

"Jingle Bells" played on the overhead speaker
While the stale smell of smoke made each dealer's knees weaker

There were trees in the corners all covered with light
That from a great distance looked just about right

On closer inspection they lost their appeal
The branches were metal; wasn't anything real?

The pit boss was dressed in a bright yellow coat
Blue trousers, white socks and orange tie at his throat

He smiled as he said, "Good times are upon us."
Of course, he had gotten a nice Christmas bonus

The others were grumbling, and most with good reason
They would get no days off through the holiday season

But still there was something to make them feel perky
A gift for each worker: a big frozen turkey

Just then there arose on the roof such a clatter
Guards sprang up the stairs to uncover the matter

A call was relayed to security's chief,
"You better get up here; we've caught us a thief."

The chief dropped his coffee, proceeding with dread
No visions of sugar plums danced in his head

He got to the roof and threw open the doors
His guards had their guns drawn, and down on all fours

Was a fellow in red with a smile on his face
And fluffy white whiskers clear down to his waist

A bag full of presents lay next to his side
While eight snorting reindeer stood venting their pride

They were all strapped together and hooked to a sleigh
    That couldn't have been more than two feet away

"On your feet," cried the chief to the jolly old gnome
    "And just why are you parked in a no-parking zone?"

The man touched his cheek with a red-mittened hand
    "I am Nicholas," he said, "and I come from a land

Where Christmas is special and truly unique
    And those who believe find the things that they seek."

The chief fell to silence and took a step back
    Saint Nick gave a grin as he opened his sack

"Now there's something for each," he said with a roar
    "And more for the people who work on the floor

"The dealers, bartenders, pit clerks and cashiers
    "The valet attendants, the maids and their peers

"In fact, gifts for all except for this note
    "That goes to the man in the bright yellow coat."

With that, Saint Nick hopped in his very old sleigh
    Preparing to go on his merry old way

The chief scratched his head as he started to see
    People opening presents and shouting with glee

And then he remembered the note for the fellow
    Who wore nothing more than a coat of bright yellow

The pit boss approached him and said with a smirk
    "Quit your loafing, you moron, and get back to work."

The chief's eyes went wide and he started to stutter
    He looked at the pit boss, his heart all aflutter

The pit boss was dressed in a bright yellow coat
  So the chief swallowed hard and gave him the note

"This letter's for you," he said nice and slow
  Then he raced to his desk for a shot of Old Crow

The pit boss unfolded the small slip of paper
  Was there money inside, or some magic vapor?

All the others had got what they wanted and more
  It was his turn to go through the mystical door

With trembling fingers he opened the note
  And that's when he started to moan and to choke

For here's what it said, and the words were quite clear
  "I'm sorry, but you get no presents this year."

Beneath that was written the rest of the letter
  "Be nice to your workers; next year might be better."

Then a shout from above him as St. Nick took flight
  "Merry Christmas to all, and to all a good night."

December Madness

IT WAS NOT that long ago when December was one of the leanest months of the year for Las Vegas casino operators. In the 1960s and early '70s, it was always a white Christmas in Las Vegas. A dealer would open his "toke" envelope, and his face would turn white. December was the lull after Thanksgiving and the lull before New Year's, and the only consolation for most casino workers was getting as much time off work that month as they wanted.

Then in 1978, things suddenly changed. The Sahara Hotel organized a casino slot machine tournament to beef up its Christmas trade, and the event was a rousing success. Not to be outdone, the Tropicana Hotel instituted a $75,000 craps tournament, Caesars Palace put together a slot machine extravaganza called "The Great Slot Round-Up," and the Golden Nugget started its annual Grand Prix of Poker. Today practically every casino in Las Vegas offers some kind of year-end event, and now December has become one of the hottest months of the year for tourism. In fact, recent studies show that the month of December ranks as the fourth busiest month of the year in Las Vegas, and much of the credit must go to a little-known entity called Las Vegas Events.

Exactly what is Las Vegas Events? "It is a separate, private, non-profit corporation funded by the hotel room tax," explained Herb McDonald, Executive Director of the Las Vegas Events staff. "We're not an arm of the Las Vegas Convention and Visitors Authority, although we cooperate with it." Founded in 1981, Las Vegas Events has proved to be a vital force in bringing major special events to the city, including these events in December of 1992: the National Finals Rodeo, the Las Vegas Rugby Challenge, the Inaugural Las Vegas Bowl, the World Doubles Cup and U.S. National Table Tennis Championship, Kool Vegas Nites, and the 16th annual Holiday Prep Basketball Classic. With over 90,000 rooms in Las Vegas , the aim of this eleven-member staff is really quite simple. It is to help keep those rooms filled.

McDonald, former senior vice-president of the Del Webb Corporation, said that Las Vegas Events was formed "because Atlantic City took a million tourists away from us." He added, "A craps shooter will shoot dice anywhere. And as long as he could save anywhere from five to ten hours in traveling time, he started going to Atlantic City rather than coming here. As a result, we created Las Vegas Events."

Without question, the biggest event of December is the National Finals Rodeo at the UNLV Thomas and Mack Center. "Overall, it brings between 20,000 and 32,000 people here," McDonald said. "We seat 17,120 people every night, and those tickets were sold out nine months ago." McDonald said it is easier to get tickets to the World Series or the Super Bowl than to the National Finals Rodeo. "I get offers of a thousand dollars every day for a ticket," he laughed. In fact, he even received an offer of an all-expenses-paid fishing trip to New Zealand, including first-class airfare, just for tickets to the rodeo.

The ten rodeo performances attract some of the top names of the rodeo circuit. It is entertainment at its rawest level, and everyone—with the exception of the People for the Ethical Treatment of Animals—loves it. As writer Hank Whittemore described it: "The rider straddles his bull. The chute blasts open, and he is catapulted into the arena. There is no past or future, only the eruption beneath him. He holds on with one hand, the other stretched out as he leans back and begins a duet with the bucking bull."

Economically, the impact of each rodeo means as much as $50 million to the city of Las Vegas, and that does not include gaming revenues. One December, for example, local shopping malls saw sales climb an additional ten percent while the rodeo was in town.

"Traditionally, Las Vegas has always been slow from Thanksgiving to Christmas," explained Rossi Ralenkotter, Director of

Marketing for the Las Vegas Convention and Visitors Authority. "And what we've done through Las Vegas Events is to institute as many activities as we can to bring people to our city." The Las Vegas Bowl, which pits the Mid-American Conference champion against the winner of the Big West Conference, is a perfect example of how this works. "The Mid-American Conference is good for Las Vegas because it's in the Midwest," Ralenkotter said, "and that's a very strong market for our city. When you consider the fact that the third week of December was a very slow week for Las Vegas, this is an event that's going to help all of us."

Monetarily, the combination of all these December events has a $70 million impact on the city of Las Vegas. The best part is that special events such as these retain more people on the city's payrolls. "We keep 10,000 people working during the month of December," McDonald said. "And the payroll alone has to be somewhere between 15 and 20 million dollars."

As interesting as the strategies involved in luring people to Las Vegas is the story of Herb McDonald himself. McDonald, who came to Las Vegas in 1946, recalled a town that was mostly desert, and his experiences bring back memories of a younger and more reckless Las Vegas.

"Bugsy Siegel was housing with me at the El Rancho while the Flamingo was being built," he remembered. "For a long time, though, I only knew him as Ben Siegel. One time I played a little gin rummy with him and won 28 bucks. About two weeks later, he saw me by the front desk and said, 'Hey, kid, I want to get my money back.' I said, 'Anytime.' He walked away, and then a casino guy came up to me. 'Do you know who that was?' he asked me. I said 'No,' and he said, 'That's Bugsy Siegel, president of Murder Incorporated.' And that's how I learned who Bugsy Siegel was."

Even with a skyline of flashy theme resorts, McDonald isn't worried about the future of gaming in Las Vegas. "I think anytime we can broaden our base, the better off we are. When I was at the El Rancho, I tried to get them to build tennis courts. They said, 'No, people would be outside playing tennis; they playing tennis; they wouldn't be gambling.'

"Then Wilbur Clark built a golf course at the Desert Inn, and people said, 'That's crazy; people will be playing golf.' Well, now we've got 40 golf courses and we've got tennis courts, and we've got all kinds of other things." As an example, McDonald cited the Mirage, with its dolphins, white tigers and exploding volcano. "They've got 3,000 rooms and 6,000 people there at one time," McDonald said. "And yet they're not all in the casino. People are going to gamble when they want to gamble, but it's been proven that 70 percent of the gambling they do is in the hotel where they stay."

McDonald once mailed out a brochure which advertised the proximity of such scenic wonders as Hoover Dam, Death Valley, the Grand Canyon and recreational parks in Utah. "I got all kinds of hell," he said, "for sending people out of town. Now it's the other way around. We are the hub to all these places now." According to McDonald, this even includes Disneyland. "There are people who fly to Las Vegas, check into a hotel, go to Disneyland for two days, and then come back here. You've got to have everything. Theme parks are just another hook to get people to come here. And fortunately, our county fathers have kept McCarran Airport up to where we have the best air service per capita in the United States."

Much of the credit for the continuing success of Las Vegas must go, however, to the heretofore unheralded Las Vegas Events staff. Thanks to these hard-working people, Christmas in Las Vegas is one of the busiest and most profitable times of the year.

Home

CHARLEY settled comfortably into the old wooden chair, tilting it back against the wall the same way he did when he was a kid. The smell inside of ham frying in a cast iron skillet and the clatter of plates being set at the table eased his spirits even more. If only there was a porchlight on at the Youngs' place, the scene would have been complete, but no one had lived there for a long time.

Off in the distance he could hear the lazy clamor of frogs bickering over squatter's rights, and that made him think about the water, which was something he didn't want to think about right now. Still, that was the reason he came back to his childhood home, and why he had been trying to reason with his father for the last three days. So far, though, he was the only one taking part in the conversation.

"Charley, you can talk to him till you're blue in the face," his aunt told him when he first drove up in the U-Haul. "But he won't pay you no mind."

Oh, he saw that his father couldn't use his left hand anymore, and that he walked with a limp, but it would take more than a stroke to ruin that man. Charley's aunt only knew what the doctors told her, and his opinion of doctors had never been all that great—not since the time he was diagnosed as having stomach flu and wound up nearly dying of appendicitis.

Suddenly the screen door opened with a squeak, and his aunt announced that supper was ready. He washed his hands at the sink, then joined the others at the rickety kitchen table. His father ate slowly, staring patiently into space, while Charley and his cousin went over things for the last time with his aunt.

They would load the trailer in the morning. "The big stuff first and then the china," was how his aunt put it. Las Vegas

(Right) In 1931, construction began on Boulder Dam, one of the engineering marvels of the world. Renamed Hoover Dam in 1947, the dam spans the Colorado River in Black Canyon. The reservoir (Lake Mead) which was created hides a lost city under its waters. This photograph, probably taken in 1933, shows construction from inside the dam; this site is, of course under water today.

---

was less than a hundred miles away and Charley's father would be happy there. Well, maybe not as happy as he would be in St. Thomas, but St. Thomas was doomed.

Charley was away at college when the trouble started. His father had written him a long rambling letter about Highway 91 being rerouted, cutting off St. Thomas from the outside world. Land values were down, his father wrote, and the only places still open for business were the Gentry Hotel, Seller's Cafe and Hannig's Ice Cream Parlor.

It pained Charley to hear the old town was dying. His high school prom was at the Gentry, and Lord knows how many chicken fried steaks he had wolfed down at Seller's Cafe. Hannig's Ice Cream Parlor was where he asked Kathleen Landis to go steady, and when she said "maybe" he got so excited he couldn't finish his cherry phosphate.

Now she was on her second marriage, and Charley was still single. He wasn't worried, though. With any kind of luck, the right woman would come along sooner or later. At least, that was what his father used to tell him before he got sick, and he'd sure found a good one.

The years blurred by. When a letter came from home there was always bad news inside. Money was scarce, and his dad was trading this for that just to stay in business. The Colorado River was flooding the crops one day and neglecting them the next, a hot Nevada sun burning the brave buds to a crisp. Then his mother died, and when he went home for the funeral he was surprised to find that his father had become an old man. Suddenly Charley realized that he wasn't someone's boy anymore. He was on his own now, and the only home he had was in his heart.

The morning dawned chalky gray. Charley poured himself a cup of coffee and went out to the front porch, hoping to sneak

a smoke before breakfast. His father looked up from the rusty porch swing, and for a moment Charley thought he saw a flash of recognition in the old man's eyes. His cigarette forgotten, he moved across the porch and dropped a hand on his father's shoulder. "Good morning," he said softly, knowing there would be no answer, and bitter at the world because there wasn't.

His father's mouth tightened, as though he too were caught up in the same swirling current. Then he turned to gaze out at the morning landscape, while Charley stood there feeling lonely and helpless. He wanted to shake the old man by his poor thin shoulders and make him laugh or cry or do something, but instead he just sat down across from him and stared into his coffee cup.

It was going to be hard on his father, pulling up stakes after forty years and moving to a city with skyscrapers and traffic lights. He would have his sister to help him, of course, and that was a blessing. The old man's days might not be easier, but at least they would be tolerable.

Charley's aunt came to live at the house in St. Thomas soon after his father's stroke, and if ever there was a martyr in the family she was it. She was the one who got rid of that live-in nurse, and started fixing some decent food with salt and bacon drippings in it. She was the one who wrote Charley and told him about the dam being built in Black Canyon. Boulder Dam it would be called.

The only problem was that St. Thomas stood right in the path of the big dam, so the government began buying up the land with what the town people called "settlement money." Most of the homeowners moved out as soon as the checks cleared, while Charley's dad sat on the front porch and quietly watched them go. When his aunt told Charley that his father had also gotten a check from the government, and never cashed it, he knew it was time to go home.

Now here he was, getting ready to cram all his father's possessions into the dusty backside of a banged-up rental trailer, and hoping the old man wouldn't hate him for it. "Dad," he said impulsively, staring hard at his father. The old man's eyes reluctantly moved from the floor to the wall and then settled on his son.

"Today's the day," Charley said gently. "We're going to put all your things in that big trailer out there, and then we're leaving this old house for good."

His father was silent, but his eyes stayed on Charley.

"I know you've got some wonderful memories of this place, but the water's coming, and we've got to leave." A pause, and then, "It's what mom would want us to do."

His father leaned forward, his right hand slowly moving towards Charley's face. For a brief moment Charley thought the old man was about to strike him, but then his fingers brushed at Charley's cheek . . . and wiped away a tear.

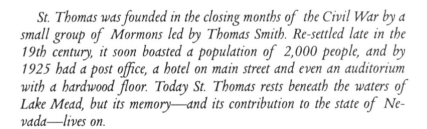

St. Thomas was founded in the closing months of the Civil War by a small group of Mormons led by Thomas Smith. Re-settled late in the 19th century, it soon boasted a population of 2,000 people, and by 1925 had a post office, a hotel on main street and even an auditorium with a hardwood floor. Today St. Thomas rests beneath the waters of Lake Mead, but its memory—and its contribution to the state of Nevada—lives on.

Famous Quotations

"YOU CAN'T judge a book by its cover."
"Two heads are better than one."
"Beauty is only skin deep."
We all like a good quotation. One crisp, well-turned phrase can turn any ordinary clod into another Daniel Webster, and since it practically came from the bible everyone else is forced to agree with him. After all, what can you do when somebody says, "Yessir, behind every cloud there's a silver lining." People have been saying it for years, so it must be true.

My grandmother had an expression for all occasions, but unfortunately it was always the same one. "Don't put all your eggs in one basket," she would say.

This never bothered my uncle. He would come right back with, "Yeah, but the squeaking wheel gets the grease." Of course, he worked in a garage and sold mufflers, shocks, struts, springs, brakes, lube jobs and retreads.

Presidents procure plenty of praise from the press for such pertinent parables as: "A chicken in every pot," "The only thing we have to fear is fear itself," and "Ask not what your country can do for you, but what you can do for your country." Give me Teddy Roosevelt any day. All he did was speak softly—and carry a big stick.

The best slogans are the ones trying to sell us things we don't need that aren't even good for us by making us think that if we buy them we can spend all day running on the beach without gasping for breath because we'll be just like all those young people in the commercials.
"The Pepsi generation."
"Weekends were made for Michelob."
"I'd walk a mile for a Camel."

When the same slogans are used to promote healthy products for regular middle-aged humans, the old pizzazz just isn't there. "The yogurt generation." "Weekends were made for buttermilk." "I'd walk a mile for a Brussels sprout."

Remember when the shortest distance between two points was a straight line? Nowadays, it's a cellular telephone. Many other sayings are outdated as well, which is reason enough to either toss them aside or reword them to fit the times.

OLD QUOTE: A man is judged by the company he keeps.

NEW QUOTE: A man is judged by the company he owns.

A good slogan for Las Vegas in 1947 could have been "The Town That Cowgirls Call Home." These five worked for the Last Frontier, which changed its name in 1955 to the New Frontier. Today it's just the Frontier.

OLD QUOTE: What this country needs is a good 5¢ cigar.

NEW QUOTE: What this country needs is a good 5¢ floppy disk.

OLD QUOTE: If at first you don't succeed, try try again.

NEW QUOTE: If at first you don't succeed, file for bankruptcy.

It's the same with Las Vegas. First there was: "Las Vegas, the entertainment capital of the world." Next was: "Las Vegas, gateway to the great southwest." Then came: "Las Vegas, the American way to play."

Convention officials spent $8 million concocting and promoting this snappy little logo. It was short, simple, and to the point. The only problem was that no one knew what it meant.

What was wrong with "entertainment capital of the world?" People don't go to Las Vegas because if they stay on the same highway they will eventually wind up in the Pacific Ocean. They don't go to Las Vegas because it is more patriotic to gamble in America than it is to gamble in the Bahamas. They go because of free drinks, cheap rooms, the idea of winning a fortune and the outside chance they might bump into a celebrity.

In fact, the four most popular phrases in Las Vegas, according to a recent survey, are:

(1) "Can I have your autograph, Mister Bogart?"

(2) "Bring me a glass of cigars and anofer drink."

(3) "How do you play this stupid game?"

(4) "Let's get married."

The problem, as I see it, is that the people heading up these publicity blitzes have forgotten what it feels like to roll into Las Vegas on a Saturday night. Someone seeing this place for the first time is not going to say, "Wow, it's the American way to play." He is not going to say, "Wow, we're out where the west begins." All he is going to say is, "Wow."

Yet if we must have these hollow aphorisms clanging about the universe, then we taxpayers demand the right to coin our own. (For $8 million, we should be able to come up with some real doozies.) So send in your favorite original slogans, and the best ones will be forwarded to the proper authorities. In the meantime, I offer several of my own—just for starters.

"A hundred dollars in every pot." "Speak softly, and carry a big billfold." "A die in the hand is worth two on the floor." "An ounce of Las Vegas is worth a pound of Atlantic City." "What this country needs is a good 49¢ breakfast like you get in Las Vegas: 2 eggs any style, bacon or sausage, toast, juice & coffee."

Oh, and don't worry about your share of the next eight million. I'll see that you get it—even though "money is the root of all evil."

Who's Who

PEOPLE WHO WORK in Las Vegas casinos do not have jobs. They have titles. With pencil in hand and tongue in cheek, see how many you can define from our list below:

(1) Shill
(2) Keno Runner
(3) Change Person
(4) Security Guard
(5) Dealer
(6) Boxman
(7) Floor Supervisor
(8) Pit Boss
(9) Shift Boss
(10) Eye In The Sky

ANSWERS

(1) A shill is a casino employee who acts like he is gambling so that other people will also gamble. When he goes on his lunch break, he acts like he is eating the food in the staff dining room—so that other casino personnel will also eat it.

(2) The keno runner is the person who "runs" keno tickets for people who are so busy gambling at other games that they do not have time to stop and walk all the way to the keno lounge, which is always about four miles from where all the other casino games are located. The keno runner can move through a crowded casino faster than a speeding bullet, and spends her days off trying to explain to friends what a "way" ticket is.

(3) The change person disperses change to slot machine players along with such words of wisdom as: "You're wasting your time on that machine, dearie. Someone just hit it three months ago." There is no doubt, though, that change persons

255

Everyone seems to be having fun at Sam's Town—even the dealer!

carry their weight in the casino industry—usually in nickels, dimes and quarters.

(4) The security guard patrols the casino looking for slot machine cheats, drunks, underage gamblers and people taking pictures. He is fond of the modern invention known as the "two-way radio," and spends his break communicating on one with his fellow security guards—much to the chagrin of those seated within a three-block radius.

(5) The dealer is a respected member of the Las Vegas community who deals the various casino games. Many dealers go on to become boxmen, floor supervisors and pit bosses. Others grow old gracefully.

(6) The boxman sits at the dice table and puts all the money in the box, hence his job title. He also watches the players, watches the dealers and watches to make sure none of the buttons on his coat sleeve fall off when he leaves the table.

(7) The floor supervisor watches the dealers and the boxmen, settles disputes, supervises payoffs, signs markers and evaluates players. The floor supervisor knows everything. "Who won the big eight conference in 1967?" "Oklahoma." "How many home runs did Reggie Jackson hit in 1980?" "Forty-one."

These are the showgirls at the Maxim Hotel's Comedy Cabaret in 1991. There are lots of showgirls in Las Vegas. They have curvaceous figures and smile constantly. They wear feathers and plumes and fancy stockings. Sometimes they don't wear anything on top. Their job is to entertain you and make you glad you came to Las Vegas.

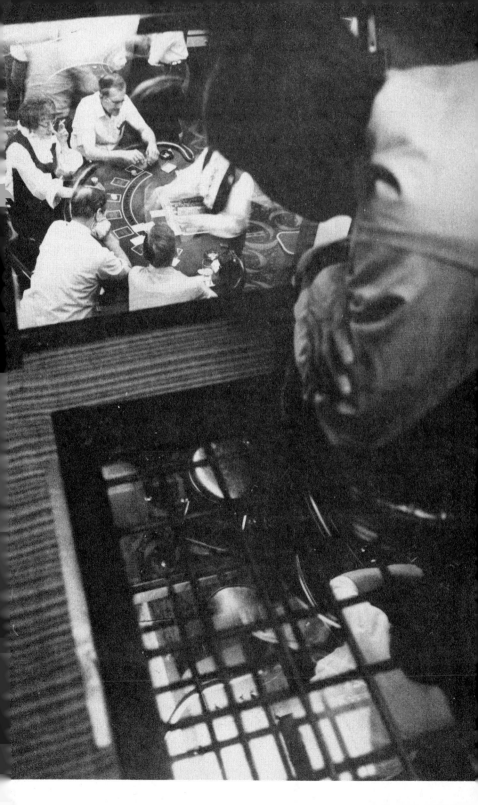

(Left) This 1970s photograph at Harolds Club shows a surveillance man at work. His job was to crawl through a maze of ceiling tunnels and look through two-way mirrors for anything out of the ordinary. Today, due to modern technology, this same person sits in an air-conditioned room and studies the action on a bank of television monitors. The cameras can fit anywhere and can be zoomed in and out at will.

"Who won the first Super Bowl game?" "The Green Bay Packers, 35-10." "Who's got the dice?" "Uhh, I think it's—uhh— the guy in the—uhh—no, it's the—uhh—the woman with the—uhh . . ."

(8) The pit boss watches the dealers, the boxmen and the floor supervisors. His duties are as varied as the designs on his trousers, and as far-reaching as the lapels on his sports jacket. Without pit bosses, the entire casino would run aground like an old ship—and probably still make money.

(9) The shift boss watches the dealers, boxmen, floor supervisors and pit bosses. His job is to enforce casino policy and make top executive decisions. "What happened to Table Six last night?" "The cards went bad." "What happened to Table One?" "The dice went bad." "Okay, change the cards, change the dice, and—phew!—change your aftershave."

(10) The "eye in the sky" is the surveillance employee who watches all the shills, keno runners, change persons, security guards, dealers, boxmen, floor supervisors, pit bosses and shift bosses. Thanks to modern-day casino technology, he is no longer known as the "eye in the sky." Nowadays, he is just called the "eye."

SCORING

None correct: You have never been to Las Vegas and probably flunked sandpile in kindergarten.

1-4 correct: You tell your friends you have been to Las Vegas because you flew over it once in an airplane.

5-7 correct: You have a cousin who used to date a cocktail

(Next Page) Struggling downtown Las Vegas casino owner Herb Pastor decided enough was enough. He traded in his slot machines at the Golden Goose Casino for girls. This young lady, one of the "Girls of Glitter Gulch," is a splendid personification of the other side of gambling.

waitress at the Stardust.

8-10 correct: Not only have you been to Las Vegas, but you have also visited the state capital, which is located at—uhh—let me think—it's up near—uhh . . . oh, well, cheer up. At least you can always get a job as a floor supervisor.

Once Upon A Time

ONCE UPON A TIME there was a lovely princess. Her name was Glitter Gulch, and she lived in the fairest castle of the kingdom. Hers was a carefree and wondrous world, with subjects who flocked at her feet to gaze upon her jeweled crown.

Alas, youth and beauty are such fleeting things. There is always another to catch the people's fancy. In the case of Glitter Gulch, it turned out to be a hefty stepsister with a bottomless purse. Big Mama was her name, and she was ten times the size of the maiden who lived down the hill. Big Mama had money, and Big Mama had connections. Soon she was ruling the roost from her flowery palaces all over a piece of neighboring land.

Slowly the hot neon where Glitter Gulch lived began to light up empty stores, greasy sidewalks, seedy bars—and vendors and hawkers, hookers and bums. "Yuck," said Glitter Gulch. "I don't feel good."

Poor Glitter was all alone, and even cheap weddings and quickie divorces would not bring her subjects back. Sounds of revelry could be faintly heard from Big Mama's estates, while Glitter Gulch was left with nothing more than a few stragglers down on their luck.

Yes, Big Mama had all the good things in life now—the top entertainers, the fur sales, the champagne brunches. Her suitors came from near and far, their satchels brimming with silver and gold.

Then came a rumbling across the countryside. Word trickled into the kingdom of something called a national recession. Profits began to backslide. "It's only temporary," Big Mama exclaimed. "Come back, come back."

Carefully worded press releases carried terse messages to the worried populace. "Some of our palaces are suffering, but these were marginal operations in the best of times . . . the strong mansions are holding up . . . we aren't recession-proof but we are recession-resistant."

It all sounded splendid, but the enemy seemed to be everywhere. To the east, a new prince was gathering forces. His name was Atlantis, and by 1981 twenty million people were forsaking Big Mama to court his favor. To the west, Sunday horse racing was introduced, and weekend tourism started to plummet. Then a dastardly plague known as lottery fever took root in almost half of the nation's colonies.

Big Mama was in big trouble. "Move over," she said to Glitter Gulch. "You've got company."

In the dark of night, the two made a pact. "Let us not quarrel with one another," they pleaded, "but instead trample those other snakes in the grass."

"Done," whispered Glitter Gulch. "Done," grunted Big Mama, and an uneasy truce prevailed. The alarm was sounded, and up rode the royal horses. Knights in dark blue suits dismounted, their saddlebags filled with facts and figures and small IBM computers.

"Let the high roller go," advised one. "Our contentions are to have more conventions," added another. Piped a voice in the background, "Our Town, the American way to play." "We like it," chimed the rest.

The gamble paid off. Family packages were offered, and bargain airfares. The economy grew stronger, interest rates went down, gasoline prices tumbled, terrorism overseas frightened people into vacationing on their own shore. Our Town grabbed every major sporting event it could, and once again the kingdom was the talk of the land.

Big Mama began to rest easy, and soon even Glitter Gulch was trying on new clothing. "I'm going to have a shuttle system," she bragged to Big Mama. "And a mall with landscaping and street furniture. And a civic plaza that's nine blocks long."

"Whoop de doo," mumbled Big Mama. Then, noticing the crestfallen look on her little step-sister's face, she quickly added, "You'll be beautiful, dear. Just like me."

Suddenly the phone rang. It was Count Igor calling from Washington. "Bad news, girls," he said. "Regulation 6A becomes effective today."

"What is that?" cried Big Mama and Glitter Gulch.

"It's a new rule requiring that you report to the king the names of all revelers whose transactions in gold exceed ten thousand pounds a day."

"Oh, why would the king do such a thing?" asked Glitter Gulch, wringing her hands.

"To stop large sums of gold from being laundered by the gnomes," answered the Count.

"But what if the king doesn't stop there? What if he lowers the gold ceiling to five thousand pounds? Or twenty-five hundred pounds?"

"You're such a worry wart," scolded Big Mama. "Why, if the king did that, it would mean his story about dirty money was just a dirty trick."

"I suppose you're right," Glitter Gulch said, feeling better already. "Would you like to split a shrimp cocktail?"

Ouch!

SOFT MUSIC—flickering candlelight—intimate surroundings. What could possibly go wrong? Suddenly the showroom captain grimaced painfully as he pried the cork from the wine bottle.

(Result: Sprained wrist, four and a half months off work.)

At another Las Vegas hotel, a Christmas party turned to tragedy when a casino hostess playfully lifted a youngster into the air. The hostess bumped her elbow.

(Result: Permanent partial disability award, $15,000 settlement.)

Taking the steps two at a time, a change girl rushed up the stairs to begin her shift. That was when she banged her wrist against the railing.

(Result: Eight and a half months off work, permanent partial disability award, $17,000 settlement.)

These are not isolated incidents of work-place injuries. Over 125,000 claims are handled in Nevada each year, where 1 in every 6 Nevada workers are hurt on the job every year. Accordingly, a whopping $4.29 billion is spent each year on state health-care. Sixty percent of those claims come from the Las Vegas area, where casinos dot the landscape like twinkling lights in an operating room. The more employees that are on the payroll, the longer the list of work-related injuries.

A fry cook cuts his thumb while dicing vegetables; a housekeeping supply person accidentally sprays herself with chemicals; a restroom porter hurts his neck carrying towels; a busboy injures his arm when he steps on a lemon peel. A paint foreman cuts his finger with a razor blade; a maid gets something in her eye while vacuuming a room; a fry cook injures his back when he slips in some pickle juice; a kitchen worker hurts his wrist lifting a tray of dishes.

In one recent month, 42 injuries requiring medical attention occurred in just one medium-sized Las Vegas casino. Multiply this by nearly 60 casinos, and the result is a sobering argument why safety and loss-time prevention are stressed so much in these days of sky-high medical care.

Every state has a no-fault insurance system, including Nevada. In simple terms, this means that a worker has little chance of suing his employer if he is hurt on the premises—and no matter what caused the accident, the hotel is seldom held responsible. The hotels are either self-insured (in-house or through a third-party administrator) or insured through the State Industrial Insurance System.

Since each Las Vegas hotel is a miniature city—many with their own print shops, paint shops, boiler rooms and kitchens—the idea of an accident-free environment is highly unlikely. Consequently, many hotels turn to the training and consultation section of the Nevada Division of Occupational Safety and Health. At no additional cost to the hotel, this regulatory agency identifies all hazards and makes suggestions on how to hold injuries down.

But even the work of this agency, and the training films many are forced to sit through, are not enough to keep accidents from happening. In one Las Vegas resort, a man working with an electric drill lost an eye when a sliver of metal flew into his face. Hanging neatly nearby was his pair of protective goggles. Medical costs in this case, including rehabilitation and partial disability, came to over $200,000.

The sad truth is that most injuries in Nevada casinos are caused by simple carelessness. A cook slices his finger while cutting chicken; a slot floorman slams his hand in the door of a poker machine; a hotel maid bangs her hip climbing out of a wet bathtub; a sous chef douses himself with hot sauce.

Disability benefits and medical rehabilitation are the state's ways of easing the pain, but two-thirds of one's salary doesn't always compensate. A hotel waitress, who injured her back when she slipped on a wet ramp, started collecting $200 a week until she was able to go back to work. Several days after getting her first check, a part-time banquet worker in the same hotel hurt her back picking up a tray. Much to her surprise, her compensation came to $4.40 a day.

"This isn't enough," she complained to the insurance company representing the hotel. The insurance company tried to explain that she was only a part-time worker, and not entitled to more than a percentage of her average weekly salary.

It failed to impress the banquet worker. "My friend is getting $200 a week," she said. "And that's what I want."

According to one insurance company spokesman, most accidents occur during the Christmas holidays, when school is out, or just before strike negotiations. No one knows how many of these claims are fraudulent or exaggerated, but the following case history shows how some scenarios begin.

A hotel kitchen worker hurt her back lifting a stack of dishes. "When the neurologist got the report," the spokesman said, "it was two stacks of dishes. By the time it reached an orthopedic surgeon, it was a large crate of pots and pans. Meanwhile, this person has been out of work for seven months and had over 100 treatments from a chiropractor. The only thing we've heard is that she is 'somewhat improved.'"

On the other hand, a baccarat dealer at one Strip resort suffered a concussion when a two-way mirror fell from the ceiling and landed on her head. She was back at work before the end of the week. After all, a concussion is just a concussion, but a baccarat dealer's tips are another matter.

Cases such as this, however, are few and far between. Most of them read like a clip from an old Laurel and Hardy movie. Showroom server injures head on gate lowered by bartender— stack of plywood falls on carpenter's foot—banquet waitress burns thighs when coffee urn tips over—porter hurts back when cart's brakes fail.

Other cases never make it past the investigation stage. A woman in one casino was given the job of recording the cash drop on all the slot machines. After a week of rushing from machine to machine, she filed an on-the-job injury report stating that her new job left her, dizzy, disoriented, too tired to even have sex. Her claim was denied. Another case involved a hotel porter. He claimed he was mugged while walking to work, losing $250 in cash and suffering severe head injuries. An investigation showed he had been involved in a fight with his girlfriend's ex-boyfriend that same morning.

I had an on-the-job injury once. A new management team had come to power in the casino where I was working, and its first order of business was to cancel the employees' dental insurance. Shortly afterwards, I bit down on an alien substance in a bowl of beef stew, and wound up with a $1,600 broken bridge.

I learned two things from that experience. One: my injury was covered by worker's disability. Two: never eat beef stew in the staff dining room.

Play Ball

HELLO, SPORTS FANS, and welcome to Cashman Field in Las Vegas. I'm Red Blazer, all set to bring you tonight's exciting baseball game between the Las Vegas Stars and the visiting Tucson Toros. Sorry for that screeching noise in the background, but we are experiencing technical diffic — . . .

Hello? Okay, I think we're all right now. Our engineer accidentally had us patched into the P.A. system. WHACK. There's a single into center field, and this ball game is underway. Let's see, that was Dab Timberlane, who came to the Toros from the Wichita Pilots of the Texas League after 14 seasons with the Houston Astros. You may remember Dab from the 1974 All Star game when he—WHACK. There's a hard-hit grounder down the first base line by Brick Smith, and the Toros have runners on first and third with nobody out.

We certainly didn't expect to see the Toros banging the ball quite this well, especially with that 30 to 35 mile an hour wind blowing in from left field. Then again, the 112 degree temperature could be taking something off Smithberg's sinkerball. Roger can usually put that ball anywhere he wants to, but tonight he seems to be throwing it right over the plate.

Stepping into the batter's box for the Toros is Hub Savage, whose .790 batting average is the seventh best in the Pacific Coast League. This'll be the test right here. There's Smithberg's first pitch, and Savage is down! Looks like Smithberg hit him on the right elbow with a fast ball, but he's all right. He's giving the crowd the high sign. No, wait a minute, he's giving Smithberg the high sign. Well, we won't go into that, because here comes manager Russ Nixon out of the Stars dugout.

That gives us a chance to remind you folks listening in that tomorrow will be Funny Nose and Glasses Night here at Cashman Field, and that's good news for all you hungry sports fans. Everything at the concession stand will be going at half price for this big night of baseball, which means you can enjoy a cold beer and a tasty hot dog with all the fixings for just $17.95. So come on down and join the fun when the Stars take on the Colorado Springs Sky Sox, who are just 14 games out of first place after beating the Phoenix Firebirds last night 26 to 19.

On the mound for the Stars now is relief pitcher Tack Treadway, making his first appearance since June 12th, when he held the Portland Beavers to only 7 RBIs in two and a third innings with an ERA of 3.27. He'll face Stone Harris, who leads the Toros in walks, squeeze bunts, stolen bases and dropped fly balls.

While Tack goes through his warm-up pitches, we'll take a commercial time-out. This is Red Blazer on the Stars Radio Network.

Hello, and welcome back to Cashman Field, where the Tucson Toros are leading the Las Vegas Stars 3 to 0 in the bottom of the first inning. During that commercial break, Treadway walked Stone Harris, Drum McKeever and Tide Morgan to bring in three runs. Then Dip Robbins hit a fly ball to Bip Roberts at second base, who stepped on the bag and tagged out Morgan for a triple play to retire the side. The Stars opened the bottom of the first with back-to-back singles by Stick Thompson, Lance Murdock and Boomer Salazar. That was it for Toros pitcher Dirk Portugal, who was replaced by left-hander Flame Stevens.

As we get back to live action, Stevens is taking his warm-up pitches. So while we have a moment, let's introduce our special guest tonight, former Las Vegas Stars first baseman Deke Davis. Good to see you again, Deke.

Thanks, Red. It's great to be here.

You left the Stars in '91. Where did you go from there?

I spent six months at Huntsville, Red.

That's double A ball?

No, it's a rehabilitation center near Houston.

Oh. So what are you doing now?

I'm in telecommunications, Red.

Sounds exciting.

Yeah, we sell pens and matchbooks over the telephone, and give away some real neat prizes like speed boats and home alarm systems. It's a lot of fun.

Well, thanks for being with us, Deke. Right now the fans are giving a big round of applause to Fuzz Stillwell, who just banged a grand slam home run to put the Stars ahead of the Toros 4 to 3. What a great night of baseball here at Cashman Field, where we've got to take a quick commercial time-out. When we return, we'll announce the winner of tonight's inflatable seat cushion, courtesy of Hospital Health Plan.

This is Red Blazer on the Stars Radio Network . . .

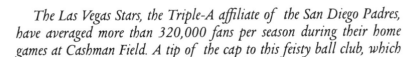

The Las Vegas Stars, the Triple-A affiliate of the San Diego Padres, have averaged more than 320,000 fans per season during their home games at Cashman Field. A tip of the cap to this feisty ball club, which has brought the flavor of major league baseball to Las Vegas.

Memories

THE TROUBLE with Las Vegas is that it never seems to get any older. As soon as a building acquires some touch of character or personality, up roll the bulldozers to tear it down so something else can be put in its place.

Those who live here take it all in stride, and hardly notice the spindly cranes that hover over the landscape like prehistoric insects. Fallen casinos are yesterday's news. Dunes, Marina, Silver Slipper, Mint. New resorts catch the eye, crowd the sky, do or die. Mirage, Rio, Excalibur, O'Sheas.

But when it's late, and the traffic's thin, and the workday's over, some of the old-timers still meet for a cold one before heading home. They are all that is left of a bolder Las Vegas, and they can tell you how it used to be.

There was the Grace Hayes Lodge, and the International, and the Cinedome. There was the Daydream Ranch, and the Village Pub, and the Playpen Apartments. There was Forrest Duke, and Paul Price, and Bob Joyce. There was the Jungle Club, and the Colonial House, and a neat cafe called the Dive.

A fellow named Lou owned the Dive, and his hamburgers were a work of art. If you blanked at work, Lou would trust you for a meal—just as long as you didn't stuff all your change in the pinball machine. The problem was that Lou trusted too many people. His old place became Battista's Hole In The Wall, and the present owner is a millionaire.

You took a right on the Strip to get to the Castaways. Built on a pie-shaped piece of ground across the street from the Sands, it consisted of a casino, two wings of rooms, a radio station out back, and a replica of an Indian temple that had something to do with "transmigration of the soul." Then somebody came up with the idea of putting a 1,500-gallon fish tank behind the bar. It didn't have fish in it, either. A nude showgirl swam lazily through the water three times a day, holding her breath while everyone watching held theirs.

Maybe the tourists zipped right past the Castaways without slowing down, but the locals loved it. It was the only place in town where you could play a penny slot machine, and maybe win the big jackpot of ten American dollars. The bartender knew your name, and what you were drinking. The waitress dished out advice as well as menus. "You've got to have a bite to eat, dear. You're going to be on your feet doing a lot of gambling." Breakfast was 59¢, and a steak was $1.95.

Most of the dealers were greenhorns, but at least they smiled sympathetically when you lost a bet and your chips went down another notch. They weren't there for the long haul anyway, but just putting in time until a good job came along. Consequently, every spring a new crop of dealers would show up at the Castaways for that curious Las Vegas ritual known as the job audition.

It was an unwritten law. You started downtown, then you got on at the Castaways before summer started, and you pestered the good places on the Strip until you got a job making some decent tokes. Passing that first Strip audition was the big test, and over the years it turned many a man to stone.

There was the time a dealer auditioned at the Castaways wearing a toupee. By the time the smoke cleared, his hairpiece had slid around sideways and his shirttail was hanging out in the back. All he could say to those who would listen was, "I blew it, I blew it."

Another dealer showed up early for his audition at a Castaways blackjack table. He stood anxiously to the side, watching with awe as the dealer on the game deftly arched the cards through the air. His eyes followed them as they landed in neat little stacks, and if somebody asked him later how many players were at the table he wouldn't be able to say. All he saw were fingers and chips and beer bottles.

Suddenly the pit boss nodded, and it was the young dealer's

The Castaways was one of the most intimate places on the Las Vegas Strip. Tourists zipped right past it, but the locals loved it. It closed in 1987, and is now the site of the Mirage Hotel and Casino.

turn. The weeks of practice and study were blurred in his head as he took the deck from the other man. He cautiously stole a look at the pit boss as he began to deal the cards, and saw with alarm that there were now *two* pit bosses watching him. With that, the young dealer's eyes rolled back and down he went in a dead faint.

Instantly two elderly security guards broke into action. One dragged the dealer away from the table, while the other hobbled to a nearby office where a tank of oxygen was kept for such emergencies. Together they worked frantically over the fallen dealer, one holding his limp body down while the other inserted a dusty mouthpiece and turned on the oxygen.

Success! The dealer's feet began to move, slowly at first, then faster and faster, and now his hands were clawing at the air—hands that had abruptly turned bright blue!

"Check the oxygen," hollered one guard to the other.

"Oh, no," replied the second. "The damn thing's empty."

The Castaways is gone now, victim of the times. It turned out the land was worth more than the hotel, and that's the name of that tune. Memories die hard, though, even in Las Vegas.

It would have been a little more fitting to serenade the Castaways' demise with a somber refrain by Mozart, or even some rip-roaring New Orleans Dixieland. Instead, an announcer said in a dull flat voice, "That's all, it's closing. Thank you." It seemed so cold and impersonal, like tearing down the Alamo to build another shopping mall.

In tiny groups the people filed out, while gaming agents methodically taped over the coin slots and men in hard-hats began hammering posts along the property lines. Inside a car, a woman cried. Then she slowly drove away, past where the Bonanza used to be, past where the Thunderbird used to be, past where the El Rancho used to be.

Another little part of Las Vegas was gone for good. July 20, 1987.

The Classifieds

THERE ARE TWO daily newspapers in Las Vegas—the *Sun* and the *Review-Journal*. My wife reads the *Review-Journal*. It comes in the morning, which is when she wakes up, and it has color pictures, Dear Abby, and a cooking section. I like the *Sun*. It comes in the afternoon, which is when I wake up, and it has controversial editorials, a crossword puzzle I can nearly finish, and Steve Roper on the comics page.

As far as the classified sections are concerned, let me read you a couple of "personals" from each and you tell me which one sounds like the best newspaper for a quarter.

From the *Review-Journal*: "Four basketball tickets, Center Court, Section 302, Call before Friday." "FREE TO GOOD HOME. Three kittens and mother." "Want to speak to people who have injuries they can trace to long-term use of computers. Call Ken."

From the *Sun*: "Let my girlfriend and I make U smile. Call Adrian." "HOT TUB PARTY, XX movies, 24 hours. Visa, MasterCard." "College girl, out of school and out of work. Call Julie." "Wanted, deaf or hard of hearing female for lifetime companionship and love."

When it comes to the want ads, however, both papers are about the same. Just turn to the "D" section of the *Sun*, or the "E" section in the *Review-Journal*, under "Employment Opportunities."

"1950's Pink Poodle Girl. Have tons of fun greeting our casino customers wearing a fantastic 50's Poodle Skirt Costume. If experienced, apply in person at Golden Goose Casino."

"Ranch chef for Furnace Creek Inn and Ranch operation remotely located in the heart of Death Valley National Monument. Must have at least five years food preparation experience."

"Parking Lot Striper, Seal Coater. Experience preferred."

One thing I've noticed is that you hardly see the word "Salesman" in the newspapers anymore. Most of these companies must be so busy looking for account executives, sales associates, marketing directors, promotional reps and tele-marketing motivators that they haven't even had time to name themselves yet. There is usually just a phone number, and some ungodly hour to call, like eight o'clock in the morning. It must be worth it, though. Selling an "inexpensive alternative to bottled water" netted some guy named Dennis a third month paycheck of $7,340.

Oh, well, let's turn the page and see what else is available.

"Psychologist for outpatient facility dealing with industrial injuries. Emphasis on psychological testing (MMPI, WAIS, MCMI, MBHI), counseling, chronic pain management and biofeedback. Doctorate in psychology or closely related field required."

"Clark county combination inspector. Requires a combination of education and experience equivalent to ICBO certification as a combination inspector plus four (4) years of relevant work/construction technology educational experience."

Darn. That last one sounded good, but I only have two (2) years of relevant work/construction technology educational experience. I was in a wood shop class in junior high.

Experience seems to be a prerequisite for just about every job listed in the classifieds, but that's no problem. Just look under "Schools and Instruction" and you, too, can LEARN & EARN.

"In just weeks have the skills you need to begin a career as a qualified electronic gaming machine technician." "Train to be a travel agent." "Become a casino dealer." "A computer career in less than a year." "If you've had dreams of becoming an interior designer, attend our FREE SEMINAR." "Command a big rig and a big salary as an MTA truck driver." "Become a paralegal." "Bartending & Cocktail Serving, Day and Evening Classes."

In order to land the really big jobs, though, you must have a low cost, well presented, attention getting, professionally printed, custom written, military converted, quality typed RE-SUME.

Consequently, you need the services of American Resume Service, Professional Resume Service, Kinko's Lasertype, Let Gerri Do It, Wordpro, Wordsmiths, The Winning Edge or Mrs. T's.

Then again, it might be easier to go to an employment agency. Just make sure the one you contact is screened, tested, insured, bonded, reference checked and security cleared. That way, you get the RIGHT person for the RIGHT job RIGHT now.

The only problem is that employment agencies are not called employment agencies anymore. Consequently, you have no idea whether you're signing up for a job or a trip on a cruise ship. Creative Beginnings, Careers Plus, Heritage, Medi-Girls, The Resource Network, Spectra, Acutemps, Key Temps, Pro Temps, Toma.

And guess who pays the employment agency, and the resume writer, and the training school? Why, the person who doesn't even have a job in the first place!

Fortunately, there is always:

"INSTANT CASH. No credit check. No interest. Money in 15 Minutes. Loan Secured by your Car, Truck, Boat or RV. Call Instant Auto Pawn . . . Today."

The Time Capsule

RUTHERFORD B. HAYES was in the White House and the railroad was pushing west when one of the nation's first time capsules was buried. It was done by a group of college students at Amherst, Massachusetts, and when the capsule was unearthed 114 years later all that was found inside were some old documents that were hardly readable.

But it started a craze that eventually wound all the way to Las Vegas. In fact, the Sands Hotel celebrated the end of its first year in business by burying a time capsule in 1953. The idea got some much-needed publicity for entertainer Tallulah Bankhead, who was starring in the Copa Room at the time.

At a special ceremony, Tallulah placed one of her studio photos inside the capsule. Other nostalgic relics included Bing Crosby's pipe, Ray Bolger's dancing shoes, Sugar Ray Robinson's boxing gloves, and a wax impression of Jimmy Durante's nose. Then the twelve-foot capsule, in the shape of a small rocketship and dotted with stars, was lowered into the earth. There it is expected to remain until the middle of the next century.

That got me to thinking. What would happen if a Las Vegas resort decided to sink a time capsule into the ground today? What rare and unusual artifacts would be left behind for the next generation of historians?

With that thought in mind, let us imagine we are burying another time capsule—circa 1995—at one of the hotels on the Las Vegas Strip. Here's our master of ceremonies, nightclub comedian Jackie Fargo.

Thank you, thank you. Sorry I'm late but I went jogging today, and it's the last time I'm going to jog in Las Vegas. The ice cubes kept bouncing out of my drink.

But as I stand here looking into your faces—and believe me, some of your faces need looking into—I want to thank you for coming outside in this heat. That wasn't the sound of drums when the band was playing a minute ago. Those were cars blowing up on the freeway. And just wait till summer gets here!

In fact, we had a near-tragedy this morning. The governor fainted, but we revived him. We threw a bucket of quarters in his face. The first thing he did when he came to was pardon the mayor, pardon the city council and pardon me. Must have been the pizza I had for breakfast.

But as you know, today is a big day for our hotel. I'm pleased to announce that the owner is even here, and I want to thank the warden for letting him out. In appreciation, we're going to put slot machines in the state penitentiary next week. The only difference is that when a prisoner hits the jackpot, he doesn't get any money. He wins a get-out-of-jail-free card.

Seriously, folks, today's the day we bury our time capsule, so without any further fanfare let's get started. As you can see, this time capsule is made of aluminum and designed to withstand almost anything, except maybe three songs in a row by Carol Channing. I'll just open the little door on the side here and—whoops. Anybody got a Phillips screwdriver? The first item to go inside our time capsule is Dean Martin's shot glass. Careful, don't spill it. Let's wedge it up against this next piece of memorabilia: the kickstand from the motorcycle Elvis Presley's stuntman rode when he went over the side of Hoover Dam in *Viva Las Vegas*. We also have the valve cap from the motorcycle's front tire, which the stuntman later used for a helmet.

The next object to go into the time capsule is Wayne Newton's mustache. I'd pass it around so you could see it better, but it's very fragile. Besides, the dye comes off on your fingers if you're not careful.

While the lieutenant governor and the attorney general are putting Siegfried and Roy's stuffed white tiger "Shasadee" inside the capsule, I'd like to introduce a few of the celebrities in

The Sands Casino is pictured here, just prior to opening night, December 15, 1952. Casino development on the Strip was at a feverish level at this time. Those are DELUXE CLUB CHIEF slot machines in the background, manufactured by the O.D. Jennings Company of Chicago.

the audience today. Without anyone's help they climbed the ladder to stardom, making it to the top on sheer talent alone, and I think that personifies what Las Vegas is all about. Ladies and gentlemen, a big round of applause for Nancy Sinatra, Charlie Sheen, Liza Minnelli, Candice Bergen, Elizabeth Montgomery, Gary Crosby, Natalie Cole, Lorenzo Lamas, Jamie Lee Curtis, Marlo Thomas, Carrie Fisher, Michael Douglas, Jane Fonda and Hank Williams Jr.

The softball that we are now putting inside the time capsule is the very one used by Kenny Rogers to inaugurate the first annual Las Vegas celebrity softball game. I'll put it in here next to these other two softballs, which were donated by Dolly Parton. That's funny, I didn't even know she liked sports.

Going into the capsule now is one of the strings from B.B. King's guitar, a string from Steve Martin's banjo, a string from Arturo Romero's violin, the string from Tom Smothers' yoyo, and the hamstring of former football great Alex Karras. Thanks for your contributions, fellows, and also to singer Robert Goulet for this 50-gallon drum of Max Factor hair spray.

While the vice president and the Soviet premier are putting Siegfried and Roy's stuffed lion "Mombassa" inside the time capsule, I'd like to—hey, guys, what are you doing? This isn't funny. Come on, put me down. Hey, it's dark in here. Don't close that door!

HELP!!!!!

The Name Game

TWO DEALERS struck up a conversation in a bar. "Where do you work?" one asked the other.

"I'm in BJ on swing at the Riv," the other said. "How about you?"

"I work the wheel on grave at the Shoe."

"Tokes good?"

"Not this week. Too many stiffs. In fact, we blanked yesterday."

"Too bad. We made a score last night, but it was only because there were two naturals on the game."

"Real georges, huh?"

"Yeah, you didn't even have to cut into them. I was dealing a double deck when a king kong on third base caught a snapper. He shoved out this barberpole, and when I started to color it up he said, 'No, that's for you.'"

"The same thing happened to me in a joint downtown. This george started up a dead game, and the next thing you know I dumped the whole rack. He gave me a hand-in, and just as I locked it up the pit boss hollered, 'Hey, where are going with that sleeper?'"

"Instant heat."

"You said it."

Every occupation has its own slang expressions, but the casino industry leads the way with colorful words and phrases. To a tourist, the preceding dialogue would have made no sense whatsoever. To a Las Vegas insider, it was a simple everyday conversation about players who were making bets for the dealers (naturals, georges, king kongs) and players who weren't tipping the dealers (stiffs). A "dead game" is a table game with no players; "BJ" is blackjack; the "wheel" is roulette; "third base" is

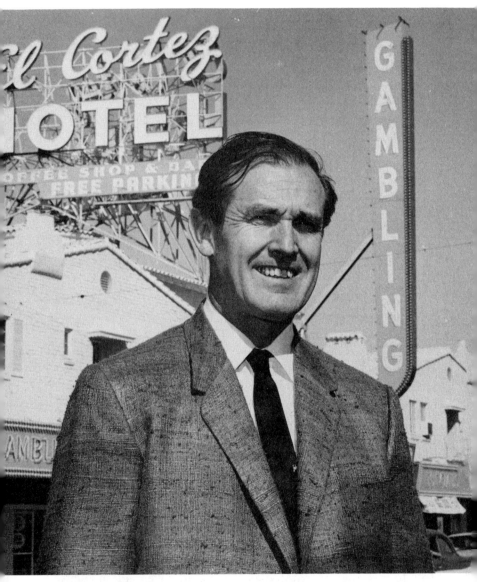

Jackie Gaughan is one of the few Las Vegas locals who still owns a casino; most of the gaming properties have been taken over by huge corporations. Gaughan was the third owner of the El Cortez Hotel and Casino in downtown Las Vegas. He purchased and took over operations on January 4, 1963. He still owns it, and the hotel looks much the same as it did when it first opened in 1941. This photo was taken in the early-1970s.

the position to the dealer's right on the table; a "joint" is a casino; a "snapper" is a blackjack; a "sleeper" is money left behind by a player; a "hand-in" is a tip; and a "barberpole" is a stack of chips ("checks") of various denominations mixed together.

"Tokes" are tips; a "blank" is not making any tokes; a "score" is making a lot of tokes; cutting into a player is hustling tokes; and "heat" is close scrutiny or constant criticism by a pit boss—who is not to be confused with a pit bull. (Pit bulls can be house-trained.)

Since casino people like to shorten the names of everything whenever possible, some pieces of their conversations come across almost in shorthand. The reason for this is because most dealers only talk to one another while they are working, which is known as "crossfiring," and that is one of the pit boss's biggest peeves. By using short words in place of long words, a dealer can crossfire for quite a while before a pit boss catches him and has him executed.

As a result, the names of just about every casino in Las Vegas are shortened to the absolute minimum number of syllables. A grunt is the only vocal expression that is shorter. Hence the Riviera becomes the Riv, the Horseshoe becomes the Shoe, and so on. Others include the Tropicana (Trop), Showboat (Boat), Stardust (Dust), Desert Inn (D-I), Barbary Coast (Barbary), Golden Nugget (Nugget), Union Plaza (Plaza), Caesars Palace (Caesars or the Palace but not both), and my very favorite: El Morocco (Elmo). It makes one wonder why the Excalibur is not called the Excal and why the Imperial Palace is not called the Imp. For some reason, those places never did get short nicknames.

The ingenious American game of craps has produced some notable slang words that have lived through the ages. Dice are called "bones," probably because the first games in prehistoric times used animal knuckles as dice. A "duke" is a big hand at the table. "Skinny Dugan" is a loser 7. "Boxcars" is a 12, and aces is "snake-eyes." That brings to mind the story of the young woman who threw a chip to the stickman during a game. Wanting the others at the table to know how knowledgeable she was, she screamed, "Gimme a dollar on snake lips!"

"Ace-deuce" is a roll of the dice where one cube lands on a one and the other lands on a two. That makes sense, but what doesn't make sense is how this same terminology is used by Las Vegas people to mark all kinds of dreadful events. For example, someone will say, "Too bad about Joe Blow. He caught ace-deuce last week." Joe didn't roll a one and a two at the dice table. Poor Joe died. And if a person's IQ is in question, he is "buffed on the ace-deuce."

Introduced in New Orleans over a century ago, craps is the only game in Las Vegas where participants stand while they play. I am told the reason for this is because the game was against the law until Nevada legalized it, and players could exit faster during a raid if they were standing up. It turned out to be one of those unwritten laws that never changed.

Las Vegas insiders never refer to chips by denomination, but rather by their various colors. You would never hear a dealer say, "I was dealing $100 checks all night." No, he would say, "I was dealing blacks all night." Or greens ($25 chips), or reds ($5 chips), or silver ($1 chips). In some downtown casinos, there are 25¢ dice tables that are called "bird games." And if there was ever a game that was for the birds, this is it. Ask any dealer who has ever worked on one.

Dealing the bird game is enough to make anyone hang up his apron. By the way, did you ever wonder why dealers have to wear those stupid things? Management will tell you it's to keep the dealer's slacks from wearing out, but I am sure you can think of a better reason.

Here are some other colorful Las Vegas expressions. When someone is eavesdropping on a conversation, he is on the "Erie Canal." If the boss tells you to "dummy up and deal," he wants you to keep your mouth shut and your eyes on the layout. A full moon is not what a disgruntled player gives you as he walks away, but the time of month when dealers believe all stiffs and turkeys show up at their game.

The most important slang word in Las Vegas, however, is "juice." Not to be confused with competence, proficiency or skill, juice is the ability to get a good casino job through a friend, or a friend of a friend, or in some instances because of being able to hit a golf ball 300 yards down the fairway. Yes, life can be a piece of cake—if you've got juice. Just ask some of the bosses working in Las Vegas.

2093—A Las Vegas Odyssey

THE OLD MAN shuffled out to the front solarium as a bright sun burned through the afternoon smog. Easing into his hydrolounger, he looked at the date on his wrist computer. It was the 34th of April already. Summer would be here in a few more weeks, and he hadn't even waxed the blades on the family hovercraft.

He pushed a button, and the Las Vegas skyline appeared on the solarium wall. The casinos glowed like miniature cities: Slotboat, Lots O' Slots, Arcade Hilton, Slotstown, Video Palace, Slot Machine Island, Reel Experience, Golden Slots. With a sigh, he watched the Bullet Train from the Arizona coast speed toward the Las Vegas Strip.

He never got used to looking at the Strip without remembering the days when cars clogged the intersections. Of course, that was back in the 20th century, before automobiles were banned by the government. Now there were so many hovercraft and balloon ships in the sky you needed a flash-gun to find your way to the mandatory drug screening every week.

Yes, the state of Nevarizona had certainly changed since the Great Earthquake. Everyone got enough to eat now, thanks to greenhouse farming, but the 75 percent sales tax left little money at the end of the month. Fortunately, the federal income tax was ruled unconstitutional by the former Supreme Court. Otherwise, most of the citizens would probably be deported to Jupiter, where all the federal prisoners and gang members lived.

Suddenly the old man heard the hiss of the school ship, and then his two grandchildren were at the solarium door. "How was school today?" the old man asked, hoping the two weren't thirsty already. Now that Lake Mead had dried up, each family was allotted only one mega-gallon of water a day.

"It was okay," answered his granddaughter, tossing her paper jacket into the trash compactor.

"Did you learn anything?"

"Yeah, we learned the names of all the presidents," she answered, then closed her eyes as she recited. "Washington, Jefferson, Lincoln, Roosevelt, Jodie Foster."

The old man chuckled. "You left out a few, but at least you know more than you did yesterday."

His grandson approached with a stick of turkey in his hand. "My class was neat, grandpa," he said. "We learned all the payback percentages on the slot machines. The teacher said if I quit school, I could probably be a casino manager by the time I'm 16."

"You stay in school," the old man said. "Or do you want to spend the rest of your life working around a bunch of robots?"

"No, sir."

His granddaughter tugged excitedly at his sleeve. "Grandpa, tell us about how Las Vegas used to be."

"You mean when I was young?"

"Yes," his grandson cried. "Please?"

"Well, all right," he said, impulsively reaching for his pipe and then remembering that tobacco had been illegal for the last 35 years. The two children sat at the old man's feet, looking up at him with expectant faces.

"When I came here, Las Vegas was a real special place. Of course, that was before gambling was legal all over the world. Back then, it was against the law in most places, and I guess that's why this town was so unique. Why, there were all kinds of attractions that used to bring in tourists by the millions."

"What kind of attractions, grandpa?"

"Well, table games for one thing."

"What were table games, grandpa?"

"They were gambling games, most of them played with cards. There was blackjack, baccarat, poker. They had a spinning wheel game known as roulette, and one with dice that was called craps."

"You said a nasty, grandpa."

"No, that was the name of the game. Now listen, kids. I

know you've never heard of anything except slot machines, but these table games were really something. People used to bet real money on them, none of that plastic stuff like you see nowadays—and they had human dealers, too."

"You mean there weren't any robots?"

"Nope, there weren't any robots in those days." The old man's eyes clouded. "Of course, that was before the government disbanded the corporations and took over the casinos. The first thing they did was get rid of most of the humans, because salaries and insurance just got to be too expensive."

"So what did you do, grandpa?"

"I did what any other red-blooded Nevarizonian would do. I went to slot machine school. Why, I could dismantle a Megatrillion ten-reeler and put her back together in less than a micro-minute. Robot mechanics hadn't been perfected yet, and I made enough money to retire by the time I was 120."

"Las Vegas must have been fun in those days," his grandson said wistfully.

"Oh, it was. You wouldn't believe it, but I remember when every casino had a showroom. People would sit out front, and all the big stars would come out on stage and sing songs."

"You mean like on MTV?"

"Well, in a way. But like I said before, it just got too expensive. So the government ripped out the showrooms and put in more slot machines."

"Gosh."

"And a lot of things were free back then. You parked your car free, you got in the casino free, and if you played any of the games you got free cocktails and sometimes even a free meal."

"What's a cocktail, grandpa?"

"It was a drink made with alcohol."

"You mean like that junk we put in the hovercraft?"

"Yeah, but this tasted a whole lot better," the old man chuckled. "I never did understand why they outlawed it."

"What else was there, grandpa?"

"Well, there were human bellhops in all the big hotels, and they used to carry people's luggage up to their rooms. Then the hotels put in automatic luggage chutes, and that was the end of that. And back before GlobalCop, every casino was staffed with real human security guards. It was really something."

Suddenly the door of the solarium slid open, and the old man's son peeked in. "I thought I'd find you kids in here," he said. Looking at his father, he added, "Dad, you weren't telling them about the old days again, were you?"

"I'm sorry, son," the man sighed, climbing slowly to his feet. "But sometimes it's hard to keep it all inside."

"Well, come on back to the dining module. The food drinks are almost ready."

"Food drinks?" the children cried. "I thought we were going to McDonald's."

The old man smiled. Some things never changed.

Nuts & Bolts

THANKS TO STATE LOTTERIES, gambling is losing its shady stigma and becoming one of the nation's juiciest sources of revenue. And as more and more states institute casino and riverboat gaming, Las Vegas casino workers are finding themselves in an enviable position. Every state with legalized gambling wants people with experience, and so Las Vegas is becoming a virtually untapped marketplace for casino personnel. For example, in one recent issue of a Las Vegas newspaper there were ads seeking experienced personnel for casinos in Missouri, Wisconsin, Colorado and Illinois.

In some instances, however, leaving Nevada for a lucrative position elsewhere can be a dangerous move. For example, a shift manager at the Mirage gave up her job and home to take a similar post at the Lummi Casino in Bellingham, Washington. Less than six months later, she and ten other out-of-state supervisors were fired in what the casino owners termed a "disagreement in management style."

The ousted workers say that was not the case, and have filed a lawsuit charging the casino lured them from jobs elsewhere with false career promises. The suit charges the casino only wanted their expertise and know-how in starting up the gambling operation and then replaced them with local workers.

So if the corporate policies of Las Vegas are getting you down, and those out-of-state jobs are starting to look rosy, take it from an ex-Mirage and now ex-Lummi shift boss. Sign a contract first.

A dealer in a Las Vegas casino approached the pit boss and asked for two weeks off. Since a holiday weekend was approaching, the pit boss turned down his request. The following day the dealer called in sick. His punishment? The pit boss suspended him for two weeks.

Do you know why all the casinos in Las Vegas are always so packed with tourists? It's because no one can figure out how to get out of them. My suggestion is that these casinos install signs that point out such features as exits and telephones. Otherwise, casino employees are going to spend more and more of their break time working as tour guides. One woman recently asked a dealer where the exit was.

"Which one?" he asked.

"You know," she answered. "The one that goes outside."

Another tourist asked where the entrance was. "Straight ahead, ma'am," the dealer said, pointing to the front door. The tourist said, "But that says exit."

Two baccarat dealers were fired for stealing from a Las Vegas casino. Were the two guilty? We will never know, but it didn't deter the two from making a living. They opened a Mexican restaurant called "Bandito's."

A woman was watching her boyfriend play roulette in a Las Vegas casino. He handed her a $5 chip and told her to bet it on one of the numbers. "Which number should I pick?" she asked nervously.

"Bet it on your age," he said nonchalantly.

She placed the chip on number 25. The roulette ball landed on number 33—and the woman fainted!

When Mark Twain first moved to Carson City, he wrote to a friend saying that Nevada was a den of "booze, wild women and 24-hour gambling." He added, "Certainly it is no place for

Craps is considered by many to be the most exciting game in the casino. Others feel the game is dying out, but they forgot to tell all those players who crowd around the dice tables in Las Vegas.

a good Presbyterian. So I no longer am one."

A Las Vegas bartender placed a large stack of napkins on the counter just as one of the hotel vice-presidents walked by. "Do you know how much those napkins cost?" the vice-president said angrily. "Get rid of them right now."

The bartender watched the vice-president walk away. Then he shrugged, and tossed the stack of napkins into the garbage can.

If you have ever wondered where our tax dollars go, read the following true story. A man, who had already lost $10,000 in markers, bet a stack of currency at a Las Vegas dice table. He lost that bet, too, which came to $4,300. Then the man bet another stack of bills totaling $1,070. This time he won, and as the dealer counted the money he noticed an official-looking certificate stuck to one of the bills. The dealer examined it closer. What was it? Why, it was one of California's guarantees that a destitute person would always get enough to eat. It was a food stamp!

A Las Vegas junket came to town, and the dealers manned their stations in anxious anticipation. Here came a junketeer to the dice table. "Give me five hundred," he said to the dealer. When the dealer got the okay, he slid $500 in $25 chips to the junketeer.

"Give me a hundred in nickels," the junketeer said, tossing back four green chips.

Next time you are in a casino, look up. Those dark domes house video cameras—and they are looking at you. At this security center at Harolds Club, a security employee watches several table games. Security measures such as this have substantially reduced cheating in Nevada casinos. The small sign just above the employee's right hand in this photograph is a message from the late "Pappy" Smith and reads: "Beware of the Unusual."

The dealer did as he was told, but the man shook his head. "No, I want *nickels*," he said. "They're for the slot machine!"

It would have made a great story. The sign on the truck read "Las Vegas Chips." The driver was making his rounds when suddenly he was forced to the curb by two masked men in a nondescript car. The driver was forced to open the back of the truck, then was pistol-whipped when the bandits discovered the truck was carrying chips all right, only these were of the potato variety. Not to miss such a golden opportunity, the potato chip company immediately launched an all-out advertising campaign. Then came a phone call from police headquarters. The truck driver failed a lie detector test, and later pleaded guilty to attempted embezzlement. Another dream dies hard in Las Vegas.

The parents of a Las Vegas baccarat dealer owned a small Chinese restaurant in one of the city's suburbs. The dishwasher had just quit, so their son agreed to help out by washing dishes when his baccarat shift ended at the casino.

After work, the son parked his white Cadillac convertible in front of the restaurant. As patrons idly watched, he stripped off his tuxedo jacket and strolled toward the dishwashing equipment.

One of the patrons approached the owner. "If that dishwasher ever quits," he said, "I would like to apply for his job."

In the days before sophisticated surveillance equipment, a Reno casino owner used to spy on the help through a small hole drilled in the ceiling. One day he spotted his bartender take a silver dollar from a customer and drop it into his shirt pocket.

Before the owner could react, the bartender retrieved the coin from his pocket and flipped it in the air. "Heads I keep it," the bartender said. "Tails, and it goes in the cash register."

The casino owner smiled as the coin landed on tails, then gasped in horror as the bartender dropped it back into his pocket.

"Put that dollar in the cash register," the owner screamed from above. "I won it fair and square!"

A Las Vegas dealer was arrested for shooting a bald eagle. The judge said to him, "Don't you know that the eagle is an endangered species? Why, I could fine you $10,000 and put you in jail for that."

"You don't understand, judge," the dealer explained. "I was lost in the desert, and hadn't eaten in over a week. I only shot that eagle because I was starving to death."

The judge nodded. "Well, in that case I'm going to dismiss the charges, but I don't want to ever see you in this courtroom again."

As the dealer turned to leave, the judge looked up. "By the way," he said. "What did that eagle taste like?"

The dealer replied, "Oh, it was kind of a cross between a spotted owl and a condor."

A drunk wandered into a downtown casino, only to be escorted to the door by a security officer. Moments later the drunk staggered back inside, and was once again taken away by the same security man. Five minutes passed. Here came the drunk again, only this time he stumbled through the side door of the casino. As the same security guard approached him, the drunk wailed, "I don't believe it! Do you work at every joint in town?"

(Right) Harolds Club in Reno was the first casino to use "Eye in the Sky" surveillance. One-way mirrors, designed into the interior decor of the casino, provided security personnel with a subtle means of watching both players and dealers. This mid-1970s photograph through one of the mirrors shows the detail the security employee saw.

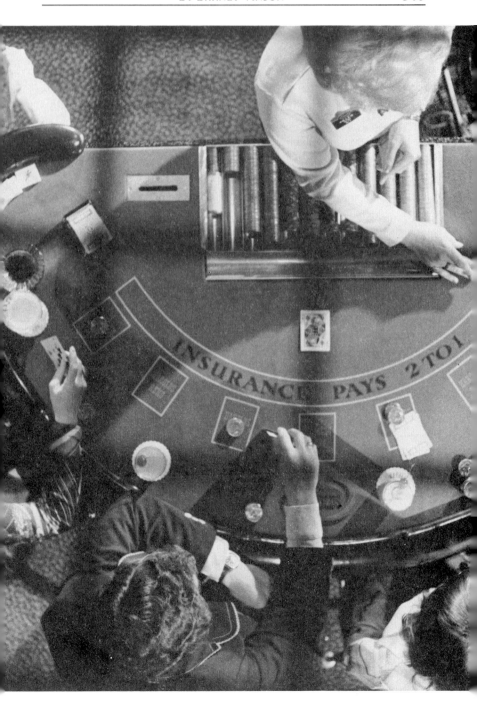

Las Vegas writer Brian Sprinkle pens the story of a gambler who returned to his room after losing $4,000 at the tables. He asked his wife how she did on the slot machines. "I lost $300," she said.

"How could you lose that much money on a slot machine?" the man cried.

"Well, you lost $4,000," she answered.

"Yes, but I know how to gamble."

Then there was the man who dropped a bundle at the dice table. He looked skyward and said softly, "Please, God. Just let me win $30,000, and I'll be even."

Suddenly he heard the voice of another man a few feet away. "Please, God," the second man was saying. "Help me win back my $40."

The first man reached into his pocket and took out $40. "Here," he said to the second man. Then he looked up again. "Now, God, pay attention. Thirty thousand dollars . . ."

At a Las Vegas casino, a woman boarded an empty elevator clutching a large cup of quarters. Just as the elevator doors began to close, two large men entered. As she stood nervously at the back of the car, one of the men suddenly said, "Hit the floor."

She dove to the floor of the elevator, her quarters flying in all directions.

One of the men looked down at her. "Are you all right?" he asked her.

"I only did what you told me to do," she cried.

He laughed. "I was telling my friend to hit the button for our floor," he explained.

The elevator doors opened and the embarrassed woman hurriedly gathered up her quarters and left. Upon checking out of the hotel the following morning, the desk clerk informed her that her bill had already been paid. Along with the canceled bill was a note.

"I'm sorry I frightened you," the note read. "Please accept my apologies, but you gave me one of the biggest laughs I have had in a long time."

The note was signed by Arsenio Hall.

A local dealer tells the tale of a well-heeled gambler who was winning big in a Strip baccarat game. The gambler, sporting an ill-fitting toupee, had not made a bet for the dealers all night, and after stiffing the cocktail waitress it became apparent the dealers could expect the same treatment.

As the cards were being shuffled after the last hand, it came time for the toupee-clad gambler to pay his vigorish. "Sir?" said the stickman in a booming voice. "How would you like TO PAY your marker?"

The dealers may not have made any money that night, but they did get the last laugh.

It happened at a plush resort on the Las Vegas Strip. A South American millionaire was playing craps when the shooter rolled a winner 6 the hard way. The gambler had bet $10,000 on the pass line with $20,000 odds, receiving a payoff of $34,000. Apparently, however, it was not enough.

He spoke quietly to the dealer, who turned to the boxman and said, "The gentleman says that we owe him another $27,000."

"For what?" the boxman cried.

"Well, he said that he meant to bet another $3,000 on the hard 6, but he accidentally placed the money on the 8 instead."

The game was stopped while the boxman talked to the floorman, who then talked to the pit boss, who naturally had to talk to the shift boss, who had to call someone else on the phone. Meanwhile, the millionaire gambler talked happily with his friends. After all, he was stuck almost a million dollars, and there was no way he would lose this argument.

The shift boss hung up the phone and nodded to the pit boss, who nodded to the floorman, who nodded to the boxman. "Pay him," the boxman said to the dealer, and a beautiful stack of $1,000 chips was shoved to the gambler.

Just as the game was about to get underway again, a player at the other end of the table shouted. "Hey, I meant to put $50 behind my bet. How about paying *me*?"

It was just another day in Las Vegas.

A Las Vegas dealer was down in the dumps. He had been out on the town, he told a friend, and somewhere along the way he lost his car.

"Do you remember where you went?" his friend asked him.

The dealer scratched his head. "Well, I started out at the Flame, then I went to the Night Gallery, and then I had a few drinks at a bar on the Boulder Highway."

His friend smiled. "Well, why don't you go to those same places again tonight? Maybe by retracing your steps you'll find your car."

The dealer acknowledged that this was a good idea, and borrowed a friend's motorcycle to repeat his previous night's escapade.

"How did it go?" his friend asked him the following day.

"Well, I did like you said," the dealer replied. "I had a few drinks at the Flame, then a few more at the Night Gallery, and wound up at that same bar on the Boulder Highway."

"Did you find your car?"

"Hell, no," the dealer exclaimed. "In fact, I lost my friend's motorcycle!"

It was graveyard shift in a Las Vegas Strip casino. One of the blackjack dealers did not show up for work, so the pit boss called her at home on the telephone. "It's two o'clock," he said angrily. "How come you're not at work?"

"Oh, I've been in California," she answered sleepily. "I guess

I forgot to set my clock back on Nevada time."

The late Benny Binion once took a cowboy from Texas on a tour of his ranch near Las Vegas.

"How big's your ranch?" the cowboy asked Benny.

"Oh, it's about a mile in one direction, and about half a mile in the other," Benny replied. "How big's your place?"

"Well, Benny," the cowboy replied proudly, "if you got on your horse at dawn and rode in any direction, by nightfall you'd still be on my land."

Benny nodded glumly. "Yeah, I used to have a horse like that myself."

Paul Sebastian might be one of the best colognes on the market, but there is one pit boss in Las Vegas who can't stand it. In fact, he reprimanded a dealer recently for wearing the stuff. You guessed it. The following night every dealer in the casino reeked of Paul Sebastian cologne.

Here is another true casino story. A man walked up to a Las Vegas dice table, presented a player's card to the floor supervisor, and wanted to know how much credit he could get. A quick check on the computer, and the floorman told him, "You can get another $14,000, Mr. Blackwell."

"Thank you," the man said. "I'll take all of it."

The man was given $14,000 in $100 chips, which is how he requested it, and the first thing he did was give the dealers $1,200. Then he started gambling.

The floorman, who had given the man a marker to sign, suddenly appeared at his side. "Mr. Blackwell, there seems to be a problem here. Your signature doesn't match the one on file. Do you have any identification?"

"No, I left it in the room."

"Well, what's your birth date? That should take care of it."

"Two—fourteen—forty-eight."

The floorman scratched his head. "No, that's not right, either. Maybe you'd better give us those chips back."

The man frowned. "You're in a lot of trouble," he said. "I've got a microphone in my pocket, and the place is completely surrounded by FBI agents."

It was the floorman's turn to frown. "No, you're in a lot of trouble," he said, motioning to two nearby security guards.

The man paled. "Isn't there any way we can settle this thing peacefully?"

There wasn't, and the man—who apparently found the player's card on the floor—went to jail for fraud.

—————

From John Alcamo's book *Atlantic City Behind The Tables* comes the story of a high roller in Atlantic City who sat down at a blackjack table with his young blonde girlfriend. After several hands, the young blonde rose to her feet.

"What's the matter with you?" the man asked her. "What did you stand up for?"

The blonde paused for a second. "Well, honey," she finally answered. "You told me to stand if I got a 17."

—————

While we're quoting from other books, how about this true tale from *Lifestyles Of A High Roller*, by Phyllis Wolff. Her husband, who was the inspiration for the story, stopped at a craps table in an Atlantic City casino. "Twenty-five dollar minimum," a sign read at the table. Wolff placed 50 dollars on the pass line, only to see an obviously inexperienced dealer push the money back to him.

"I'm sorry, sir," the dealer told him. "This is a $25 table."

The Regulars

YOU WILL FIND THEM in every city and hamlet in America. They are known as the regulars, a group of people who congregate every day at the same time in the same location. In my home town it was at Pop's Place, a hamburger joint just off the main drag and in the shadows of the county's tallest building: a ten-story skyscraper that loomed over everything in sight.

In New Orleans, I spotted the regulars playing dominoes in front of the old courthouse in the French Quarter. In the small towns that make up the Deep South, they get together in front of the general store, sipping pop and swapping yarns. On television, they meet at Cheer's or at Mel's Diner. In Las Vegas, they show up at one of the casinos every day—and each casino has its own group of regulars.

The downtown regulars were a special breed. Most of them did a little gambling, but it was more of a social thing than a way to eke out a living. A former pit boss at the El Cortez said, "Most of them would buy a five dollar stack of quarter chips, not with the idea of how much they would win, but how long they could stay in action." He remembered one 80-year-old regular who had a 25¢ chip in action at the dice table. When a burly young man accidentally picked up the old man's chip, the 80-year-old shouted, "Drop that chip or I'll break your neck!"

The big dream of every dealer was to work on the fabled Las Vegas Strip, but even the classy places on that famous thoroughfare had their own bands of regulars. One of them was a former airline pilot named Oscar. At least, he told everyone he used to be a pilot, and if he was telling the truth then I can see why so many people take the Greyhound. Apparently, Oscar broke the sound barrier once too often, and now he was hard-pressed to scrounge up enough money for a meal. So he hung around the casino until he spotted a friendly face, which usually got him a free ticket to the buffet.

George was an ex-judge who dressed like an ex-convict. Unruly hair sprouted from under a faded baseball cap, but there was an innocent glow in his eyes that belied the loneliness he must have felt inside. He knew all the dealers on a first-name basis, and passed out candy as he made his rounds every day. Occasionally he would make a bet at the tables, but it was a small price to pay for being accepted as one of the guys.

Doc's claim to fame was that he performed the first successful muffler transplant on a '76 Ford Pinto. Doc, who owned a service station outside of town, was one of those rare individuals who could sleep and gamble at the same time. In fact, the only time his eyes opened was when he won a bet. Then he would collect his winnings and nod off again.

Sidney was another regular. When compared with the others, Sidney was almost a celebrity. In his earlier years, Sidney invented an electric bubble machine which he sold to musician Lawrence Welk. Later on, he became an extra in the movies and then hosted his own children's TV show in Florida. When that bombed he headed for Las Vegas, which was one of the few places where there was still a little glamour left around the edges. We didn't call him Sidney, though. We called him Bubbles.

Most of the regulars had nicknames. They didn't know they had nicknames, but out of earshot they were Alfred Hitchcock, Wheelchair Ralph, the Grim Reaper, Tugboat Annie, Mortimer Snerd. "Here comes Mortimer," one of the dealers would say, and the rest of us knew who it was without even looking up.

You could almost set your watch as to when Up-A-Unit would appear at the dice table. We called him Up-A-Unit because that was the way he gambled. He would bet the minimum amount on all the numbers, and go up one unit every time one of his numbers came up. "Up a unit," he would say over and over, and after 30 or 40 minutes of this it became almost like Chinese water torture.

There was System Smitty, who got his nickname because of

If you pass the same table at the same time every day, it's possible you will see the same people. They are the regulars, and each casino has its own circle of them. This group congregates at Sam's Town.

all the systems he tried on a regular basis. It didn't matter whether the dice were hot or cold; Smitty had a system that sometimes actually worked. On one such occasion, he amassed enough in winnings to buy a brand new Cadillac. Since he didn't trust banks, he kept the rest of his bankroll in his pocket. With no permanent place to call home, he slept in the back seat of his Cadillac. This went on for almost three weeks, until his system finally backfired and he was forced to sell the car. Then it was back to the streets for System Smitty.

Next to Smitty, the most colorful regular I ever heard about was Suitcase Murphy. Murphy sold shirts out of a suitcase, and a three-shirt sale meant that he picked up a quick eight buck commission up front. Murphy may have been a gambler, but he was an honest man, and if you put in an order for some shirts you would get them sooner or later. Meanwhile, he had eight dollars of your money—enough to chase a dream which usually turned into a nightmare.

Then there was Coathanger. Coathanger got his nickname because he hung coathangers on his belt with complete changes of clothing on them. Coathanger looked like a walking dry goods store. He wore three or four sweaters over his shirt, carried saddlebags on his shoulders, and kept his money and other personal effects in an old Army ammo belt strapped around his waist. Coathanger wasn't what you would call a high roller. He would bet ten dollars on the pass line and another 15 to 20 dollars on long-shot proposition bets, so he usually lost all the money he brought with him. Still, you could say that Coathanger never lost his shirt when he gambled. There were too many sweaters on top of it.

One regular without a nickname was Marvin. A former pit boss at the Sands, Marvin had become one of the very things he detested in his working days: a true dyed-in-the-wool grinder. Marvin was no slouch. He could actually get markers, which was something most regulars only knew about through the rumor mills. Marvin would make a conservative bet at the tables, usually five dollars on each number. If he lost he would raise his bets to ten dollars on each number, then $25, and then $100. On the rare occasion when he did manage to win something, he would bore everyone to tears:

"Yeah, I was down almost two grand. Then this lady picked up the dice and rolled for half an hour. If I hadn't taken my bets down after I caught that ten, I would have owned this place."

I never could understand people like Marvin. He was in the casino business all his life, and probably could have written a best-seller about what the Sands was like when Sinatra and the rat pack were filling the showroom. Yet all he wanted to do after he retired was hang around another casino, putting his life savings on the line while trying to grind out an insignificant profit.

Maybe it is loneliness, or maybe it is that creeping sickness we know as compulsive gambling. Grocery Store Bob could tell us what it's like, but he won't. He gets his paycheck from the grocery store every Friday at three o'clock, and by 3:30 he's at the tables, betting as though there's no tomorrow.

In the meantime, he's just another of the regulars. You can feel sorry for him if you want, but in his own world he is as happy as any of the rest of us. And when you get down to it, I guess that's all that really matters.

The Morton Downey Show

MY APPEARANCE on the Morton Downey Show began with a simple telephone call. The conversation went like this:

"Hello?"

"Vinnie Barnson?"

"Who?"

"Er . . . Barney Vinson?"

"Yes?"

"I'm calling for the Morton Downey Show."

"What is this—some kind of survey?"

"No, no, no. We want you to be on the show."

"Oh! It's my favorite show!"

At the time, I didn't even know that Morton Downey was back on the air. The last I heard of him, he claimed to have been attacked in an airport washroom by a gang of skinheads, and shortly after that his show was canceled. Now he was back again, and I was to be his next victim.

According to the caller, I would fly to Palm Springs, be met at the airport by a limo, be whisked to the hotel where I would spend the night, relax by the pool for a couple of hours, be whisked to the studio, have dinner with Morton Downey, go over the format with the producer, tape the show, then be whisked back to the hotel. The upshot of the whole thing was that Morton Downey's new show was seen nationwide, and would be a tremendous boon to "flat book sales"—to quote my publisher.

Still, the idea of appearing on television was frightening because I was completely at the mercy of the person doing the interview. Previous interviews always produced the same questions: how much money had I seen anyone win, and why

315

didn't dealers ever smile? On one occasion, a television interviewer scanned my book while putting on her make-up, and it took three takes before she even got the title right.

The Morton Downey Show was to be taped on a Saturday night, and that afternoon my wife and I headed for glitzy McCarran International Airport. As we filed onto the tarmac, a long sleek jetliner sat poised on the runway. Suddenly the line of people in front of us veered around the long sleek jetliner. Behind it was a two-engine prop plane that looked like something out of an old Indiana Jones movie. It was our plane, of course.

Soon we were airborne, and just as we finished our meal of pretzels and Sprite the aircraft bounced to a landing at the tiny Palm Springs airport. I searched in vain for a limo, but all I saw was a young woman in a mumu standing in front of a Ford Bronco. Suddenly she spoke. "Mr. Vineyard? I'm here to take you to your hotel."

Well, I certainly couldn't complain about the hotel. It was a beautiful place right in the middle of downtown Palm Springs. Unfortunately, the pool was the size of a ping pong table, and it was hot enough outside to fry eggs on the sidewalk. I retreated to my room, changed clothes, and two hours later was back in the lobby for the three-minute ride to the studio.

The studio turned out to be a combination bar, restaurant and auditorium. We were escorted to a table in the restaurant, then a waitress came to take our order. The menu listed our choices: fried zucchini, fried cheese sticks, fried shrimp and nachos. Morton Downey, meanwhile, entered the restaurant and without a look in our direction took his seat at a long table with a group of other people. While we studied the menu, we could hear Downey and his group ordering their meal. "Medium." "Medium rare." "Well done." "Medium."

So that's how it worked. Morton Downey and his boys got steaks, and I got nachos. "Excuse me," I said to the waitress as she turned to leave. "Do you serve alcoholic beverages?"

"Yeah."

"Cancel those nachos, and bring me a grapefruit juice and vodka."

Author Barney Vinson was invited to make an appearance on the *Morton Downey Show*. The highlight of the program came when Downey tore one of Vinson's books in half and threw it on the floor. Forewarned, the publisher of this book has used stronger paper so that television hosts will have to work harder to do their jobs.

I was on my second drink when the producer of the show approached our table. There was the faint aroma of Worcestershire sauce on his breath. "Mr. Vinton?"

"Vinson."

"You'll be the first guest tonight. Mort will ask you a few insider questions, such as how much money you've ever seen anyone win, and why dealers never smile. He's more laid back than he used to be, so the show should be a lot of fun."

"Great." I held up one of my books. "And maybe he can mention my book."

"Book?"

Yes, book! After all, that was the reason I was here. He took the book gingerly. "I'll see what we can do," he said. "In the meantime, we need you in make-up and then we'll get you miked up."

Make up. Miked up. All I know is that half an hour later there was a microphone clipped to my tie, some kind of electrical transmitter in my back pocket, and enough pancake on my face to stop a bullet.

The show itself was a blur. Morton Downey, whom I had never even met, came bounding out. The studio audience began their Downey war chant ("Mort-Mort-Mort-Mort"), and I was introduced by an off-camera announcer. Wonder of wonders, he even said my name correctly.

Then Downey was in my face. "How much money have you ever seen anyone win in Vegas?"

"A million dollars." (Gasps from the audience.) "Of course, the same player lost three million the next day."

"Well, I want to know something," Downey screamed. "Why do the casinos in Vegas bar card counters? I mean, the minute someone learns enough about blackjack to get the odds halfway in their favor, YOU GUYS THROW 'EM OUT!!" (Cheers from the audience.)

"You're talking about something that happened 20 years ago," I answered, finding it hard to be intimidated by this guy when I had a couple of vodkas under my belt. "They don't bar card counters anymore."

"Oh, yeah?" Downey bellowed. "Well, here's what I think of Las Vegas—and your book!"

With that, Morton Downey ripped my book in two and threw it on the floor. The camera zoomed in for a close-up.

If I had known what he was going to do, I could have come up with a snappy comeback. "That just tears it," I might have said. Or "That'll be $5.95." Instead, I just looked down at the floor with a goofy grin on my face.

Later I would get even. Toward the end of the show, Downey wanted to know about the mobs and their link with modern-day Las Vegas. That's when I called him Howard Stern. Did I do it on purpose, or was it a slip of the tongue? I am still not sure, but I do know one thing.

I will never do another television interview. Unless Jay Leno calls me. Or David Letterman. Or Oprah Winfrey. Or Hard Copy. Or . . .

Today's Fashions

ONE OF THE BIGGEST CHANGES in Las Vegas is not the city's new dramatic skyline, nor the corporation takeover of locally-owned casinos. It is the subtle appearance of a whole new type of customer. The high roller is gone, and in his place is what casino moguls refer to as the medium roller. This new breed of customer is easy to spot. He roams the casino with packs of other medium rollers, drinking margaritas out of Dixie cups and looking for the nearest restroom. He can also be recognized by the camcorder strapped around his neck, the rental car contract sticking out of his pocket, and by his ultra-casual attire.

I can remember a time when male customers wore suits and neckties, and their female counterparts were adorned in flowing gowns and ermine stoles. Of course, I understand that few women wear furs anymore, and I don't fault them for that. We have all seen the stark pictures of baby animals being clubbed to death for their pelts, and who in their right mind would want to wear a fur coat after seeing something like that? But there are alternatives, such as cloth.

New lifestyles, however, have made the dress code of the nineties an almost indifferent afterthought. This is not a problem only in Las Vegas, but throughout the civilized world. On Broadway, for example, "the audience looks as if it's coming out of a movie or a Red Lobster restaurant," writes Woody Hochswender in *Esquire Magazine*.

Nowadays, the only people who dress up in Las Vegas are

(Next Pages) *Question:* What's wrong with this photograph, taken in 1962 at the Riviera? *Answer:* Everyone is wearing suits and cocktail dresses. But look at the dealers!

the people who work there. If you walk through a casino wearing a suit, someone will surely stop you and ask for directions.
Chances are the person stopping you will be wearing either a
baggy pair of Bermuda shorts or one of those new-fangled
warm-up suits that have become so popular.

I don't know who started this latest craze, but everyone is
wearing them now. The pants have zippers on the legs, so you

can put them on after you've tied the shoelaces of your $150 tennis shoes, and the jacket usually has some kind of logo on it that doesn't make sense. The jacket also has two very skimpy pockets that will not hold anything larger than a roll of Life Savers, so consequently the wearer has to tote everything around in a leather purse.

Another item that is popular today is the personalized T-

shirt. Years ago, T-shirts were white and they were worn either by teen-agers or professional athletes. Today everyone wears T-shirts. They come in two sizes: extra small and extra large. They come in every color except the color you are wearing, and they all have messages on them: "Busby's Barbecue." "Here Comes Trouble." "Hard Rock Cafe." "I'm With Stupid." "Davy's Locker." "I Love San Francisco." "Jeremiah's Chili Cook-off." "Pebble Beach Country Club." "B.U.M. Equipment Company."

Today you can't go into a restaurant without passing a counter filled with T-shirts. It's not enough to pay $14.95 for a plate of ribs and two lukewarm beers. No, you've got to spend another $17.95 announcing to the whole world that "I Ate At The Coral Reef Cafe, Davenport, Iowa."

There are also T-shirts that expound the brave feats of the owners, such as one I saw an elderly man wearing at a Las Vegas dice table. "I Flew The Grand Canyon," his T-shirt proclaimed. (I was thinking to myself that if this old geezer flew the Grand Canyon, it was from inside one of those Flight For Life helicopters.) At the other end of the table was a man wearing a T-shirt that read "I Skied The Summit." The floorman watching the game was an affable Latin named José Jimenez. I said to him, "José, look at these guys. One skied the summit; the other flew the Grand Canyon. What have *you* ever done?"

He thought for a moment, then said, "Well, I swam the Rio Grande."

Writer Michael Paskevich of the *Las Vegas Review-Journal* gives one half-hearted excuse why slovenly attire is so much in evidence these days. "Vegas is an adult Disneyland," he writes, "and visitors stuck in the button-down workaday world literally want to take out the starch and relax a bit." But in an interview with a Las Vegas casino executive, he was told:

"I know this sounds like an old lounge joke, but some of these people look like they've left their pickups running in the parking lot."

Another casino executive put it even more bluntly. "It's not important how people dress," he told me. "It's what they are carrying in their pockets." He did not elaborate on whether he

Casual wear is encouraged at Sam's Town and accepted at all other Las Vegas casinos, with few exceptions—but don't forget to bring money.

was referring to money—or guns.

In an unofficial survey of my own, I counted 500 tourists coming through the doors of one fashionable Las Vegas resort. Of that number, only two women were wearing dresses. Everyone else was wearing either faded blue jeans or slacks of various colors, styles and sizes. I only counted eight people wearing ear rings, and six of those were men!

My question is that if this is the way people dress when they go out of town, what do they wear the rest of the time? No wonder C&R has a sale every other month. Nobody buys suits anymore.

There was a time, however, when evening wear was a way of life in Las Vegas. Photographs from the fifties and sixties show everyone dressed to the hilt: men in dark suits and women in simple yet elegant dresses, their ensembles gently accentuated by white gloves and sequined purses. The way people dressed in those years lent an air of carnival revelry to the Las Vegas ritual of casino-hopping—and every night was special.

Unfortunately, that era has come to a jean-faded end. Today it all goes, and that means acid-washed jeans, sweat shirts, T-shirts, football jerseys, leotards, bathing suits, shorts, stretch pants, cutoffs, mini-skirts, bell bottoms, tank tops, sweat sets, overalls, hot pants, jogging suits, lounging pajamas, pedal pushers, bathrobes and anything else short of absolute nudity.

I remember when letting your hair down meant wearing a polo shirt with a little alligator over the pocket. And if you were really a rebel, you wore your shirt with the back of the collar turned up. Today you would stand out in a crowd for doing something like that. Not because your collar was turned up, but because you were wearing a shirt at all.

Greener Pastures

I **AM OFTEN ASKED** by Las Vegas outsiders what it is like to work in a casino. Usually I make a joke about it, because most people think of the casino industry as one of the most glamorous businesses in the world. Mention gambling, and right away visions come to people's minds of lavish surroundings, celebrity parties and high-stakes action.

Unfortunately, Las Vegas is more a state of mind now than an actual city. The reckless abandon of the fifties and sixties is nothing more than a memory, and the big conglomerates that run the town today have changed the whole concept of what Las Vegas was once all about.

Still, this is an exciting time in Las Vegas with new theme parks sprouting up like mushrooms. After all, more and more areas of the country are turning to legalized gaming as a way to pay for state government, and the uniqueness of wide-open gambling is making Las Vegas just another whistle stop for the endangered high roller.

That leaves the American family, so the resorts get 'em here with roller coasters and water slides—and if a casino worker doesn't like it there are a dozen people itching to take his place. The adjective today is "team player," against which the standards of yesteryear—skill, speed and efficiency—don't stand a chance. "Team player" sums it all up. If you're a team player, you wind up with a fancy title and a fancy salary. If you're not a team player, your future is as cloudy as a 50¢ martini and you might as well start looking for another job.

True story. A casino worker's job performance was being evaluated by the casino manager. "You're not a team player," the casino manager told him.

The worker replied, "Sure I am—when I have the right

coach!" But exactly what does being a team player signify? Does it mean what the words imply: working with others as a team to make the workplace a happy and profitable environment for all concerned? Or does it mean blindly following orders without question, no matter which direction they take you. The Dunes Hotel was filled with team players, many of whom are still out of work due to inept and bungling ownership that sent the property reeling into bankruptcy.

These are the nineties, though, and team play is now the order of the day. Here is an employment ad that appeared recently in the *Review-Journal* that paints a clearer picture of this new age of corporate lingo:

"WANTED. TEAM LEADER. This individual will be responsible for ensuring that the highest level of guest room and casino area cleanliness is achieved and maintained. Also responsible for promoting the success of the company's team concept. This position requires previous supervisory or team leader experience. Must possess strong customer service, communication, organizational problem solving and team building skills."

In other words:

"WANTED. RESTROOM ATTENDANT. The man who gets this job better keep the men's room clean, and if he sees another restroom attendant goofing off he should report him to the boss pronto, and if the boss doesn't do anything about it report both of them to corporate security."

Another problem facing us today is the changing attitude of casino customers. Years ago there weren't enough casinos to go around, and many would-be customers found themselves being turned away. That's all changed. Now there aren't enough customers to go around. So the casinos have begun massive courtesy campaigns—killing the customers with kindness before killing them at the tables.

It started at the Tropicana back in the mid-eighties. All the other casinos were up to their usual tricks: throwing people out for getting disorderly, refusing to explain the games to novice players, gouging diners in the coffee shops and gourmet restaurants. But then the Tropicana splashed the following message on its marquee: "55 Smiles An Hour Only At The Tropicana."

Once again, it was "follow the leader" time in Las Vegas, as other casinos began their own courtesy campaigns. Dealers who once were reprimanded for talking to players got reprimanded now if they didn't. And just as an animal knows that winter is coming, the customer sensed—by some half-buried primal instinct—that he had finally risen to royal status in this desert domain.

As a result, a note of thanks from a customer meant accolades from management, and dealers began hustling letters instead of tips. On the other hand, an unhappy customer could get almost anyone fired by filing a complaint, and it has happened more than once. "Try another table," one dealer told a player. A complaint was made, and the dealer was out of a job.

On another occasion, a dealer was explaining the game to two tourists when a woman—with $10 on the table—complained that the conversation was distracting her. She and her husband filed a complaint, and four hours of paperwork were eaten up by the dealer, floor supervisor, pit boss, shift boss and games manager.

Maybe that is why so many casino employees are going back to school and learning new skills. Or they are doing other jobs on a part-time basis until enough money rolls in to make it a full-time endeavor. If the casinos in which they work will not reward them with job security or retirement benefits, then hopefully they can do it on their own.

Pegg Wallace started in the casino business as the first woman craps dealer at the El Cortez. Years later, Pegg would give up a career as a casino executive to go into business for herself, and now she is a senior director and national trainer for BeautiControl, an image consulting corporation.

Don Murphy was casino manager of the Treasure Island Hotel and Casino on the island of St. Maarten, and before that was executive host at the Frontier in Las Vegas. Now he is a crackerjack realtor for ERA Western Properties.

Vic Taucer was a casino supervisor and gaming class instructor. Now he is a teacher at Community College of Southern Nevada and the owner of his own company called Casino Creations. Willie Stark bounced from casino to casino as a dealer and boxman. Then he won the annual Las Vegas rib burn-off, and now has his own barbecue joint called "Chili Willie's."

My wife Debbie was a blackjack dealer for ten years. After brushing up on her typing and shorthand, she became a Clark County court clerk, and she has never been happier.

I'm still in this crazy business, but hoping that someday one of those locked doors will open for me. In the meantime, whenever I see somebody digging a ditch or driving a delivery truck, I think to myself:

Hey, this business isn't so bad after all.

Remembering Red

WHEN I MOVED to Las Vegas in 1967, the city was a lot smaller than it is today. In those days, one could actually travel from one end of the Strip to the other without celebrating a couple of birthdays along the way.

Still, it was a big city as far as I was concerned. I remember circling around Hoover Dam at night, then driving through Boulder City. Suddenly, down below, there was Las Vegas, spread out as far as the eye could see. It looked like an overturned pirate's chest, with precious stones scattered everywhere. In my mind, every twinkling light was a priceless jewel, and all I had to do was go down in that valley and scoop them up.

To make a long story short, I almost starved to death trying to get to those jewels. Try explaining this land of opportunity to someone who has less than $300 to his name. How close was I to the brink of disaster? By the time fate smiled on me, or at least blinked in my direction, I was broke. Phone calls were 10¢ then, so I used my last dime to call the manager of a local radio station about a part-time job. His secretary said, "I'm sorry, he's in a meeting right now. Call back in an hour."

People like to talk about the good old days, but I still shudder when I think about those times. Just as I was ready to throw in the towel, however, I got a job—as Johnny Holiday on KENO radio. I didn't particularly like the idea of being called Johnny Holiday, but the station already had its jingles made up. So Johnny Holiday it was.

The grainy years of rock and roll were fading into history, and all the new songs were about peace and flower power. A boring new musical era had dawned, and the air waves were assaulted with the likes of *Rubber Duckie, Candy Man,* and *A Boy*

Named Sue. After Elvis and the Beatles, it was a dreadful letdown, and that was when I hung up my earphones for good.

It was just as well, I suppose, because Johnny Holiday never quite achieved the stature of such prominent radio personalities as Hal Morelli, Chuck Manning and Red McIlvane. Hal has since given up the business, Chuck is still spinning records around town, and Red McIlvane died recently. But when I first came to Vegas, Red was about as big as radio personalities got. Everybody listened to him . . . even other disc jockeys.

I think the secret to his success was that his voice came across on the air as folksy and down-to-earth. His timing was flawless, tuned by years of stage work, including six seasons as the announcer on the old Horace Heidt radio show. After a stint in the air force, he took a radio job in Phoenix, moved on to Los Angeles, then came to Las Vegas.

In an interview with Red several years ago, he laughed as he recalled his first day in Las Vegas. "I pulled into the station parking lot, and all I could see were brand new Cadillacs." It turned out that the other announcers were giving free plugs to the local Cadillac agency, and in turn they were getting new cars to drive. That was Red's initiation to life in Vegas.

Back in those days, there was always a photo of a scantily-clad showgirl in the newspaper. "It attracted the kind of people who were colorful and interesting," Red said. "And it attracted customers." This gave Red an idea. If he could obtain a motorhome, and a photographer, and a couple of showgirls, he could go on a national tour. He could make stops in every major city along the way, and garner all kinds of free publicity for Las Vegas.

Red set to work. He already knew how to get a free Cadillac. Maybe he could use the same principle to get a motorhome. He approached the local dealership. Without so much as a fanfare, they agreed to loan him one, as long as he promoted the company during his travels. He also promised to promote Holiday Inns, and in return got free rooms along the way. He promised to promote every major resort in Las Vegas, and got free vacation packages to distribute on his trip. The whole thing was turning into a dream come true. It would be a

December 5, 1973, was opening night for Kirk Kerkorian's MGM Grand
Hotel. Jane Powell, Fred MacMurray and Barbara Eden did the ribbon-cut-
ting, but in this case the ribbon was a strip of motion picture film. That's Red
McIlvane in the background with the microphone, right behind Jane Powell.

crazy stunt for a crazy town: the Las Vegas Fun Bus!

Now came the hard part. Red needed a final okay from the
Las Vegas Convention and Visitors Authority. The board listened patiently as he made his pitch. When he was finished,
the chairman said, "It sounds fine, but where do we come in?"

Red hesitated. This was the moment of truth. "It will cost
$13,000 dollars," he said meekly.

The board members huddled for a moment, then the chairman said, "You've got it."

Two things happened in quick succession just before Red's
Fun Bus hit the road. The temperature went to 100 degrees,
and the *Las Vegas Sun* newspaper went on the streets with this
headline: "Why Should Las Vegas Pay For Red McIlvane's Va-

cation?"

Red got a phone call from the Convention Authority. "Go," the chairman told him, "but go quietly." Red swallowed his pride and headed out of town. There were no marching bands, no parting speeches, no television news cameras. There was just Red, his photographer, and his showgirls, off to chase a dream that was slowly starting to unravel like a cheap blanket.

Maybe it was just coincidence, but the Fun Bus rolled back into Vegas just as summer sizzled to an end. Red immediately called the Convention Authority. "Hi, we're back," he said brightly.

"That's nice."

"Well, don't you want a report?"

"Is it necessary?"

"Yes. We came in $375 *under* budget."

"Keep it."

"But—"

CLICK.

Okay, so the Vegas Fun Bus wasn't a rip-roaring success. But it was a great idea—until the *Las Vegas Sun* newspaper got hold of it. Irony of ironies, Red would wind up in later years writing a weekly column for the same newspaper. Before that would happen, however, he would host a local television show, work as a news anchor, become a casino publicist, start up a magazine and form his own advertising agency. He would also become widely-known for his humanitarian efforts, one of which was a tradition of serving holiday dinners to the homeless and disadvantaged.

It was his sense of humor, though, that made him a household name. One incident that comes to mind was the time he conducted a survey to determine why the shoreline of Lake Mead had a reddish glow. He said it was from 785 pounds of Max Factor makeup being washed down the drains of Las Vegas after the midnight shows and into the waters of the lake. "Where else," he said, "can you catch pink bass?"

And when I questioned him once about the future of Las Vegas, at a time when Atlantic City was its arch-rival, he pondered for a moment before saying, "Nothing can stop Las Vegas. Not even a silver bullet."

His sense of humor got him through the worst of times when he was battling cancer with radiation and chemotherapy. In one of his columns, he shared with his readers the observation that he was beginning to glow in the dark.

Red is gone now, and only his memories remain. Memories, and accolades. Phyllis McGuire said, "His death is a great loss to the community." Shecky Greene said, "He had the soul of a comedian." Stardust executive Jim Seagrave said, "He could touch our hearts; he was in a class by himself." A longtime friend said, "He charmed us. He entertained us. He moved us." But Red's greatest memorial came from Red himself, shortly before his death. "The greatest gift," he wrote, "is the ability to cherish our days—one day at a time."

Progress

YOU SAW IT on the TV series *Vega$*. It was in *Fever Pitch*, *Viva Las Vegas*, *Rain Man*, and just about every other film that was shot on location in southern Nevada. You've glanced at it a hundred times from your car, and it was probably the first landmark you saw when you came here.

I am referring to the diamond-shaped sign on the south end of the Las Vegas Strip that spells it all out in big bold letters: "Welcome To Fabulous Las Vegas, Nevada."

The sign is small, and maybe it seems out of place now in a town gone mad with frenzied construction. Yet there is something about that sign to which most of us can relate. It is almost like going back in time and touching the past, when Las Vegas was younger and a whole lot simpler.

The sign was there when the Strip was a narrow highway threading the needle from L.A., and the sign was there when Las Vegas resorts had storied names like International, Bonanza, Thunderbird and Dunes. I always thought that as long as that sign stood, a little part of Las Vegas would stay the same. But I didn't reckon on something called progress.

You see, what happened was some of the hotel owners on the Strip got together recently and hired a fancy consultant to come up with some ideas on how to modernize this fabulous boulevard. Sure enough, one of the first things the consultant recommended was to get rid of the sign that has stood there for almost 40 years.

A public uproar, however, resulted in a quick revision of plans, so the sign will stay. But it is being overshadowed by a $30 million improvement project along the Strip that calls for palm trees, flowers, wide sidewalks and plenty of lighting. Such things are more in keeping with the new carnival-midway image of America's favorite sandlot.

Meanwhile, Las Vegas folklore got another slap in the face when the Flamingo Hilton demolished the building which housed Bugsy Siegel's original suite. Twenty years ago there was talk of erecting a statue in honor of Bugsy Siegel. Ten years ago there were plans afoot to name a casino for Bugsy. Now a complete about-face and the ultimate coup de grâce: Bugsy took a one-way ride out of town. Never mind that it was Bugsy's imagination and fortitude that put Las Vegas on the map. The Las Vegas of today is geared toward the rosy-cheeked American family, and there's no room at the inn for gangsters of Bugsy Siegel's ilk.

So all the rumors about hidden rooms at the Flamingo filled with bundles of hundred dollar bills, and secret passages, and bodies buried in Bugsy's rose garden have finally been put to rest. Instead, the Flamingo is treating us to an expanded buffet, a remodeled swimming pool, and a slew of new rooms. It will mean more business for the Flamingo, because there will be more people staying on the property. Of course, the first thing they will want to see when they get there is—the Bugsy Siegel suite.

Oh, there are other things to see in Las Vegas:

Circus Circus has opened a $75 million climate-controlled water theme park called Grand Slam Canyon.

The $1 billion MGM Grand Hotel & Theme Park lights up the Strip with a playground almost the size of Disneyland.

The $450 million Treasure Island Resort is now open next to the Mirage, with pirate ships doing battle on their own lagoon.

The $400 million Luxor has opened next door to the Excalibur, featuring a pyramid-shaped hotel for tourists—and a landing light on top for UFOs.

I just wonder how tourists will react to all these waterfalls, pirate's coves, rushing rivers, white-water rapids, lagoons, creeks, pools and water slides—and with all this water, why can't the rest of us use our sprinklers in the afternoons? No one in charge seems to realize that Las Vegas is right in the middle of the Mohave Desert, so how will tourists know they're supposed to bring wet suits, scuba gear and waterproof matches?

No one is against progress, but the historical sites that set Las Vegas apart from other cities must remain. They are our link to the past, and our beacon to an even-brighter future. If the "Welcome to Las Vegas" sign goes, what piece of Las Vegas will fall next?

Will it be Vegas Vic, that lanky cowboy on Fremont Street from another time and another place? Will it be the gingerbread wedding chapels that no longer fit the image of Las Vegas gone legit? Or will it be Glitter Gulch itself, where even a glitzy $63 million canopy will not make things how they used to be.

Will it be Lake Mead, a dangerous waterhole full of sheer drop-offs and man-eating carp? Will it be Mount Charleston, where death from a wayward pine cone can come at any moment? Or will it be Hoover Dam, that colossal eyesore and traffic hazard?

Many casino workers have already fled to quiet suburbs in Illinois, Indiana and Mississippi, and in a lot of ways the idea of living somewhere else has become more appealing in this hectic age of change and confusion. After all, there is something to be said about living in a comfortable little town where nobody locks their doors, where everyone knows your name—and where all the casinos close at nine o'clock every evening.

Game Starters

THE STORY GOES that if you ever find yourself hopelessly lost, just start playing a game of solitaire. Before you know it, there will be somebody peeping over your shoulder saying, "That red nine will go on the black ten."

The same principle applies to casino games. All it takes to start a game of blackjack, for example, is a dealer standing behind an empty table with his arms folded. It doesn't matter if there are seats open at 15 other tables. It doesn't matter if every player at every table is winning. It doesn't matter if the dealers are using shovels to pay the bets!

There will always be one player looking for his own private Eden—a table where he will be the center of attention. If it costs him every dollar he has in his pocket, it will be worth it just to utter one of the following time-worn phrases:

"Are you open?"

"You look lonesome."

"Doesn't anybody like you?"

"Did you take a shower this morning?"

"I'll give you something to do."

Or every dealer's very favorite:

"Shuffle the cards. I'll see if I can get your game going."

It's the same story at games which require more than one dealer: namely baccarat and dice. Baccarat, however, is too intimidating for most people. The dealers' tuxedos and the fancy chandeliers scare everyone away. If I owned a casino, I would let baccarat dealers wear T-shirts and blue jeans. Willie Nelson would be on the stereo, and the waitresses would serve beer in those long-neck bottles you see everywhere but Las Vegas. And I'd change the name of the game. After all, who would want to play a game with a fancy French name when they could play

"Closest To Nine Wins A Whole Bunch Of Money."

That leaves dice. The only difference is that a game starter won't show up at a dice table until a dealer has spent five minutes telling a funny story to the other dealers. Then, just as he gets to the punch line . . .

"Hi, is this table open?"

Ditto for major sports events such as the Super Bowl or World Series. Score tied, two out, bottom of the ninth, runners at first and third . . .

"Hi, is this table open?"

Or:

Everyone at an empty table listening attentively as the floorman says, "Did you guys hear about the change girl they arrested this morning? She was walking down the hallway behind the showroom when two big security guards came around the corner. She started running and dropped her purse. One of the guards picked it up, and it was full of . . ."

"Hi, is this table open?"

Even worse is the game starter who has to announce to the whole world that he is gambling in Las Vegas. "ALL RIGHT, BE NICE, DICE, COME ON AND ROLL ME A SEVEN!! COME ON, SEVEN, COME ON, COME ON . . . BABY NEEDS A NEW PAIR OF SHOOOOZ!!!"

This, of course, brings a host of other people to the table, racing up to see what all the hollering is about. You would think they would shake their heads and walk away when they discovered that it was just another idiot on the loose. Not so. In fact, the table will soon be jammed with players—and no one will ever know what was in that change girl's purse.

Meanwhile, now that the game is crowded, take one guess as to where the game starter is. Why, he's gone, of course. It's no fun now that he's just another participant, so he's off to find another empty table where he can be king of the mountain again.

Almost as bad is the novice who has never played before. He will usually have a list of bets he is supposed to make, but he doesn't want to go to a table where other people are gambling. He might make a fool of himself in front of all the players. So he goes to a table where he is all alone, and makes a fool of himself in front of all the casino employees.

"Excuse me. I want to bet five dollars on the pass line, and I want to back it up with the odds when I get a point. Uhh, what is a point and what are odds and where is the pass line and can I get a drink and anything else that's free??"

There is also the game starter who wants to be everybody's friend. He will walk up to an empty table, dig out a wrinkled 20 dollar bill, and while waiting for change will go into the following mind-numbing dissertation:

"Do you guys know Tony? He's a bellhop at the Flamingo. No? Well, anyway, he told me yesterday I should bet the number 36 on the roulette wheel, because it comes up more than the other numbers do for some reason, and I should've listened to him because last night I walked by a roulette wheel just in time to see number 36 come up, and then this morning on my way to breakfast I walked by the roulette wheel again, and you'll never believe it but . . ."

According to psychological studies, most gamblers are either pessimists or masochists who enjoy the chase more than the kill. Tell one who approaches an empty table that the dice or cards are cold, and the invariable answer will be, "Good! I'll change that." He loses, of course, but not before getting a crowd of others to the table.

Then there is the odd-ball gambler, who not only talks to himself but answers himself on occasion. He is liable to do anything, which is one reason why hotel security guards should be allowed to carry nuclear weapons. One such player showed up at a dice table at the old Bonanza Hotel. He placed $300 on the pass line, stuck both dice in his mouth, and spit them to the end of the table. "Winner seven," said the stickman. "No roll," said the pit boss. Too late. The player was already out the door with his winnings.

In days of yore, each casino in Las Vegas had a couple of shills on the payroll. Their job was to pretend they were gambling, which always lured other people to the games. It was sort of like big-game fishing, only the casinos used humans as bait. Nowadays, with record crowds of tourists piling into Las

Vegas every month, the casinos don't need shills. All they need are a few tourists with no friends, no money and nowhere to go.

Take the one who spotted an empty Las Vegas dice table and came running. Placing a five dollar chip on the table, he announced to dealer Bob Myers, "I hate to see people not working."

Bob replied, "I wish I was a lifeguard."

Slot Shots

THERE IS SOMETHING about a carnival that borders on larceny. Lead bottles defy gravity, nickels skip across shallow plates and thud in the sawdust. Moving cardboard ducks glide casually to safety while mis-sighted rifles pop frantically in the cool night air.

Las Vegas has that same carnival atmosphere. Dice skim down a green felt table, and the crowd goes wild. The Big 6 wheel clacks past a 40 . . . slows on a 20 . . . stops on a 1. Money goes into a slot machine; occasionally something comes back.

In a sense, slot machines are a throwback to that era of side shows and come-ons. At one time, casinos could hardly get anyone to play them. That all changed in 1975 when payouts were loosened, jackpots were increased, and the machines themselves were adorned with such space-age features as computerized screens and musical chime boxes.

During this formative period, a Las Vegas casino executive received a letter from an irate player, who complained that one of the machines was serenading its customers with Hitler's marching song. "We are of the Jewish faith and lost many friends in the holocaust," the letter read. "How could you do such a thing?"

The executive turned the letter over to his slot manager. Out of curiosity, the slot boss opened the back of the machine and triggered the music. Sure enough, the tune, from one of Beethoven's classics, was the same used by Adolf himself in World War II.

It seems a slot machine salesman had rigged one of these new chime boxes to the machine, hoping this would boost profits and consequently increase sales. "There were about 20

Mechanical slot machines lingered in northern Nevada until well into the 1980s. Here is an interesting mix of electric and mechanical slot machines— along with a priceless collection of antique weapons—at Harolds Club in Reno. The photo was taken during the late-1970s.

different songs that could be programmed into it," said the slot manager. "We had it set to play *Old Susannah*, but somebody from our drop department started fooling around with it. And he liked this song better; he thought it had a snappier beat."

Needless to say, *Old Susannah* got back on the hit parade in a hurry.

Yes, it was a time of trial and error, but Las Vegas was still innocent enough to get away with a few mistakes. Legalized gambling in Atlantic City was three years down the road, and the only thing we knew about that town was that some bathing beauty contest was held there every year.

Meanwhile, casinos in downtown Las Vegas were hoping to draw big crowds with a new slot machine called Big Bertha. The size of a Sherman tank, this giant contraption never really caught the public's fancy. It was big and it was bold—but, the problem was that no one ever won anything while playing it. To quote an old proverb, it gave no quarter.

It also required a lot of upkeep. One of the first Big Bertha machines, for example, kept "eating" coins. The mechanic, a tall husky woman named Jo, told the slot manager not to worry. "I'll get inside," she said. "You put the money in, and I'll find out what's wrong."

As the slot manager pushed quarter after quarter into the

Slot machines are the casino's largest producer of revenue. Once considered an amusement for wives while their husbands played at the tables, slot machines are now just as much a man's game as craps and blackjack.

machine, he noticed that he was attracting quite a crowd. Suddenly, a muffled voice was heard. "Okay, that's enough!"

With that, the back door of the machine swung open and out stepped the disheveled mechanic. "Who's that?" cried one of the onlookers.

The slot manager never blinked. "That's just our pay-out unit going on a break. She'll be back in 30 minutes."

The crowd studied the woman in awe, then moved on to ex-

Downtown operator Herb Pastor takes a walking tour of his Coin Castle in this 1981 photograph. Pastor also owns Sassy Sally's and Girls of Glitter Gulch, formerly the Golden Goose.

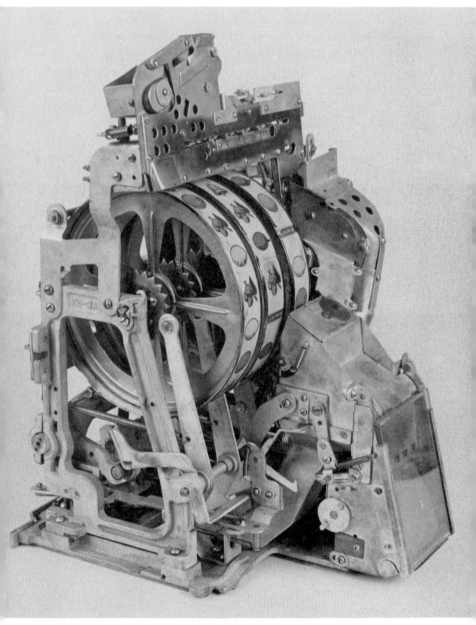

The old mechanical slot machines were an awesome combination of levers, springs, gears, cams and ratchets. This mechanism, from a Jennings DELUXE CLUB CHIEF, is a model that many Strip hotels offered their guests.

amine all the other slot machines. They appeared to be gingerly examining each one, looking for some sign of life inside.

A slot mechanic tells the next story. Narrated in his own words, it is a tale wrought with all the elements of a best seller. It even has a happy ending.

"I was up north in Reno," he began, leaning up against a dead slot machine and looking off into space. "We had some four-reelers on the floor at the Horseshoe Club that paid up to five thousand coins. Well, the owner didn't like it when some-

body hit one of them things. He liked to drink champagne and pass buttermilk, if you know what I mean.

"Then one day, sure as hell, this lady hit the dime machine for five hundred dollars. Procedure was we had to check everything out and if it was a good jackpot, we'd call the owner. So I give him a holler and he says, 'Aww, hell, these things aren't supposed to happen.' I said, 'Yes, sir.' He said, 'Well, check it out again.'

"So I did. I went over that dad-blamed thing with a fine tooth comb, then nodded again to the owner. He give me a look that would drop a mule, but he had the change girl pay the lady, and last I saw of that machine it was being hauled down to the basement for an auto-topsy.

"Well, I got to talking to this lady, and come to find out she was a schoolteacher from up San Francisco who had never won anything in her whole life. She said she was thinking about staying in town for a while, so I wind up buying her a drink on the house figuring maybe I'll get myself a nice tip out of it—only she don't know no better.

"Next night I come in to work, and there she is back at the slots pumping them handles for all she was worth. This went on for quite a spell, I'm talking December right on up through the following February. And I noticed something strange happening to this woman. It was like she was disintegrating right before my very eyes. She could barely walk upright, her hair looked like it come out second-best in a Georgia taffy pull, and her breath could've stopped a cross-country Greyhound.

"Well, it weren't my place to say nothing, although I did feel partly to blame for buying her that drink in the first place. I'd see her stagger in and I just had to duck my face.

"Then the last time I saw her she come walking in dressed to the nines, and she had a gentleman on her arm. She'd met

(Left) These specially-built "Double Dollar" machines, shown in this 1959 photograph at the Horseshoe Club, offered a whopping $10,000 jackpot. Two Mills "High Top" mechanical slots were bolted together, and the handle operated both machines when two silver dollars were played. Gimmick machines such as this one were commonly built in the casino's own slot shop during this era.

(Left) Did you ever wonder what the first automatic-pay slot machine looked like? Here it is . . . the LIBERTY BELL, built by Charles Fey in 1898. Serious slot machine players should cut out this picture and carry it with them at all times. Only four of these rare slot machines exist today, and each is estimated to be worth up to $100,000! Many people enjoy collecting old slot machines, which can be purchased for as little as $600.

him there at the club, and went and got herself married. She told me she was going to stay in Reno the rest of her life, and the only place she'd do her drinking and gambling from then on was at the Horseshoe Club."

Without another word, the slot mechanic stubbed out his smoke and went back to work. Another casino success story had gone into the archives, this one under the heading of true love.

No Smoking

IT TOOK THE INDIANS 500 years to do it, but they finally got even. They introduced Columbus and his men to tobacco, and eventually cigarettes became one of the most peculiar phenomena in American history.

Actually, inhaling the smoke of dried plant material started in Central America more than 2,000 years ago. After the sun went down, there wasn't much to do except propagate the species. Afterwards, it was either eat vegetable matter or smoke it.

The Mayans smoked tobacco in pipes, and then came loosely-wrapped cigars. By the way, if you've ever wondered why cigars come with a band around them, it's because women smoked cigars centuries ago. The bands kept their dainty fingers from touching the tobacco leaves, and the custom of cigar bands persists to this day.

In the late 1800s, an American industrialist named James Duke invented the first cigarette-rolling machine. This resulted in the formation of the American Tobacco Company, which became so powerful that the Supreme Court, in a smoke-filled room, ordered it to be disbanded. By this time, cigarette smoking was a national craze, and Trinity College in North Carolina changed its name to Duke University out of appreciation.

The entertainment world, however, was the catalyst that sparked the craze to dizzying heights. Humphrey Bogart smoked cigarettes even when he was kissing some dame, and other actors who didn't even smoke in real life smoked on the screen because it was the thing to do. Even a young Ronald Reagan smoked in the movies, although everyone knew he was just puffing and not really smoking. When a real actor smoked a real cigarette, he did it with a sense of wisdom and disdain and the smoke came out his nose. Actresses smoked, too, and that made it acceptable for every other woman in the country to light up.

Songs on the jukebox endorsed cigarette smoking in hits like *Smoke Rings* and *Smoke Gets In Your Eyes*. Lyricists had a field day with such immortal lines as "a cigarette that bears the lipstick traces," "smoking cigarettes and watching Captain Kangaroo," and that all-time favorite: "Tell Saint Peter at the golden gate that you hate to make him wait . . . but you just gotta have another cigarette."

There were cigarette ads on the radio and in magazines and on billboards all across America. Who can ever forget Johnny the bellhop and his "Call for Philip Mor-rr-rr-is." That was one commercial I never understood. When I was a kid, everyone said that smoking stunted your growth, yet here was this four-foot dwarf in a little red hat expounding the virtues of Philip Morris cigarettes. Maybe it was because Philip Morris came in king-size, so things kind of balanced out.

Lucky Strikes were toasted, and doctors walked a mile for a Camel. Throat dry? Smoke Kools. In brightly-colored 18¢ packages, each brand was your passport to a netherworld of glamour and intrigue: Chesterfield, Old Gold, Wings, Raleigh, Pall Mall, Viceroy. Even President Roosevelt smoked cigarettes, although back in the thirties there was something almost sissyish about puffing on a smoke through a five-inch cigarette holder. Roosevelt could get away with it, though, because he was the president. On the other hand, if Bogart had done it, it would have ruined his career. "Of all the gin joints in all the— uh, have you seen my cigarette holder, sweetheart? It was right here next to my gun."

World War II sent American GIs into Europe, where they routed the Germans and showered the populace with Hershey bars and cigarettes. Those who didn't get hooked on chocolate got hooked on nicotine, and cigarette smoking became an international fad.

Then television came into our living rooms, and so did Edward R. Murrow. Murrow, who gained fame by covering the war and uncovering McCarthy, was constantly veiled in a cloud of cigarette smoke and to this day no one is exactly sure what he looked like.

Automobiles didn't have air conditioning yet, or power steering, or power brakes. But they did have push-in cigarette lighters. Most people spent their vacations driving to California or the beach or the Grand Canyon. And what souvenir did they always bring home with them? Why, a personalized ash tray, of course.

In Las Vegas, there was a box of free cigarettes on every blackjack table. Everybody smoked while they gambled. It was just like the movies. It was the thing to do.

Slowly, however, the price of a package of cigarettes was going up. Fifty cents a pack, a dollar a pack, a dollar-fifty a pack. Even the casinos were starting to fret, and so the boxes of free smokes started to disappear.

The time finally came when cigarettes were kept in a locked drawer inside each gaming pit. Policy was that if a player wanted a pack of smokes he told the dealer, who told the boxman, who told the pit boss. The pit boss would then unlock the drawer and get the cigarettes. It was easier to get a $5,000 marker!

It was about this time that the Surgeon General's office came out with the bad news that smoking was unhealthy, and cigarette packages began to carry such dire messages as: "Smoking causes lung cancer, heart disease, emphysema and may complicate pregnancies." The only thing they didn't say was, "Hey, these things'll kill you."

The tobacco industry retaliated by coming out with more cigarettes, only now the names were more wondrous than ever: Misty, Lark, True, Now, Alpine, Heritage, Belair, Salem, Merit, More. And they all had filters, so put that in your pipe and smoke it!

More bad news from the Surgeon General. If smoking didn't get you, then secondhand smoke would. Restaurants began segregating smokers and non-smokers. Those who didn't smoke sat near the window. Those who did smoke sat near the kitchen.

Airliners banned smoking on all flights, and nicotine addicts were thrown in jail if they were caught sneaking a cigarette in the plane's restroom. All this time you thought those metal detectors in the airports were scanning passengers for weapons? No, they were looking for cigarette lighters!

Breathing secondhand smoke was a violation of a person's constitutional rights, or so said the Supreme Court. Of course, that started the lawsuits, the most asinine of which concerned a Nevada prisoner who sued the state because he was forced to share a cell with a five-pack-a-day smoker—and thus was be-

---

Smoking, drinking and gambling; there's nothing like it. But at the Silver City Casino on the Las Vegas Strip, the smoking lamp went out several years ago. The big question, however, is what happens if a player betting big bucks wants to smoke? It's a choking question.

ing subjected to cruel and unusual punishment. Oh, by the way, he was in prison for beating a car salesman to death with a rock.

Too bad the car salesman couldn't sue.

Meanwhile, back in Las Vegas, things were getting serious. What would happen if casino employees got together and filed a mass lawsuit on the same grounds? Better safe than sorry, so each casino instituted non-smoking areas, and one even went so far as to outlaw smoking altogether. This gladdened the hearts of many, but sent chain-smoking gamblers off to browner pastures. In fact, my mother-in-law won't even patronize the Tropicana any longer—simply because her pet deuces-wild slot machines are now off-limits for smokers.

That brings up an interesting question. What if a highrolling gambler with a cigarette parked himself at a no-smoking black-jack table and wanted to bet a thousand dollars on the next flip of the cards? We posed this question to four Las Vegas pit bosses, and these are the answers we got:

"We would make it a smoking table."

"He could play. After all, we're in the gambling business."

"I'd let him play."

"Sure he could play. This is a casino, not somebody's living room."

See what happens when a person's constitutional rights bang heads with a company's profit-and-loss statement? Poet Graham Hemminger put it this way almost a hundred years ago:

"Tobacco is a dirty weed. I like it.

"It satisfies no normal need. I like it.

"It makes you thin, it makes you lean,

"It takes the hair right off your bean.

"It's the worst damn stuff I've ever seen.

"I like it."

Celebrity Tales

Even with the spread of legalized gaming, Las Vegas is still synonymous with glitz, glory, glamour—and celebrities. When I first moved to Las Vegas, I spotted celebrities everywhere, but there was a secret to finding them. You made the rounds early in the morning, around two or three o'clock. That was when all the big stars finished their performances. Then they would head for the lounges, and a chance to unwind while somebody else did all the work. Back then, all the major casinos had lounges, and I never understood why most of them were phased out. Corporate logic, I suppose, since a keno parlor generates more income than a cocktail lounge. It's a shame, though, because the lounge shows helped make Las Vegas what it is today.

There was the Blue Room at the Tropicana, where Si Zentner's orchestra backed up singers like Julie London and Helen O'Connell. There was Nero's Nook at Caesars Palace, where the Checkmates played to capacity crowds. At the Frontier, there was the Gay Nineties Bar, and such entertainers as the Mary Kaye Trio, Jack E. Leonard and an earthy comedienne named Belle Barth.

In the beginning, hotel lounges were little more than adjuncts to the casinos—geared to keep the gamblers from wandering too far from the tables and slot machines. The lounges gave the hotels star-power. It was great to have Johnny Carson in the showroom at the Sahara, but even better if there was Shecky Greene or Don Rickles in the Casbar Theater.

The Sands brought it all together better than anybody. With Frank Sinatra in the Copa Room, there was always a cluster of celebrities in the audience: Marilyn Monroe, Humphrey Bogart, Judy Garland, Jack Benny. Add to that the famous

Winner's Circle Lounge and entertainers like Louis Prima,
Keely Smith, Sam Butera and the Witnesses and—well, you
had something magical.

Actually, Prima and his gang started out at the Sahara. "December 26th, 1954," Sam Butera will say without a moment's
hesitation. "Everything was happening then. Everybody was
staying out late. And all of the stars from all of the different
hotels would come in and catch our shows at the Sahara. Everybody—Sinatra, Dean Martin, Howard Hughes, Marlene
Dietrich, Martha Raye, Ray Bolger, Danny Thomas, Sammy
Davis. Every night the joint was jammed."

Sinatra! The name alone conjures up an image of what Las
Vegas was all about. Visualize a smoky showroom with drums
rolling and hot little spotlights probing the stage. Suddenly:
"Ladies and gentlemen, Frank Sinatra." The curtains parted,
and out stepped a thin man with hard eyes and a crooked
smile. Applause crackled through the air like bursts of electricity, and you got a little shiver inside, because for a moment in
time you were breathing the same air as Frank Sinatra, and because ever since you were a teenager desperately looking for a
girlfriend there was the music of Frank Sinatra. Now here he
was, right in front of you, in the flesh!

Las Vegas columnist Ralph Pearl wrote that the most profitable three weeks in the history of the Sands Hotel came in
January of 1960 when Sinatra opened his "Summit Meeting at
the Sands" with Dean Martin, Joey Bishop, Sammy Davis Jr.
and Peter Lawford. Twice nightly during that three-weeker almost every big star in show business made a visit to the Sands,
and eventually wound up on stage at the mercy of Sinatra and
his clan. From Pearl's book, *Las Vegas Is My Beat*, here's what it
was like:

Suddenly Frank Sinatra dashed over to slightly bewildered
Sammy Davis Jr. He picked him up bodily as though he were a
bundle of laundry, then rushed to the mike. "Ladies and gentlemen," Frank said as he held up Sammy, "I want to thank all of
you for giving me this valuable NAACP trophy." Then Sinatra,
still carrying Davis in his arms, walked over to a prominent-looking gent at ringside and dropped his trophy in the man's

lap. The prominent gent? None other than Senator John F. Kennedy of Massachusetts, already being groomed for the White House. Davis looked up into Kennedy's face and meekly said, "It's perfectly all right with me, Senator, as long as I'm not being donated to George Wallace."

More howling as Joey Bishop and Peter Lawford retrieved Davis from Senator Kennedy, then disappeared out the door. Moments later they came back onstage without Sammy. Noticing their sad expressions, Frank and Dean asked, "What happened to the trophy?"

Joey Bishop: "We played it on the hard eight, and lost."

That was the magic of Las Vegas at the moment-in-time when Sinatra was its greatest ambassador. So much has been written about the man that it is difficult to separate fact from fiction, but you are about to read a genuine Frank Sinatra story never told before. So treat it for what it is—a rare personal look at this century's most famous singer.

In the old days there was an unwritten law that nobody bothered celebrities inside the casinos. So when Frank Sinatra and nightclub comedian Sonny King strolled into the Cal-Neva coffee shop, nobody gave them a second glance. They sat down at the counter, and when the waiter appeared they both ordered the same thing: ham sandwiches on whole wheat bread—the ham cut paper thin, with mayo, lettuce and tomato on the side.

The waiter disappeared into the kitchen and moments later set two sandwiches in front of the entertainers. Sinatra took one look at the wedge of ham on his plate and politely said to the waiter, "Would you take this back, and have the chef cut the ham paper thin?"

The waiter returned shortly with Sinatra's sandwich. And yes, the ham was still too thick. "Paper thin," the singer repeated.

Another trip to the kitchen, but the ham was still not thin enough. "Tell the chef to come out here," Sinatra roared.

"Yes, sir."

The waiter headed into the kitchen for the fourth time, and in a few moments he was back—alone. "Where's the chef?"

Sinatra asked him.

"He said to tell you to go screw yourself," the waiter answered. That did it. Sinatra and Sonny King headed for the
hotel's time office. There they waited for the chef to get off
work and punch out—after which a certain singer was going
to punch him out.

In the meantime, two dealers walked by. One said to the
other, "That looks like Frank Sinatra."

"Are you crazy?" his friend replied. "What would Frank
Sinatra be doing here?"

Two cocktail waitresses approached. One nudged the other.
"If I didn't know better, I'd swear that was Frank Sinatra."

"You need a vacation," her companion laughed. "But the
little guy's kinda cute."

Finally the waiter who served the ham sandwiches walked
by. "If you're looking for the chef, forget it," he hollered to
Sinatra. "He sneaked out the front door about an hour and a
half ago!"

The Light Of The Luxor

NOT SINCE KING TUT'S tomb was uncovered were the circumstances as mysterious: a strange telephone call in the dead of night, a clandestine meeting in the desert with strangers in attendance, and veiled references to a sinister enterprise called "Project X."

Then after everyone was seated, a set of curtains suddenly parted. There, and for their eyes alone, was an artist's rendition of a giant pyramid with a dazzling shaft of light emanating from the top.

"That's when I smiled," remembered Zachary Taylor, president of G-Force International Entertainment Corporation of Beverly Hills. "I didn't know any of the other people, or why they were there, but I knew why I was there." Taylor, and G-Force, were to design and install the brightest light on earth at the top of the Luxor pyramid on the Las Vegas Strip.

Luxor architect Veldon Simpson called the meeting on December 2, 1992, and now the Luxor's "Beam of Light" is pointing the way to Las Vegas' flashiest new theme resort. In fact, thanks to G-Force and production designer Tyk Phillips, the Luxor can rightfully brag that it is the world's most visible building. With the installation of 45 high-tech xenon lights, the resulting effect is one mighty shaft of light rising into the night sky. "It is quite literally the brightest light ever created by man," Taylor explained. "One will be able to see it from ground level, very clearly, over 15 miles away."

According to a Luxor press release, the light beam—on a clear night—is also visible at cruising altitude from Los Angeles, some 250 miles away. And if that's not impressive, you can read a newspaper by its light ten miles into space!

There was little doubt in anyone's mind that G-Force was

The Luxor Hotel is perhaps the most radical of all the new theme resorts on the Las Vegas Strip. The light on top is said to be the brightest ever created by man, with an output of 36 billion candle power.

the right company to top off the Luxor. In addition to introducing architecturally-sculptured lighting systems to Las Vegas, G-Force has provided high-intensity lighting and special effects for events at Disneyland, Hollywood and Palm Springs; the Olympics and Pan American games; and concerts by Barry Manilow, Neil Diamond, the Who Tours, Motley Crue and Moody Blues.

Taylor praised the Circus Circus corporation for showing the foresight to take on the Luxor project, but admitted there were a lot of challenges along the way. "We had a very unique situation here," he said. "We had to set a platform grid on top of a pyramid. Then there were a lot of considerations about the glass. Finally, the people at Circus Circus agreed that we should have clear glass at the top to allow the beam (of light) to come through unencumbered."

The result is "an absolutely pure white beam of light" that generates 40 times the candle power of a strong searchlight, or an equivalent peak output of 36 billion candles. This is comparable to every man, woman and child in the United States holding 150 candles skyward—or each person on Earth holding up seven candles.

How does the system work? The globe of each 7,000 watt bulb is vacuum-sealed and charged with xenon gas. Inside each bulb are two large tungsten diodes. By means of a strobe ignition system, direct current is sent from one tungsten pole to the other, forming an electrical arc. The direct current excites the xenon gas, turning it into a plasma-like state, and that becomes the light source. This is reflected into a parabolic reflector and directed upward into individual beams, which are then aligned to constitute one gigantic ray of light.

According to Taylor, the whole system was conceived "along the lines of your grandfather's Model T. You crank it, and slowly it coughs up into full operation." It's the same with the super light at Luxor. The strobing, which is programmed by computer modules, lasts for about 30 seconds, then fades away as the light beam rises into the heavens.

And so the unlikely merger of the pyramids (2686-2181 B.C.) and the incandescent light bulb (1879) has resulted in one of the most spectacular light shows in the history of Las Vegas. "It is another first for Las Vegas," Taylor said, "but I suspect it won't be the last."

Vendetta

HE GAVE HER a cocky grin as he struggled out of his beach robe. Then he turned and ran toward the pounding surf. She sat on the warm sand, watching him splash out of sight, and then the smile on her face slowly faded.

She was born in Italy, but her memories were American. Growing up in a crowded smelly ghetto near downtown Chicago, she could remember burying her head underneath the pillow every time a train rumbled past. Oh, why did they leave the lush vineyards and cobbled streets of home for this?

The complicated English language was bad enough, especially since her parents and two brothers spoke nothing but Italian. Every time she tried out her English, all she got for her efforts was a thump on the head and a cold stare.

"But papa," she would exclaim, the tears welling hotly in her eyes. "We are in America now."

"America, yes. Americans, no. We are the blood of our ancestors, and you don't forget it."

Her brothers were no help. They slept until noon, then vanished into the swarming streets with their young Sicilian friends. She was at the kitchen table early each morning, poring over her homework, then quickly she would set the books aside when her father strode through the room on his way to work. Even her mother's patient encouragement did little to ease the guilt, and the pain.

He surfaced twenty yards from shore and waved to her clumsily as he tried to stay afloat. The sea sparkled under a brilliant Hawaiian sun, while lazy humps of land gave off the appearance of some prehistoric monster snoozing at the water's edge. He pulled the mask over his face, biting down tightly on the snorkel's rubber mouthpiece, then ducked his head beneath the water.

Chicago's a nice town if you like ball games and good-looking women and the best politicians money can buy. But when you're fresh out of school, and trying to break into journalism, you've got to start in the sticks. Either that, or be a messenger boy for the rest of your life.

So he crammed everything he owned inside the trunk of his old Plymouth, and started looking for a small-town newspaper that might be looking for him. He found one in Las Vegas.

It was a tourist rag that came out once a week, full of topless ads and two-for-one coupons. The pay was lousy, the working conditions worse, but he was a newspaper reporter, by God, and someday things would get better.

She glanced at her watch. Five minutes had passed since he waded into the surf, and she could still see the tip of his snorkel as he swam aimlessly offshore. A sudden breeze made her shiver, but the cold she felt seemed to be coming from deep inside her own heart.

Her oldest brother was shot to death in a Cicero spaghetti house. A Chicago police sergeant called it a gangland slaying, and among those brought in for questioning was her own father. His picture was in the newspaper, a heavy overcoat shielding his face. "Alleged Crime Boss Questioned By Authorities," the caption read, and in the months to come there were stories of other murders, and more photographs of her father.

She tried to talk to him, but he just cupped her face in his knotted hands and shushed her into resentful silence. Soon after that, the killings stopped. Still, things would never be the same—not for her, not for her family, not for the goons who patrolled the family estate day and night, chattering in Italian and flipping their cigarette butts in her lovely rose garden.

She avoided reading the newspapers because some smart-aleck reporter in Las Vegas had begun his own "investigation" into organized crime, and his stories were being picked up by the Chicago dailies. Suddenly her father was back in the news, and it made her angry.

"We must stop this," she complained to her brother.

He nodded, and handed her a small envelope. A plan was formulated, and three days later she left for Las Vegas.

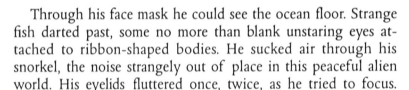

Through his face mask he could see the ocean floor. Strange fish darted past, some no more than blank unstaring eyes attached to ribbon-shaped bodies. He sucked air through his snorkel, the noise strangely out of place in this peaceful alien world. His eyelids fluttered once, twice, as he tried to focus. Everything was so . . . peaceful.

He had only been in Las Vegas three months when he got a letter from the number one newspaper in town, and when he read the contents he let out a holler that brought neighbors to their doorsteps. Thirty-six thousand bucks a year for three columns a week, and his own by-line!

It was life in the fast lane, but he loved it. Greasy sandwiches on the run, strange telephone calls in the middle of the night, rigid deadlines almost impossible to meet. Then a local television station offered him the anchor spot on its evening newscast. It increased his work load even more but gave him enough money to move into a nice townhouse and start socking away some serious change. With grim satisfaction, he noticed that his life was finally starting to click into place.

That was when he got the idea for a series of articles on organized crime. It was no secret that certain Midwest mobsters were represented in Las Vegas by some unsavory characters. Hell, he'd had a run-in with one of the them at the courthouse, and that same night his car was torched.

He wasn't worried, though. Nobody would try anything so foolish as bumping off a reporter, no matter what he wrote. It was like killing a cop.

He was getting sleepy. His arms and legs kept him afloat with almost no conscious effort, yet he seemed to be drifting further and further away from shore. The water was warm and soothing, almost holding him in a lover's embrace. Forcing himself to concentrate, he began to paddle slowly at first, then faster and faster.

She met him a week after arriving in Las Vegas. There was a small bar near the newspaper office which he was known to frequent, and she sat there for four hot afternoons sipping iced tea before she saw him for the first time. He was with several other people, but she kept staring in his direction until he finally smiled back, and then he walked over and introduced himself.

When she told him she was from Chicago, he grinned broadly and asked her out for dinner. Two weeks whirled past, and then they were winging over the gentle Pacific, on their way to the Hawaiian islands. He needed a vacation, he told her, because he was working on the biggest story of his life, and when he got back to Las Vegas things were going to get hectic.

His eyes burning with excitement, he recounted all of it: illegal labor payoffs, embezzlement, extortion, murder. A web of crime and corruption that stretched all the way to Las Vegas, where boxes of money were skimmed off the gaming tables and hand delivered to a mafia overlord in Chicago.

And who was this don mafioso, she asked, knowing his reply before he answered. It was her father, of course, a gentle and misguided man whose greatest crime was living in a country he never truly understood.

There was no use trying to reason with this brash young man. She knew him well enough by now to understand that he was as bull-headed and set in his ways as her own father was. They were two peas in the pod, these men in her life, and what friends they could have been if only life were simpler.

The sun climbed high above them as they made their way to the beach. He pointed with boyish awe at wind-bent palm trees and snowy stretches of sand, while she followed silently behind. Her mind kept go-

*ing back to that last conversation with her brother, and the small enve-
lope still inside her purse.*

*A fast-acting poison, he had explained carefully, which would para-
lyze the nervous system in approximately ten minutes. A person just went
to sleep and never woke up, and a pathologist would probably chalk it
off as a fatal heart attack. In any case, that was what her brother had
told her, and she supposed he knew about such things.*

*She spread a blanket on the sand, then slowly screwed the top off the
thermos. Pouring coffee into two plastic cups, she waited until he turned
to look out at the sea. Then, her heart thudding dully in her chest, she
emptied the contents of the envelope into one of the cups.*

*"You better drink this before you go in the water," she said, looking up
at him. "You didn't have any breakfast this morning."*

*He took the cup from her, making a face as he drank. "This makes
the coffee at the newspaper office taste like tap water," he grimaced. "But
I love it."*

*She returned a thin smile as she sipped her own coffee, idle thoughts
tumbling through her head. It was probably snowing in Chicago. She
forgot to pack her favorite dress. Her birthday was less than a month
away. She would never see her father again.*

*He gave her a cocky grin as he struggled out of his beach robe. Then
he turned and ran toward the pounding surf. She sat on the warm sand,
watching him splash out of sight, and then the smile on her face slowly
faded.*

It took him fifteen minutes to reach shore. Suddenly his feet
touched the sloping bottom, and if he had the strength he
would have shouted with joy. Instead, he waded out of the water and fell to his knees, gasping for breath.

Then he saw her. She was lying on the blanket, one arm
flung crazily across her face. Running to her side, he saw that
her skin had turned a pasty white and her eyes were staring
blankly into the sun.

"Get a doctor," he cried, and a brown-skinned youth began
sprinting down the beach. He knelt beside her, and gently
closed her eyes. As he waited for the doctor, he noticed the
two coffee cups—his discarded where he left it, hers half-full

and resting by the picnic basket.

Maybe the coffee would steel his nerves, or at least give him the strength to finish this terrible day. He brought her cup to his lips and drank the rest.

Career Move

HEY, BOB, why the long face? Well, that's a shame, but the same thing happened to me about a month ago. "Reduction in staff," they said, and after I'd been working there almost two years. That's the trouble with those big corporations. All they care about is making money.

Why, you take old man Peterson. He went to work at the canning plant right out of high school, put in close to 35 years, and he's still up there knocking out those sheets of aluminum. Then Bill Sawyer's boy takes two years of CPA school, and he's already vice-president—strutting around in that gabardine suit, and carrying that skinny briefcase. It makes me sick just thinking about it.

You know what we ought to do? We ought to hop in old Betsy here and take off for Las Vegas. My friend Lamar over at the filling station says we can get jobs out there as waiters and make a fortune, maybe even retire in three or four years time. Shoot, we probably wouldn't even have to get an apartment. Lamar says that everybody lives right in the casinos, even the people who work there. Yeah, I know Lamar's never been to Vegas, but his sister honeymooned out there and she ought to know.

Course, I don't know if I could hack being a waiter or not. You got to carry around those big heavy trays, and set food on fire and everything. Then you have to get a health card, and I can't stand it when they start taking blood out of your arm. Remember when we got vaccinated in grade school? They had to have two nurses—one to give me the shot, and one to catch me before I hit the floor.

Naw, that being a waiter don't sound like the way to go. I think I'd rather start out as a martyr d', or whatever they're called. Every fancy hotel in Vegas has one. Well, it's sort of like being a waiter, only you get to wear a starchy shirt and a red bow tie. You just stand there at the door and tell people where to sit, and they're likely to give you anything from a buck right on up to a ten-spot. Course, you got to listen to Wayne Newton for four hours every night, so you'd probably spend all your money on doctor bills.

Naw, I don't think I want to be one of those guys. It'd be nice, though, rubbing elbows with all those movie stars. The only one I ever seen up close was Johnny Crawford that time at the livestock show. You never heard of Johnny Crawford? Well, you must've used your TV for a hat rack, Bob. He's the one that played what's his name's kid on *The Rifleman*.

What's that? Naw, I never thought about being a Las Vegas dealer, but I always had real good luck playing card games. Well, when's the last time you ever beat me at Crazy Eights? Never, that's when. Sides, you can learn all those games right out of a book—blackjack, roulette, backerat. And craps is easy enough. They either make their point or they don't, and then you just give 'em what they got coming. Shoot, we could do that job in our sleep.

Course, you got all those big shots watching you, and that's enough to scare me. I can't even stand having somebody behind me in the cafeteria line, much less shuffle a bunch of cards with some joker breathing down my ear. And if you make a mistake, there's no telling what they're liable to do. Remember that picture show we saw last summer at the drive in? Boy, Bob, you got a memory like a gnat. I can't recall the name of it exactly myself, but it was all about this Vegas card dealer. And at the end of the movie he was running for his life—just because some guy won a bunch of money playing blackjack.

Naw, I don't think I want to deal cards for a living. We'd probably be better off just being bartenders. All those casinos out in Vegas need bartenders, and there ain't nothing to making mixed drinks. I mean, how hard is it to whip up a bourbon and coke? Besides, they've got all those gorgeous cocktail waitresses, with names like Stormy and Starr and stuff. Why, I bet we wouldn't be in Vegas more than two or three weeks and we'd both be going out with some real foxes. And there's all kinds of neat places to go sight-seeing out there, like Death Valley.

You heard what? Well, that must've been some kind of typical graphic error. I don't think there's no place in the country that gets that hot. Well, hand me that newspaper there on the kitchen table, and I'll look it up for you on the weather map. It ought to be back here somewhere with the want ads.

Hey, look at this!

"A-One Truck Driver Training. Be your own boss in eight short weeks. Make $30,000 plus a year. Call Hank at 1-800-493-2574."

What do you think, Bob? Why, we could pick up a bunch of computers out in California, take 'em to the East Coast, drive down to Florida and load up with citrus fruit, then on our way back we could go over to Huntsville and look up Marcia Davis, and then we could . . .

Swan Song

I **TURNED ONTO** the Las Vegas Strip just as one of those old songs came on the radio. You know the kind. One chord, one voice, one certain phrase, and suddenly your whole life shifts into reverse.

"So bye bye, Miss American Pie . . . drove my Chevy to the levee but the levee was dry . . ."

In an instant 20 years peeled away. The mournful refrain of that song was all it took to bring back blotchy sketches of Nixon and flower power, of Viet Nam and an unlikely place called Fresno. I had gone there to see an old friend, who surprised me by arranging a ski trip to Devil's Peak. Four of us piled our gear into a stuffy sedan and started up the mountain, all the while serenaded by Don McLean with his strawberry ice cream voice.

"And them good old boys were drinking whiskey and rye, singing 'This'll be the day that I die . . . this'll be the day that I die.'"

One of the guys, wearing a bright orange ski jacket, took the lift to the top of the expert hill. With reluctant admiration, the rest of us stood in the snow and watched as he disappeared from sight. Hours crept by with no further sign of him, so finally we notified the ski patrol. Just before twilight they emerged through the mist, towing a long narrow basket behind them. Strapped to the basket was someone in a bright orange ski jacket, who naturally turned out to be our hapless companion.

This ruined our whole trip. Instead of exploring the taverns and bunny havens up on the mountain (which had been our game plan from day one), we spent the rest of the weekend helping our friend master the art of hobbling on crutches.

(Left) Louis Prima sings his heart out at the Sahara lounge in March of 1956. That's Keely Smith in the background. This was the era when there was big-name entertainment at all major Las Vegas resorts. Today major performers demand big bucks, and most casino lounges have been replaced by keno parlors.

Then we drove back to Fresno in somber silence, our mood akin to that of a crew in a crippled B-29 returning from an aborted bombing mission.

It was certainly not a heartwarming experience, so why did I love the song so much? Was it because it paid tribute to a rock star who died at the peak of fame, or was it simply because the song came warbling out of the deep past—when life somehow seemed simpler and less complicated?

In the early seventies, there was no such thing as heavy metal or rap music or records with subliminal messages on them. The most controversial song I can remember from those days was *Mellow Yellow*, which was about getting high on dried banana peelings. Crack and smack didn't mean what they do now, either. A crack was something you said about somebody, and a smack was what you got when you said it.

Maybe the reason I liked *American Pie* was that it touched on all the things I remembered when I was in school. Sock hops, and James Dean movies, and real pickup trucks that didn't have personalized plates and enormous tires and fancy roll bars. If you had an accident in a 1955 pickup, the only thing you hurt was your pride.

Now here I was, cruising through Las Vegas, and wondering how everything could change so much in a few short years. Even the Strip wasn't the same anymore. Marquees that once proclaimed "Elvis" and "Liberace" and "Sammy Davis" in brilliant twinkling lights now ballyhooed names and shows out of Tin Can Alley. At the Sands, for instance, there was somebody in the showroom tonight called Melinda. She wasn't in the audience; she was the star! Quite a difference from opening night in 1952 when the headliners were Danny Thomas, Jane Powell, the Copa Girls and Billy Eckstine.

Edgar Bergen and Charlie McCarthy opened the Desert Inn

in 1950, along with Vivian Blaine, Pat Patrick, the Donn Arden Dancers and Ray Noble's Orchestra. Tonight's stars were the Gatlin Brothers and Steve Kelly—and judging from the number of horses tied up out front, the show was a big success.

When the Stardust opened in 1958, helicopters flew over the audience as the "Lido de Paris" began a 33-year run. Appearing there tonight was something gro-tesque called "Boy-Lesque," with Kenny Kerr dressed up like Joan Rivers. Scarier yet, he looked better than she did.

The granddaddy of Las Vegas resorts was the Flamingo, which opened far from town in 1946. Headlining in the show-room on opening night were Jimmy Durante, Eddie Jackson and Xavier Cugat. Tonight's program was "City Lites," a musi-cal variety show featuring four singers, eight dancers, one co-median and two whiskey sours for $17.95.

In fact, for the grand sum of $1,208.40, you and a guest could see every nightclub show in Las Vegas, including "High Voltage," "Legends In Concert," "Abracadabra," "Keep Smilin' America," "The Comedy Stop," "The Comedy Store," "Comedy Cabaret," "Bottoms Up," "Nudes On Ice," "Crazy Girls," "Sex Over 40," "Memories Of Elvis" and "Reflections Of Sinatra." This, of course, did not include gratuities, taxes or the assur-ance you would be able to see the performers without the use of highpowered binoculars or maybe even the Hubble space telescope.

So bye bye with a tear in my eye . . . to this gritty little city where the tourists would fly . . .

And them good old boys who built it up to the sky, singing "This'll be the same till I die . . . this'll be the same till I die."

Well, would you believe what happened here?
  New owners turned a deafened ear.

Soon all the stars would disappear,
  Not to mention lounge shows everywhere.

Goodbye to Satch and Prima's clan,
  The Duke, the King and Herman's band,

Who packed them in, oh, it was grand.
I wish I still heard music in the air!

Yes, bye bye, with a tear in my eye . . . to this pretty little city where the rules don't apply . . .
And them good old boys who have started to cry, singing

"This'll be the day that I die . . .
This'll be the day that I die."

Me

I BECAME INTERESTED in writing when I was young. If Franklin Dixon could bring the Hardy boys to life in my imagination, then I wanted to do the same thing. My first tentative step in that direction was when a group of us kids put together our own newspaper. We called it *The Echo*. We wrote stories about other kids, then sold the papers for a nickel apiece—mostly to the kids we wrote the stories about. A couple of years later, I landed a job with the local newspaper, reporting the results of the junior high school football games. It paid five dollars a week and my own by-line.

At the age of 16, my best friend Bobby Young went with me to the local radio station. We had an idea for a weekly show called *Teen News*. The announcer put us on the air that same afternoon, and the program ran for two years.

After graduation from high school, I enrolled at the University of Houston, where I majored in radio and television. The college had its own radio station, so I got plenty of broadcasting experience and learned such important things as pronunciation. (The German composer's name is Richard VOG-ner, not Dick Wagner.)

By now I was hopelessly hooked on radio. My first job at a real radio station paid $50 a week, plus free room, discounted meals, and a taxi to take me to and from work—all commercial trade-outs with the radio station. By 1964 I had crossed over into television, as news director of radio-television station KGBT in my hometown of Harlingen!

A year later, I won the Texas Associated Press Award for "Best Documentary Program." It was for the story of Dykes Simmons, a Texan sentenced to death in Mexico for allegedly killing three members of a prominent Mexican family. Lengthy interviews with Simmons were filmed in a Monterrey, Mexico prison in a story that I called "Life In A Death Cell." Simmons would later escape from the prison disguised as a woman, only to be killed in a barroom brawl in Fort Worth.

The sixties were tragic times, not only for Dykes Simmons, but for America as a nation. The war was escalating in Viet Nam, a dynamic young president was assassinated, new words like flower power and LSD reluctantly became part of our vocabulary. People with funny names and funny ideas suddenly had their pictures on television: Jack Ruby, Sirhan Sirhan, James Earl Ray. Reporting the news was no fun anymore. It was time for a change, a new beginning.

I came to Las Vegas. At first I settled into an old and comfortable routine, working as a disc jockey for a local radio station. But the action was in the casinos, where a thousand dollars could change hands on one roll of the dice and where movie stars walked by so close that you could reach out and touch them. Inside those marvelous casinos, everything stayed the same . . . except me. My life was changed forever.

First I went to one of the local dealer schools, where I learned to deal craps. There was no diploma when I finished, just a tip on who was hiring. My first dealing job was at the Mint in downtown Las Vegas. Thankfully I kept my part-time job as a disc jockey. Every time one of the casino bosses got upset with me, I dedicated a song to him on my radio show. It was enough to get me through some very hard times, and I have been in this peculiar business ever since.

I do not profess to be an expert on gambling. I can only tell you that most games of chance got their origins eons ago when there was little else to do. My advice to anyone who plans to gamble is to think of it as just another form of entertainment. Gambling should be nothing more than a diversion, a momentary escape from the turbulent times in which we live. Any time a person bets his own money to win more money, it is a bad gamble indeed.

My diversion is writing, and *Chip-Wrecked In Las Vegas* is my third book about this town. I am also the author of *Las Vegas Behind The Tables,* Parts 1 and 2, released by Gollehon Press,

Grand Rapids, Michigan. To publishers John Gollehon and Dan Mead I owe a special debt of gratitude. Among other things, they have given me the confidence to put my thoughts on paper, which has introduced me to an exciting new world— a world where I get paid for doing something I love. How lucky can a person be!

When I met John Gollehon, I was working at the Dunes Hotel in Las Vegas, back when it was one of the city's premiere gambling resorts. I was going through some hard times in my personal life, so the idea of spending a year researching and writing a book was just what I needed to get me going again.

It was during this period that an old pit boss stopped me in the hall one day. "What have you been up to?" he asked me.

"Well, for the last six months I've been working on a book," I told him.

"Oh, yeah?" he growled. "What are you reading?"

It was this type of mentality that made working in a casino so . . . interesting. Yet the truth was that many of the city's oldtimers were starting to die off, and if somebody didn't write about that era soon it would be too late. Fortunately, John gave me the chance, and among those who talked candidly with me before their deaths were casino owner Benny Binion, journalist Dick Maurice, TV personality Red McIlvane and newspaper publisher Hank Greenspun.

In August of 1986 my first book was released. I remember opening the box which contained my ten free copies, and the thrill of seeing my name in bold print across the cover. Several weeks later, the book appeared in bookstores and gift shops around Las Vegas, including the Dunes Hotel where I still worked.

I spent my breaks at the gift shop, watching shoppers circle the shelves and waiting for one to buy my book. Finally, the day came when a woman not only glanced at my book, but actually held one in her hand! I hurried to her side.

"If you buy that book," I smiled, "I'll be happy to autograph it for you."

"Beg your pardon?" the woman asked, backing away.

I introduced myself as the author of the book, and of course

Chip-wrecked author Barney Vinson sits at a Caesars Palace blackjack table with one big stack of chips and one small stack of chips. Unfortunately, he started with five big stacks of chips.

she was positive she had finally met the Boston Strangler, Machine Gun Kelly and Jack the Ripper all rolled into one.

"No, I wrote that book," I assured her. "Here, let me show you my driver's license."

Well, okay, I blew the sale. The lady left without the book, and there is probably still an all-points bulletin for me somewhere in the state of Nevada. I did learn something from this experience, however. Never introduce yourself to someone who is contemplating the purchase of a book you have written. First of all, they won't believe you. Secondly, they will want a free copy of it.

In my first book I wrote about a woman who won $1.8 million playing a slot machine. After the book was released, she came back to Las Vegas for a slot tournament, where she won an additional $55,000. That was when I met her. She proudly showed me her latest check, then said, "I understand you wrote about me in your book."

"Yes, I did."

"Well, where's my free copy?"

Here this woman had won almost two million dollars on a slot machine, and there was a check in her purse for another $55,000, yet she still wanted a free copy of my book. When I told her I didn't have any books, she walked away in a huff. Actually, I couldn't blame her, but the fact was that if somebody got a free copy of my book, somebody else had to pay for it—and that somebody was usually me. According to a stipulation in my contract, I had to pay half the retail price for any books I bought myself.

It was around this time that a going-away party was held for a friend of mine who was moving back east. My wife suggested I give him a copy of my book as a farewell gift. Since I didn't have any copies, it meant I had to buy one at full retail price. So on the way to the party we stopped at a grocery store, where my books were on display.

As I picked up one of the books, I was struck by a sudden thought. Why should I have to pay full-price for a copy of my own book? I glanced around the store, then quickly shoved the book under my shirt. After all, I wasn't actually stealing the book. In fact, the grocery store would get its commission because the book was gone; the distributor would get his commission; my publisher would get his commission; and I would get my royalty. It was one of those instances where everybody won, so how could I be doing anything wrong?

I made my way through the checkout line without any problems. Then I got into the car and slipped the book out of my shirt. My wife, of course, wanted me to march back inside and pay for the book, but I didn't. Still, it might have made a great story if I had been caught. "Author Steals Own Book," the headline could have read. There are few things more difficult than marketing an unknown writer, and any publicity is better than none at all.

At least, that is usually the case. On the other hand, there have been instances where I have found myself completely at the mercy of others—namely the news media. Magazine and newspaper reporters have misquoted me so many times that I don't even like to do interviews anymore. Russian roulette is more fun. An article in the *National Enquirer*, for example, almost cost me my job because of inept and inaccurate reporting. The *Enquirer* called me five times while writing the story; but when I asked for a retraction, I never heard from them again.

Interviews on television are even worse. I did a national TV news program once where the interviewer was in Georgia, and I was in Los Angeles. There was an earphone stuck in my ear, and I was told to look directly into the camera and not at the monitor—because there would be a five-second transmission delay. So . . . I was looking intently into the camera, listening to the question the interviewer was asking me, and my earphone slowly started edging its way out of my ear. All I heard was, ". . . Vegas . . . Siegel . . . gangster?" Thankfully, the station cut to a commercial, and some big guy walked up and poked the earphone back into my ear. Now why couldn't I have thought of that?

Book signings have always been an adventure. One took place in a Texas shopping mall on a Friday night, with my name in lights on the marquee outside. The hour for the book signing came and went, and nobody showed up. I mean, there was not one human being in the entire mall!

That was when I learned that Friday night meant only one thing in Texas: high school football.

As a result of my writing, I have made new friends—and new enemies. Among the latter are several casino managers for whom I have worked as a pit supervisor. Some casino bosses have very thin skins, stretched over miles of highly-strung and ultrasensitized nerve endings. Consequently, I have been black-balled, exiled, ostracized, demoted and given poor job evaluations, all as a result of stories I wrote which were intended to be nothing more than humorous reflections on a humorous subject. This is clearly a violation of at least two amendments to the U.S. Constitution, but it still happens.

I have received letters and telephone calls from faithful readers all over the country, and I have answered every one. It is nice to know that people actually read the things I write, and that they are moved enough to let me know.

In fact, I would like to share a special letter with you that was sent to me by Lewis and Fredell Rosen of Galveston, Texas:

"Fredell and I will never be able to thank you enough for turning us on to your two best sellers," Lewis wrote. "They have changed my life forever. I've been a nervous flier all my life, and have never been able to sleep on an airplane. Somewhere in chapter two of your first book, I dozed off and didn't wake until after the plane had landed.

"Your books are carefully stored in my carry-on bag to be read whenever I travel. With my new-found secret, thanks to you, I'll be able to arrive rested wherever I go. It might take a while for me to finish your books but hopefully more will be out by then to enable me to continue this new freedom."

Another reader, who apparently has some big misconceptions about the money that a writer makes, wrote me this letter:

"Every day I drive 103 miles to visit my mother, who is 90 years old. I am sure you know a lot of businessmen, so I was wondering if you could all get together and buy me a house. I saw one that I like for $89,000. It is nothing elaborate and needs some work, but I could do a little at a time on it. Hope to hear from you soon."

Unfortunately, I was unable to help that reader. There is another $89,000 house that needs some work—and it belongs to me.

In closing, I thank each of you for sharing these pages, and hope you enjoyed being "Chip-Wrecked In Las Vegas." This book is dedicated to my wife Debbie. Thanks, honey, for sharing your life with me.

The End